The General Prologue

by Geoffrey Chaucer:

A Critical Introduction

by

Ray Moore M.A.

Dedication:

To all of the students who sat in my classes over a period of thirty-eight years with gratitude for everything that they taught me.

A note on illustrations:

Except for the map on page 29, which is used by kind permission of the copyright holder, all images used in this book are (to the best of my knowledge) public domain and therefore non-copyright. If I am in error, please contact me by email: mooreray1@yahoo.com

Contents

Preface

Reading Middle English can be intimidating. The entire aim of this book is to take away the fear and leave you free to enjoy one of the most remarkable pieces of comic writing from any age.

The ideal Chaucerian interpreter should combine the skills of medieval grammarian, literary historian, socio-political historian, and literary critic. The author of this book does not claim to qualify fully in any of these categories. I have, however, taught *The General Prologue* frequently over four decades, and each time I have deepened my understanding of Chaucer's meaning. I have experienced students laughing out loud when they 'got' the jokes and cringing when they perceived exactly the thrust of Chaucer's satire. Sometimes it has been my own reading of the text and of secondary sources which has produced a new insight, but more often it has been a student's contribution to class discussion or a point made in an essay.

The present book is not written for the medieval scholar, but for the high school and undergraduate student who reads the *Prologue* because it is on his/her syllabus, or for the general reader who simply wants to enjoy Chaucer. The analysis offered goes beyond that found in the ubiquitous 'Notes' (helpful as these are to the first-time reader) without getting into the esoteric detail of the specialist literature. It is written to dispel the misapprehension that only scholars can understand and appreciate a text written in Middle English. The intention is to give the reader the confidence to develop his/her own understanding of a work which is an essential part of the European literary heritage.

As far as possible, I have tried to make the starting point of my analysis the text itself. Rather than attempting to place the poem in its historical, cultural, literary, philosophical, or biographical contexts in separate chapters, I have integrated these elements into the textual analysis whenever they seem to shed light on the writing. I assume that the reader has a copy of the text in Middle English – the only way to truly experience Chaucer. There are many editions of the *Prologue*, including those on-line, and they are all pretty much the same with only minor variations in wording, spelling and line numbering. I used *The Cambridge School Chaucer* edited by Kirkham and Allen.

I have chosen to give my own modernized version of the *Prologue* as an aid to reading the original, not as an alternative – please use it that way. There are so many modernized versions of Chaucer's text (sometimes erroneously termed 'translations' – Middle English is already English, so you cannot translate it!) that some justification is required for providing yet another. Here it is: I like mine better. I have made no attempt to keep to Chaucer's rhyme scheme or meter because doing so forces one to make compromises on meaning. I have chosen not to write in modern prose but to keep to the discipline of a line-by-line approach because this makes it easier to refer back to the 'real' text. For each line, I have sought to give the full meaning rather than a word-for-word modernization, and as a result I have frequently added details normally found only in textual notes [and occasionally made use of brackets to make the meaning completely clear].

All sections of the text are prefaced by a set of study questions. Do not skip these! It is important that you think about the text for yourself before proceeding to read my analysis. Several of the portraits are prefaced by modernized versions of descriptions of the same estate type written by Chaucer's contemporaries Gower and Langland. Do not skip these! They are interesting because they illustrate both just how conventional Chaucer is in his characterizations, drawing on the same traditional stereotypes as Gower and Langland, and how radically different is Chaucer's approach from those other writers in the estates satire genre.

My aim throughout has been to present a coherent reading of the text based on my current understanding of it. All critics agree that irony plays a central rôle in Chaucer's description of the pilgrims. Kittredge states unequivocally that "in the simplest language: *Chaucer always knew what he was about*" (emphasis in original 151). However, much of the irony is ambiguous, partly because Chaucer sometimes intended it to be so, but much more because the modern reader has to guess at the implications, connotations, and sometimes the denotations of words which the medieval listener/reader would have found perfectly clear. Where the interpretation of a portrait is controversial, I review the arguments on each side and give my own interpretation; I have enough respect for my readers to assume that they will take what they find convincing and reject what they find unconvincing.

Middle English can seem daunting at first, but it is actually easier than it looks. There are many commercial recordings of the *Prologue*. Get hold of one and listen to it while following along in the text; then read aloud along with it; and finally read the text aloud yourself. You will soon get the hang of it, and will find yourself able to read other Middle English texts, the obvious starting point being some of the tales which the pilgrims tell.

The Chaucer literature is vast, and any writer must be aware of 'standing on the shoulders of giants.' Wherever I have been conscious of borrowing an idea from a previous writer, I have given the source. Any failure to do so is an omission which I will immediately correct if it is drawn to my attention.

I should like to thank the staff of the Lake Sumter State College Library, Leesburg, Florida for their help.

Chapter 1: "Wel nine and twenty in a compaignie"

Introducing the Pilgrims

The dramatis personae, the "nine and twenty in a compaignie, / Of sundry folk" (24-5), do not span the whole range of Chaucer's society. None of the pilgrims comes from the aristocracy, or even the middle nobility, and none comes from the landless laboring class. Brewer explains Chaucer's focus on this subset of society thus, "The great were too  powerful to be represented, the humble were too remote from Chaucer's imaginative experience" (199).

Feudal society was traditionally divided into three estates: First Estate, the Clergy, who prayed; Second Estate, the Nobility, who fought; and Third Estate, the Peasantry, who labored. Such a simplistic tripartite structure, however, increasingly failed to capture the shifting gradations of late fourteenth century English society as the rise of an urban merchant class and of a class of university-educated intellectuals (nominally clergy but employed in secular careers), together with a peasant class demanding higher wages and greater freedom, began to break down traditional estate divisions. Gies and Gies describe the erosion of medieval feudal structures in the High Middle Ages:

> [T]he real enemy of the castle barons and their privileges was not the royal power but the slow, irresistible surge of economic change. The cloth merchants and other business men who exploited their workers, not perhaps more brutally, but more effectively than the barons did their villeins, were moving ahead in the economic race… (Gies and Gies 30)

Although accurately categorizing the pilgrims proves difficult, at least ten (the Merchant, the Five Guildsmen, the Cook, the Shipman, the Doctor, and the Wife of Bath) are representative of this new bourgeois class of entrepreneurs whose status depends, not upon birth or the filling of traditional positions, but on their individual skills in their chosen trade or profession.

The Knight is generally recognized as the highest status pilgrim, but he is a member only of the minor gentry, and he certainly does not appear to be the wealthiest of the pilgrims, nor is he the only knight. We are told of the Franklin, "Ful ofte time he was knight of the shire" (358), and "the Man of Law had probably also been knighted on attaining the rank of sergeant-at-law" (Swanson in Brown ed. 402). In fact, the feudal knight owing military service to his lord was already an anachronism. Although Chaucer is frequently contrasted with his contemporaries Gower and Langland who addressed contemporary conditions much more directly at a time when social and religious institutions and values appeared to be collapsing, it is precisely this 'middle class' surge which Chaucer captures in *The Canterbury Tales*.

Whilst the Pilgrim-narrator promises confidently to place each pilgrim in his or her "degree," or rank and place in society (40), and in his or her "estaat," or social category (718), it is not surprising that he seems concerned at the end of the *Prologue* that he has not met this obligation :

> Also I prey yow to foryeve it me,
> Al have I nat set folk in hir degree
> Heere in this tale, as that they sholde stonde.
> My wit is short, ye may wel understonde. (745-748)

The narrator's concern is understandable since the pilgrims who he sets out to classify do not exist in "an archaic and closed social order but [one] that ... reveals that order in the process of breaking down. Most of Chaucer's pilgrims are by no means content to stay in their proper places but are engaged in the pursuit of wealth, status, and respectability" ("Medieval estates and Orders"). The decline of feudalism was accompanied by the growth of a money-based economy which presented new opportunities for social advancement to the ambitious and the talented.

English society in the second half of the fourteenth century was thus in a constant state of flux. Even the social status of the individual pilgrims is not easy to identify, and critics disagree how they should be defined by status. The following classification is my own:

Minor nobility:	Knight and Squire.
Higher clergy:	Prioress and Monk.
Lower clergy:	Second Nun, Nun's Priest, Friar and Parson
Church employees:	Pardoner and Summoner (who may be either laymen or in minor orders)
Landed gentry:	Franklin
Professional class:	Clerk, Sergeant of the Law, Doctor
Urban bourgeoisie:	Haberdasher, Carpenter, Webbe, Dyer, Tapicer, Manciple, Harry Bailly
Mercantile class:	Merchant, Shipman, Wife of Bath, and Cook.
Rural freemen:	Miller, Reeve.
Freemen laborers:	Yeoman, Plowman

The historical Chaucer would fit into the professional class, but the status of the narrator is kept deliberately vague.

Though Chaucer's approach to the political and social issues of his time lacks the directness of Gower or Langland, Howard argues that Chaucer's social criticism in the *Prologue* derives from his sense of a society in crisis:

> [I]n *The Canterbury Tales* Chaucer presented social class distinctions in such a way as to point up the disparity between what people thought and what they did – between the obsolescent idea of social class which his society held and the more complicated actuality of its gradations. In the General Prologue he suggests the Three Estates ...; but he describes a variegated and mobile set of social distinctions or 'degrees.' And he sets the idea of their obsolescence in our minds with the Knight ... [T]he picture it [*The General Prologue*] provides is a fundamental medieval conception, that of a world in decline from the 'former age' or the Golden Age, growing old, becoming physically and morally weak. (Howard 100)

Indeed, the *Prologue* itself begins by highlighting the single event in English history which was most disruptive to the harmonious ideal represented by the concept of the Three Estates. The murder of Archbishop Thomas à Becket on December 29th, 1170 at the instigation of King Henry II both resulted from and further widened the schism between Church and State.

Even the concept of pilgrimage was becoming an anachronism by the time that Chaucer wrote about it:

> Everyone agreed that the institution of the pilgrimage was not what it had been in old times, and Chaucer, though he represents the pilgrimage in its ideal and symbolical form at the end, shows the pilgrims at the outset and along the way to be following an obsolescent custom 'After the newe way.' We see too, in the General Prologue, that their stations in life are changing, that the social structure and the culture itself are changing. (Howard 89)

The Pilgrims: Types or Individuals?

It was the critic Kittredge who in 1914 advanced the view that *The Canterbury Tales* should be read as a dramatic poem with fully developed characters and a degree of realism not far removed from the modern novel. That Kittredge overstated his case is now generally agreed, for Chaucer left his work unfinished and thus it is inconsistent both in its development of individual characters and in the matching of pilgrims to tales. Nevertheless, it remains true that the artistic conception of the *Tales* was something entirely new and that the effort to individualize the pilgrims was an important element of its originality.

Kittredge stresses the realism of the *Prologue* stating confidently:

> There is not one chance in a hundred that he [Chaucer] had not gone on a Canterbury pilgrimage himself. And pilgrims did, for a fact, while away the time in story-telling. (149)

Brewer reminds us that, "London was a small town, the court of Westminster of course even smaller, and so many of these characters are specific to well-known places there with limited personnel," and argues that, "Chaucer and his primary audience ... were a well-knit group" which would have encouraged the author to include portraits of individuals well known to both (199).

Writing in 1924, Manly notes the "imperfectly schematic" nature of the *Prologue* (*New Light* 73) and concludes not, as modern readers tend to assume, "that Chaucer merely described an actual group of pilgrims of which he himself was a member" (*New Light* 70), but that Chaucer includes in his fictional account "some at least of the pilgrims [who] were real persons, and persons with whom Chaucer can be shown to have had definite personal contacts" (*New Light* 73). Manly argues that Chaucer is not writing for posterity but for a small audience of nobility and gentry who would have recognized the individuals upon whom most portraits are based and "caught every sly reference to persons and things they knew" (*New Light* 76). Manly concludes that, since Chaucer draws upon his observation of the society of his time, then "Chaucer's character sketches represent not so much types as individuals – typical no doubt of their status and occupations, but typical only as the happily chosen individual may be" (*New Light* 74).

Manly identifies the Prioress with a nun called Argentyn who is known to have been at the priory of St. Leonard, Stratford-at-Bow (a priory of 30 nuns in 1354 and only 14 as recorded in the poll tax records of 1380-1) at this time. Manly's argument is summarized thus:

> So small a religious house was not likely to play an important part in the political or ecclesiastical history of the kingdom. In the 14th century, however, Stratford for a time became fashionable. The convent appears to have been the residence of Elizabeth of Hainault, and at her death in 1375 she seems to have been on terms of intimacy with the Stratford nuns. She directed that she should be buried in the chapel of St. Mary in the priory church and it has been concluded that she lived in the convent ... Elizabeth of Hainault made bequests to a nun called Argentyn who was also mentioned as one of the nuns in 1380-1; she occurs twice in Elizabeth's will. If, as has been suggested, Argentyn was the model in part for 'madame Eglentyne' in the Canterbury Tales, she must have been a woman of a certain gentility and fashion. (Cockburn, King, and McDonnell)

In a similar vein, Brewer (writing in 1978) calls the description of Harry Bailly "unquestionable true-life" (since it is known that a Harry Bailly kept an inn in Southwark in Chaucer's time); finds "broad hints" that the Sergeant-of-Law is "that [Thomas] Pinchbeck who had so annoyed Sir William [Beauchamp] and was making a lot of money by slightly dubious practice" (and who signed against Chaucer for an arrest in a debt case in 1388); identifies the Merchant with "that Gilbert Mawfield to whom most of them, including

Chaucer, owed money"; and thinks it "highly likely" that the Cook is Hodge of Ware "a well-known London restaurant owner whose food was suspect" (199). Characters who Brewer believes would have been readily identifiable to Chaucer's audience, though their names are lost to history are: the Doctor, the Friar, the Shipman, and the Pardoner. Still other pilgrims, Brewer sees as, if not provably representations of actual people, closely tied to particular places: the Prioress from the "well-known convent at Stratford-le-Bow ... evokes all the snobbish amusement of the courtly in-group at the inappropriate and foredoomed struggles of the inferior outsider" (199); the Manciple "is clearly associated with the Inns of Court" (199); the Franklin embodies "the extravagance of a country cousin and may also touch on a Norfolk gentleman associated with Pinchbeck" (199); and the "rascally Reeve of Norfolk ... [is] likely based on an official who managed some of the Pembroke estates in Norfolk" (174). This last pilgrim is the most individualized of all. He is definitively said to live in Bawdeswell which Manly calls "an insignificant village, far from London, almost in the 'ferthest end of Norfolk'" an inexplicable choice unless Chaucer had "some particular reason for interest in it" (*New Light* 86).

Other commentators have suggested individual identities for more of the pilgrims. In a note to the text, John Halverson suggests a name for the Shipman based on the name of his ship, the "Maudelaine", "There was a vessel of this name in the late 1300s, whose master, one Peter Risshenden, may have been Chaucer's model" (17). Hall writing of the Knight claims that:

> With such specific descriptions of the Knight's activities, it is probable that the Knight served as a model of persons Chaucer actually knew. It has even been purported that a certain Yorkshire family of Scrope was in Chaucer's mind as he portrayed his noble figure representative of the Age of Chivalry. Two English families, the Yorkshire family of Scrope and the Chester family of Grosvenor, claimed the same heraldic insignia - the "arms Azure, a bend Or" - as their own, and to decide the dispute, testimony was undertaken in 1386. Chaucer himself was one of the witnesses who testified in behalf of the family of Scrope. Testimony was given by those witnesses who had seen first-hand the arms displayed publicly, such as on a tombstone, or more importantly, in actual battle. Those knights and

esquires who testified in favor of Scrope described the self-same battles.

It is fair to say that both the dramatic interpretation and the effort to identify Chaucer's pilgrims with actual historical figures have been passé in literary criticism for some decades now. In the end, we can simply never know if a particular portrait is based on a historical individual, and we may question what knowing would actually add to our understanding of the text.

In 1973, reacting against both the dramatic and the historical approaches, critic Jill Mann argued that the *Prologue* belongs to the genre of medieval estates satire, works which attack the abuses and corruptions within the three traditional estates. Mann writes, "Chaucer was concerned to impose an estates form on the *Prologue* in order to suggest society as a whole by way of his representative company of individuals," and that "the estates type was the basis for Chaucer's creation of the Canterbury pilgrims" (in Patterson ed. 26 & 32). The Norton Anthology gives the following account of two examples of estates satire by a contemporary of Chaucer:

> John Gower's *Mirour de l'Omme* and *Vox Clamantis* systematically indict every estate, order, and profession. They set forth the functions and duties of each estate and castigate the failure of the estates in the present world to live up to their divinely assigned social rôles. Unlike their virtuous predecessors in the past, the estates were pursuing wealth, power, and luxury. Although Gower says that his condemnations are aimed only at vicious and not at virtuous persons - and they will know who they are - his presentation of present-day estates is almost uniformly negative.

This helps us to identify that which is traditional and that which is truly original in the *Prologue*. Chaucer uses the traditional classifications: there is *one* pilgrim for each estate, and each portrait is named for the estate and not for the name of the individual even though some pilgrims are named. The order of presentation used in the estates satire provides Chaucer with a framework with which he knows that his audience will be familiar but which he freely adapts to his own artistic ends. Benson, in arguing against the attempt to identify the pilgrims with historical figures, comments that, though the portraits purport to describe real individuals not stereotypes, "Chaucer's entire Canterbury pilgrimage probably appeared less realistic to its first readers than it does to us, for they would have had a surer sense of the unlikelihood of such a carefully diverse collection of pilgrims riding together..." (7).

The Order of the Portraits

In terms of arrangement, Chaucer ignores the norm in estates satire that all clerical figures should come before all lay figures and that all men should come before all women. Neither does Chaucer simply substitute a hierarchy based on status for a hierarchy based on literary precedent. It is true that the portraits show a general decline in status from the minor nobility to the freemen, but anomalies are introduced by the arrangement of the pilgrims into small social groupings, which furthers the fiction of the pilgrims having a real existence. Thus the Yeoman follows the Knight and the Squire because he is travelling as part of the Knight's retinue, and the Ploughman is included with the Parson, layman alongside cleric, because they are brothers travelling together.

Many critics have sought to rationalize the order of the portraits in the *Prologue*, but no theory has proved convincing, so we may suspect that the lack of order is precisely Chaucer's point. Mann, who insists that the content of the portraits is based on stereotypes and largely embodies the ideas and world-view which are typical of each pilgrim's place in society, nevertheless concludes, "The strict order of estates literature is governed by the notion of function, of hierarchy in a model whose working is divinely established. It is precisely this notion of function that ... Chaucer discards" (in Patterson ed. 26). Similarly, Leicester states that "one of the principal themes [of the *Prologue*] is the insufficiency of traditional, social and moral classifying schemes - estates, hierarchies, and the like – to deal with the complexity of individuals and their relations" (in George 94). The failure to set "folk in hir degree" is not failure at all.

Conclusions

To clarify Chaucer's intentions in the portraits and their ordering, it will be helpful to state the conclusions upon which this study is based.

This is what Chaucer does that no writer of estates satire had ever done. Firstly, he gives some of his characters names, indicates where they live, and describes them in terms of physical appearance and dress in ways which sometimes appear to have no relationship to their estate stereotype. It would be naïve to believe that in doing so he did not base some details upon people who he actually knew.

Secondly, the narrator simply describes what he sees and almost never makes overt moral judgments (the one exception is lines 661-4). Manly accurately defines the unique element of Chaucer's satire as lying in the fact that, "He does not argue, and there is no temptation to refute him. He does not declaim, and there is no opportunity for reply. He merely lets us see his fools and rascals, and we necessarily think of them as he would have us think" (*New Light* 295).

Thirdly, Chaucer develops the individual personalities of the pilgrims hinted at in the *Prologue* as they interact on their way towards Canterbury; and he makes them narrators of stories in which the reader (sometimes) hears their individual voices. Indeed, as we shall see, the careful reader even hears the voices of some of the pilgrims themselves in the descriptions given by the narrator in the *Prologue*. No doubt Benson is wise to warn the reader against seeing Chaucer as a 'modern' writer and the pilgrims, both as they are initially described and as they develop and interact, "as fully developed and psychologically complex characters, like those we know from a realistic novel or film" (in Boitani and Mann 130). He reiterates that the descriptions are based on types found in estates satires, that Chaucer's individualization is limited to "insinuations" which create "the illusion of life-like individuality" (in Boitani and Mann 130), and that there are a number of inconsistencies between the way characters are initially described and what we subsequently learn of them. Nevertheless, the fact that Chaucer does not individualize his pilgrim-narrators with the consistency of a modern novelist does not mean that he does not individualize them to a degree that was quite new in literature.

The *Tales* and their *Prologue* are a magnificent hybrid: they take from Chaucer's reading of Latin, Italian and French poetry; from his knowledge of estates satire; and from his observations of English society and of the people around him. Through Chaucer's genius, something entirely new is produced.

Chapter Two: "I was of hir felaweshipe anon"

Introducing the Narrator

The *Prologue* establishes the frame narrative for the *Tales*: Geoffrey Chaucer, beginning a solitary pilgrimage to Canterbury, quite by chance meets nearly twenty-nine other pilgrims at the Tabard Inn and is invited to join them; the Host, Harry Bailly, proposes a story-telling competition on the journey which he will himself judge; the next morning thirty people set out to Canterbury. Thus it is that  the narrator records his impression of his fellow pilgrims, the incidents which occur as the party makes its way towards Canterbury, and the tales told by each pilgrim. (*Note*: On the number of pilgrims, see next chapter.)

The result of this narrative frame is to create characters who are both audience to the tales of tellers and also tellers of their own tales creating a complex number of interrelationships which Williams describes thus:

> There is the level of Narrator who, through his reportage of the Canterbury frame story, creates pilgrims, like the Knight, who, in turn, become authors and create a third level of characters in their tales, such as the character of Theseus. And there is still another dimension. The very authors who tell these stories are the audience for them on the way to Canterbury, and there is another audience beyond them in the person of the Host who must initiate, criticize, and judge, and still another audience, Chaucer the narrator, who must listen closely both to the pilgrim authors and to Harry Bailly and do his best to report their tales. Is there still another level of audience? Of course there is. Splendidly hidden in all of this in God-like fashion is Geoffrey Chaucer the ultimate author of the Canterbury Tales, revealed in his fictional namesake and communicating, through this complicated structure, with us, the ultimate audience, hidden away, like the ultimate author, in the real world. (Williams 24)

The first-person narrator is identified as Geoffrey Chaucer, but this persona (usually called by critics 'Chaucer the Pilgrim' and by me in class called 'Little Geoffrey Chaucer') is not to be confused with the historical Chaucer, who had a position in the royal administration at court and who is the actual author of *The Canterbury Tales*. The distinction between the Pilgrim and the Poet was first proposed by the critic Donaldson writing in 1954; he defined the Pilgrim as a narrator acutely unaware of the significance of what he observes so precisely. This is to say that the character of the Pilgrim, though it borrows aspects of the history, character, and even physical appearance of the historical Chaucer, is actually as much a literary creation as are the other pilgrims, some of whom similarly are based to some degree on real individuals. For completeness, let me add that critics quite rightly insist that the Poet is no more to be confused with the historical Geoffrey Chaucer than is the Pilgrim: every writer, by the very act of creating a text, adopts a creative mask.

Probably the best view we get of the Pilgrim is in the "Prologue to The Tale of Sir Topas" when the Host addresses him thus:

> Until our Host began to jest,
> And then for the first time he looked at me,
> And said: What man are you?
> You look as if you are searching for a hare,
> For I see you stare continually at the ground.
> Come close to me, and cheer up.
> Now stand aside, sirs, and let this man have place!
> He is shaped in the waist as well as I am;
> He's like a little doll embraced in the arms
> Of any woman, small and fair of face.
> He seems abstracted by the look on his face,
> For he doesn't converse with anyone.
> (Author's modernization)

The Pilgrim is quick to assure the reader that what the Host says is only in jest, for the good reason that it is not very flattering. Indeed, the Host teases the Pilgrim constantly, a sure sign that he does not regard him as a person of higher status than himself. The story that the Pilgrim tells fully justifies his apology to the Host for not being the storytelling type; it is so bad that the Host commands him to shut up, and, since his rhyming is so awful, to tell a tale in prose which he

17

obligingly does. This is the persona which Chaucer gives to his narrator.

Donaldson's concept of the Pilgrim as a persona consistently presented throughout the *Prologue* and in the interactions with the Host is a further manifestation of the dramatic theory of the *Tales* which derives from Kittredge, and the same qualifications must be made: the *Tales* is an unfinished work which contains inconsistencies some of which Chaucer might have edited out, but (more importantly) Chaucer could have no conception of the sort of complex, consistent characters found in the modern novel. Thus, Benson again correctly warns readers that:

> Chaucer does not restrict himself to a single consistent narrative voice in the *General Prologue*, as is sometimes claimed, but is variously naïve and shrewd, devout and worldly – bluffly endorsing the murderous Shipman one moment, while slyly questioning the Physician's religious faith and business practices the next. The standards of judgement continually shift: the pretentions of the Merchant or the Man of Law produce social satire, while the Pardoner is condemned and the Parson praised in strictly Christian terms. (In Boitani and Mann 129-30)

The Poet is quite happy to adapt the Pilgrim persona to the needs of particular portraits, and, as a result, the Pilgrim sometimes appears naïve and foolish (Monk, Friar), sometimes wise and serious (Parson, Ploughman), and sometimes shocked and morally offended (Summoner, Pardoner). Notwithstanding these inconsistencies, it is important to understand that the Poet does construct the persona, the Pilgrim, who does exist as a separate character in the poem, even if he does not have the psychological consistency of a character in a modern novel.

Introducing the Poet

The content of the portraits is not based only upon the Pilgrim's impressions on that first night in the Tabard Inn, but upon the totality of his experience of his companions during the days of their pilgrimage. Nevertheless, within the fiction of the frame story, it is important to bear in mind that the only knowledge that the Pilgrim can possibly have of the other pilgrims must come either from his observations of their appearance and actions, or from their own accounts of themselves; in other words, the naïve narrator presents very much each pilgrim's own estimation of him or herself. Mann points to the importance of the "omission of the victim" from the Pilgrim's account which encourages the reader "to see the behavior of the pilgrims from their own viewpoints"; that is, by ignoring the effects of their actions, the Pilgrim is able to "present the expertise of his rogues on the same level as the superlative qualities of his admirable figures" (Bloom ed. *Geoffrey Chaucer* 29). Whilst Mann is clearly correct in that no victims are actually present on the pilgrimage, thus depriving them of a voice, I think that she underestimates the subtle way in which victims are consciously introduced into the portraits by the other voice in the *Prologue*, that of the Poet.

Many of the details about the pilgrims in the *Prologue* are obviously based upon a perspective that could not realistically be gained from a personal encounter. Whoever is telling us about these people appears to know everything about them: not just what they do, but also what they think and feel. He has the sort of knowledge and understanding associated with an omniscient narrator. This is our clue to the existence of another Geoffrey Chaucer, Chaucer the Poet. Baldwin clarifies the distinction, "The bias and inadequacies of the Pilgrim are counterchecked by the incontrovertible authority of the Poet" who is operating with "the panoramic viewpoint of unlimited knowledge and with the authority belonging to the third-person narrator" (68).

Chaucer not only has great fun re-inventing himself as a naïve observer who takes each of the pilgrims at face value and is mightily impressed by everyone he meets, but also takes delight in using the over-voice of the Poet to inject into the portraits ironic details which undercut his narrator's praise. This use of dual perspective allows the Poet to exploit the obvious distance in most of the portraits between the enthusiastic praise and admiration of the Pilgrim and the darker reality of the character being described. New Criticism terms the Pilgrim an 'unreliable narrator'.

Ian Johnston identifies one of the central themes of *The Canterbury Tales* in this way:

> While the ideals of the dedication to a traditional Christian communal society are still clearly there, it is equally evident that for many of these pilgrims, including the Church

officials, the sense of a communal duty is being eroded by a personal desire for money and the fine things money can buy. In fact, there is a strong sense throughout *The Canterbury Tales* that this money is somehow a threat to something older and more valuable.

Thus, there is normally a comic disparity between the Pilgrim's apparent approval and admiration of his fellow travelers and the implications and connotations of the words used to describe them by the Poet: in this way, comic irony is created. This irony ranges from gentle, indulgent humor to scathing sarcasm depending on how far removed a particular character is from what he or she ought to be. However, here the modern reader faces a problem that Chaucer's contemporaries probably did not face: all critics agree that, as Helen Cooper points out, "Chaucer is the master of irony by way of the superlative," but "there is no critical unanimity" on precisely when the superlatives are justified and when they are intended to be ironic. Cooper makes this helpful distinction between irony in other works of the period and the irony found in the *Prologue*:

> medieval allegories … consistently spell out what they mean: Chaucer, as ironist, does not. Judgement depends on the reader's picking up clues in the text, and some of them are deeply ambiguous. Moral certainty tends to be replaced by a semiological slither. (29)

This ambiguity was almost certainly less of a problem for Chaucer's intended audience because *The Canterbury Tales* is quintessentially performance poetry; listening to Chaucer himself reading aloud would have removed most of the ambiguity we now find in the portraits.

The Persona of the Pilgrim

It would, however, be wrong to think of the Pilgrim-narrator either as a static character or as a completely inconsistent character. Critics appear not to have noticed that the narrator's attitude changes during the course of the *Prologue*. The first portraits are (with the exception of the Yeoman) of the social elites (Knight and Squire) and the clerics whose being in religious orders gives them even higher status (Prioress, Monk, and Friar). The Pilgrim is in awe of these people and finds it impossible to criticize them – even the frankly vicious Friar. However, when he comes to pilgrims who are more on his own social level, he begins to insert the odd line of conscious criticism: of the Merchant, "But sooth to seyn, I not how men him calle" (286); of the Lawyer, "And yet he semed bisier than he was" (324); and of the Cook "But greet harm was it, as it thought me" (387). Some critics interpret these lines as the voice of the Poet breaking through the mask of his narrator, but this appears to make no sense to me.

As the *Prologue* progresses, the absolute division between Pilgrim and Poet seems to narrow because of the Pilgrim's growing awareness, and the reader begins to suspect that more of the ironies are conscious and intended. Our narrator is receiving a moral education before our eyes, and that education is completed when he describes those two wholly good men the Parson and the Ploughman. It is surely no coincidence that the remaining portraits are of the churls, the ugliest of the pilgrims both outside and in, and that the Pilgrim's descriptions pull no punches.

Finally, Pilgrim and Poet morph briefly into one when the no longer naïve, indulgent, gullible Pilgrim, stirred by the Summoner's joking about excommunication, hell and damnation, makes a definitive statement about religious and moral values, "But wel I woot he lied right in dede" (661). Even if the narrator appears not to see the greed which motivates the Summoner to lie, this is no longer the Pilgrim who said with wide-eyed admiration of the Monk's justification for ignoring the rules of his order, "And I seyde his opinion was good" (183). After this outburst, there is somewhat of a return to the two distinct voices of Pilgrim and Poet, but the distance between them is never again what it was when the narrator began the portraits.

The Interpretation of the Portraits

Every critic of the *Prologue* is agreed that the portraits can be divided into two sub-sets: a small number of the pilgrims are idealized and the rest are, to varying degrees, presented ironically or even satirically. The former establish the 'gold standard' against which the latter can be more effectively judged and found wanting. The problem is that there has never been unanimity on which portraits Chaucer intends to be interpreted as idealized.

The simplest view is that there are three idealized portraits representing the three estates: the Parson, the Knight, and the Ploughman. However, some critics find other idealized portraits. For example, *KnowledgeNote Study Guide* states:

> Four of the characters, the Knight, the Clerk, the Poor Parson, and the Plowman, are treated differently from the others in that no irony is used in their portrayal. They are portraits of perfection, standing for ideals that few could expect to achieve. The Knight stands for chivalry, the Clerk for dedication to the search for truth, the poor Parson for genuine Christian piety, and the Plowman for honesty and hard work. In contrast to these four, the other portraits reveal different degrees of hypocrisy, a quality that Chaucer treats sometimes with gentle humor, as in the case of the Prioress, whose dress and manners are all a little too self-consciously elegant for a nun. But he can also be savage in his satire, as with the Pardoner, whose greed and deceptive practices clearly disgust the poet.

Presumably the Clerk is there to represent what the new class of clerical intellectuals should be. Brewer selects exactly the same four pilgrims (with the tentative addition of the Squire and the even more tentative addition of the Yeoman) as being "the only characters whom Chaucer approves of" because they represent the "ideal three-fold order of society; knights to fight for all, clergy to pray for all, ploughmen to get food for all" (198).

This fragile consensus was challenged in 1980 by Terry Jones in his book *Chaucer's Knight: The Portrait of a Medieval Mercenary*. Jones argues that the same irony qualifies Chaucer's account of the Knight as is evident in most of the other portraits. The question is currently unresolved by scholars, although it is fair to say that the weight of scholarly opinion has come down against Jones' revisionist interpretation. However, the Knight's position amongst the ideal portraits is not as secure as it once was. Moreover, detailed analysis of the portrait of the Clerk will show that any interpretation which denies the critical irony in the Clerk's portrait must be suspect. Thus, one of our primary goals will be to establish which portraits represent the 'gold standard' against which the failings of all of the other pilgrims are to be judged.

Conclusions

To clarify the question of Chaucer's intentions in the ordering of the portraits and in his descriptions of them, it will be helpful to state the conclusions upon which this study is based.

Firstly, having abandoned the hierarchical approach of estates satire, Chaucer chose not to present an alternative hierarchy either in terms of status or morality. The most that can be said is that there is a general, though uneven, decline in the status of the pilgrims who are described from the high-status Knight, Squire, Prioress and Monk, and that this is paralleled by a general, but equally uneven, decline in their morality.

Secondly, the portraits are carefully arranged in social, status and employment sub-sets to encourage the reader to see comparisons and contrasts between the pilgrims so grouped, and within these sub-sets there is a general tendency for the immorality of the pilgrims described to increase.

Thirdly, there are only two portraits which entirely lack individualizing detail and which can be interpreted without hesitation as idealized: the Parson and the Ploughman. Every one of the other portraits is intended to be critical to some degree, though Chaucer's attitude ranges from the mildest, indulgent irony to the most biting satire depending on how far the reality of their lives is from the ideal of what it should be.

Finally, Nevo is certainly correct when she states that each pilgrim is judged by the same criterion, "The pilgrim's characteristic behaviour is defined in every case in terms of the acquisition and use of wealth … Money – pelf - is the touchstone to which each of these characters is brought, and by which he is tested. There is no portrait which does not take its orientation from an attitude to money or from dealings with money, whether in the form of illicit gain or of legitimate hire" (in Bloom ed. *Critical Interpretations The Prologue* 11). This is the unifying moral principle upon which all of the portraits are based.

Chapter Three: Setting the Scene

[11] And God said, Let the earth bring forth grass, the herb yielding seed, and the fruit tree yielding fruit after his kind, whose seed is in itself, upon the earth: and it was so ...

[24] And God said, Let the earth bring forth the living creature after his kind, cattle, and creeping thing, and beast of the earth after his kind: and it was so ...

[26] And God said, Let us make man in our image, after our likeness: and let them have dominion over the fish of the sea, and over the fowl of the air, and over the cattle, and over all the earth, and over every creeping thing that creepeth upon the earth. ("Genesis" Chapter 1 King James Version)

Lines 1-18:

1. How is the long first sentence structured? [Where does each part begin and end? Look for subordinate and main clauses, and conjunctions.] What does this structure add to the experience of reading the opening sentence?

2. Find examples from these lines of phrases and details that you consider to be realistic and those that you feel owe more to literary convention.

3. What motives are suggested for people undertaking the pilgrimage that is about to begin? In what ways are the season and nature imagery important factors? (Many details in these lines stress the re-birth of sexual energy in spring. List and explain as many examples as you can without blushing!)

> When the sweet showers of April
> Have penetrated to the roots after the dry month of March
> And bathed in moisture every vein of the plants
> Which causes the flowers to come into blossom;
> 5   When, also, the West Wind, with his fragrant breath, has
> In every wood and field breathed life
> Into the tender shoots and buds, and the young sun
> Has run half his course into the sign of Aries the Ram,
> And small birds sing melodiously
> 10   That sleep all through the night with their eyes open
> (Because Nature so urges them in their amorous desires);

Then folk long to go on pilgrimages,
And pilgrims want to seek out new places to visit
Distant shrines, well known in various countries;
15 And particularly from every part of every county
Of England, they make their way to Canterbury,
To seek the shrine of the holy blessed martyr, St. Thomas Becket,
Who helped cure them when they were ill.

The poem opens with one carefully structured, eighteen-line sentence which paints a vivid picture of life returning to the countryside after the dead, cold English winter. Technically speaking, the sentence is complex-compound: a subordinate temporal clause ("Whan that April ..."), three compound subordinate temporal clauses ("Whan Zephirus ... / ... [when] the younge sonne ... / And [when] smale foweles..."), and three main clauses linked by the conjunction 'and' ("Thanne longen folk ... / And palmeres for to seken ... / And ... to Caunterbury they wende"). Of course, the reader does not stop to analyze sentence structure, but the reader does immediately appreciate the effect of sentence structure. This long opening sentence literally wends its way towards Canterbury. Beginning in the sky above the English countryside, moving to the first stirrings of life in the soil and the animals, introducing the topic of pilgrimage in general, and only finally arriving at a particular destination, the sentence is a microcosm of the journey of the pilgrims. The assertion that Canterbury draws pilgrims from "every shires ende / Of Engelond" will be validated in the portraits by references to the origins of the travelers which range from Dartmouth in the far West to Baldeswell in the East.

The theme of these lines is the return of life after the dead time of winter, a process which is described using extended personifications and diction that have both religious and sexual connotations. The theoretical beginning of Aries, first sign of the zodiac, is the moment of the vernal equinox which marks the victory of the sun over the shade of night, and Easter, with its Christian connotations of resurrection, normally occurs in Aries. Moreover, as Wilcockson points out, "It was thought in the Middle Ages that God created the world in March" (Bloom ed. *Modern Critical Interpretations* 25), and it is therefore no coincidence that the progression by which the coming of life is described mirrors the description of creation in

Genesis. Wilcockson also draws attention to the theological connotations of the words "vertu" (4) and "Inspired" (6) commenting of the latter that, "The most common use of 'inspire' in the fourteenth century carries the implication 'infusion of the divine presence'" (Bloom ed. *Modern Critical Interpretations* 25).

At the same time, the rebirth of spring is described in frankly sexual language. Hoffman analyzes it thus, "The phallicism of the opening lines presents the impregnating of the female March by the male April, and a marriage of water and earth. The marriage is repeated and varied immediately as a fructifying of 'holt and heeth' by Zephirus, a marriage of air and earth" (Bloom ed. *Geoffrey Chaucer* 23). The word "engendered" has connotations of procreation and begetting; the sweet April showers literally inseminate the land with "swich licour" causing flowers to blossom and bloom. The personified "sweete breeth" of the West Wind suggests a human lover seducing the beloved "croppes" (7). The sun is mid-way in Aries, the first sign of the Zodiac, which astrologically represents impulsive, vital energy. Aries is, of course, "the Ram" (8) a traditional animal symbol for virility and the wild forces of nature.

The birds are mating and "slepen al the night with open ye, / (So priketh hem nature in hir courages)" (10-11), lines which will be echoed in the description of the amorous Squire "so hoote he lovede that by the nightingale / He sleep namoore than doth a nightingale" (97-8). The word "corages," meaning spirits or feelings, relates here to erotic rather than spiritual love, and Chaucer uses a bawdy pun in describing how desire is prompted in the birds: nature "priketh hem," a double entendre which suggests one name of the male sexual organ. (Compare Mercutio in *Romeo and Juliet*, "The bawdy hand of the dial is now upon the prick of noon," and see also lines 189 and 191). Thus the opening sentence presents a dichotomy: spring awakes both spiritual hunger and the physical lust for life, and the same pilgrims who go to Canterbury for religious reasons also go for social recreation. The potential conflict between serving God and serving Man, which will become a central theme in the *Prologue*, is established from the outset.

The sound of the first eleven lines is dominated by long, open vowels and caressing sibilants:

Whan that Aprill with his shoures soote… (1)
Whan Zephirus eek with his sweete breeth… (5)

And smale foweles maken melodie,
That slepen al the night with open ye (9-10)
Listen to those gentle, sweeping 's' sounds. Now contrast the sound of these lines with that of the two 'copulation' lines:

The droghte of March hath perced to the roote... (2)
(So priketh hem nature in hir corages), (11)

Hard consonants and short vowels give these lines an edge - no gentle sibilants here. Listen to the explosive violence of those 'p' sounds. There is a marked contrast in both sound and meaning between the abstract verbs "inspired" (6) and "yronne" (8) and the concreate, sexual verbs "perced" (2) and "priketh" (11).

Lines 12-18 maintain this hard energy to describe human activity. The sibilants are now harsh, the consonants sharp and the vowels short and hard:

And palmeres for to seken straunge strondes,
To ferne halwes, kowthe in sondry londes; (13-4)

By the end of the sentence, the real world truly has come back to life, an effect which is strengthened by Chaucer's manipulation of verb tense. The subordinate clauses which open this sentence are largely in the present perfect tense ("hath perced ... [hath] bathed ... Inspired hath ... Hath ... yronne"). However, a subtle change occurs when Chaucer comes to describe the birds which "maken melodie" (9) and "slepen al the night" (10). In her analysis, Bowden calls "maken melodie," "a slant-form past participle, while actually expressing the present tense." This is needlessly complicated; it seems to me to be the continuous present tense like "slepen al the night." Yet however one describes the grammar, the change in tenses takes the reader from the hypothetical to the actual (from "Whan" to "Thanne") preparing us for the unambiguous continuous present tense of the verbs describing humans ("longen folk ... to seken ... they wende" [12-16]). Let's just pause to acknowledge the pent-up energy, the sense of liberation, of that verb "longen." The shift in verb tenses supports the change in focus from the universal to the particular which is embodied in the imagery and diction.

The way that the poem opens derives from the French *reverdie* (chant of welcome to the spring) or re-greening tradition of medieval lyric poetry which had become very popular in Chaucer's time. Cannon makes the point that here Chaucer is writing in his 'high' style "with a vocabulary that is both heavily polysyllabic and recherché [i.e. consciously affected and pretentious], consisting of words that Chaucer did not use very often ('licour', 'veyne', 'holt', 'heeth', 'strondes', halwes') or that he uses here in unusual ways ('tendre', 'vertu', engendered')" (Boitani and Mann 244). The style of the opening sentence certainly stands in stark contrast to the more realistic, colloquial style of the rest of the *Prologue* in which there is not another eighteen-line sentence.

When Chaucer describes the coming of spring in England, he is drawing quite as much from literary precedent as he is from personal observation. To give a concrete example, it is simply not true that March was a dry month in England. Certainly, the April showers re-awakened vegetation, and the prevailing winds changed from cold easterlies to warmer westerlies, but objectively January, February and March each had greater rainfall than April. Although he did not know it, Chaucer was living at the beginning of the Little Ice Age, and in the second half of the fourteenth century, the problem in England was not drought, but a significant fall in winter temperatures together with a sometimes disastrous increase in rainfall. This small detail should alert the reader to question the apparent realism of Chaucer and to acknowledge the importance of literary precedent in his poetry. [Bowden supports the realism of a dry March by quoting the proverbs, "A bushel of March dust is worth a King's ransom," which actually suggests the scarcity of dust in March, and, "A dry March, wet April, and cool May fill barn, cellar, and bring much hay," which does not imply that a dry March is typical. She also refers to an article by Professor Hart, "The Droughte of March" (1962), which I have not been able to access. In it she says that Hart "gives statistics to support the fact that March in England is often a relatively dry month," which is not what Chaucer appears to be saying when he refers to "the droughte of March" (*Commentary* 317).]

The voice that the reader hears is anonymous, third person omniscient. It speaks in an authoritative way about the cycle of life: a timeless truth is being stated about the unchanging order of the universe, the verities of nature. The awakening of life is described as moving hierarchically, by a process of cause and effect, from the air to soil, to plants, to animals, to man and finally to the divine. David Williams explains how Chaucer puts man at the top of the chain of being on earth:

The author has also structured the lines so as to include in this vision of awakening the four constitutive elements of life: earth (the dry land), water (April showers), air (Zephirus), and fire (the younge sonne) ... Chaucer placed man at the center of this cosmos, as we see in the lines themselves, which are constructed so as to move toward and emphasize human awakening as the center of this process ...To animal, to man, human nature is described differently: whereas the plants and animals only come to life, as they should, in a natural physical manner, blooming and being physically fertile, man's rebirth is signified by a spiritual impulse ... Man, of course, possesses a nature that is both physical and spiritual, and by managing his lines this way Chaucer tells us that man's higher nature, while in harmony with the physical world, demands of him spiritual awakening. (Williams 27-29)

Whilst the quickening of the spring makes the flowers bloom, the crops germinate, and the birds mate, in man the regeneration takes a spiritual form. However, there is a typical Chaucerian irony in the elevated tone of this opening, for the majority of the people on this pilgrimage do not exactly illustrate "man's higher nature," as we shall soon see.

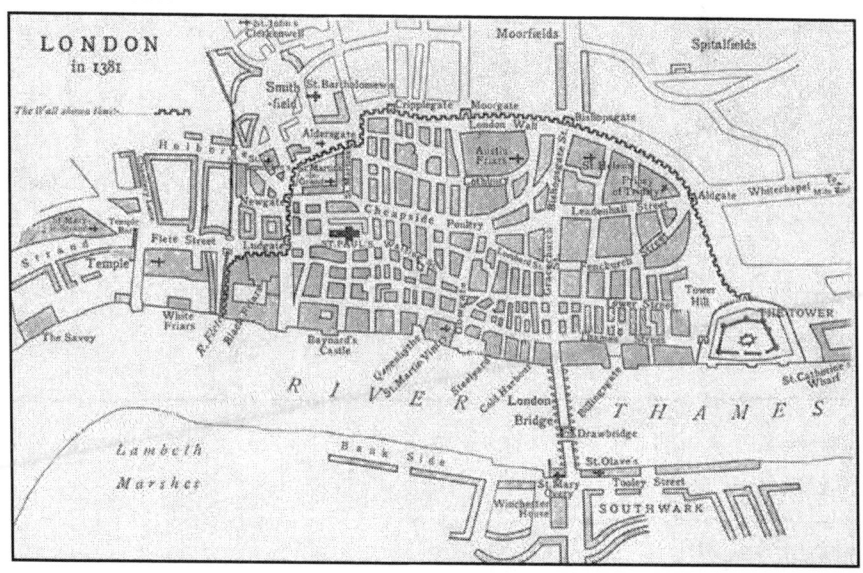

Lines 19-34:

> Pilgrims and palmers pledged together
> To seek Saint James and the saints in Rome.
> Went forth on their journey with many wise tales,
> And considered they were free to tell lies for the rest of their lives –
> I saw some that claimed they had sought saints:
> Yet in each tale that they told their tongues told lies.
> (Langland *The Vision of Piers Plowman* author's modernization)

Southwark is a London borough south of the River Thames. In Chaucer's day, there was only one bridge across the Thames, London Bridge, and it led from the still-walled city into Southwark where the Tabard Inn was situated on the only road leading south, making it a popular gathering point for those planning to ride to Canterbury. Ironically, Southwark also had a reputation for its brothels (or stews), located between Maid Lane and Bankside, particularly after 1385 when the City of London authorities took action to rid the city of prostitutes.

There is an interesting discrepancy between the number of pilgrims reported by the narrator and the number actually described in the *Prologue*. The number twenty-nine cannot possibly be right: counting the pilgrims mentioned in the text there are either twenty-eight or thirty. It all depends on the reading of lines 163-4, "Another Nonne with hire hadde she [the Prioress], / That was hir chapeleyne, and preestes thre." Is the Prioress accompanied by one priest or by three? To me, three would make no sense at all, so I opt for the Pilgrim joining a preexisting group of twenty-eight. Why, then does the Pilgrim describe that group as being "Wel nine and twenty in a compaigne" (24)? The first answer is that the word "Wel" indicates that the number is an approximation, 'twenty-nine or so'. The number twenty-nine is probably used because it was on 29th December 1170 that Thomas Becket was murdered. Chaucer is thus the twenty-ninth pilgrim – a propitious number.

1. What is your first impression of Pilgrim Chaucer, the narrator of the poem?
2. What pattern does the Pilgrim set out for his descriptions of his fellow travelers?

3. Contrast lines 1-18 with lines 19-34. What are the main differences in subject matter and style?

> It happened that in spring one day,
> 20 As I was staying at the Tabard Inn in Southwark
> Prior to beginning my pilgrimage
> To Canterbury with a very devout heart,
> There came at night into that lodging
> Roughly twenty-nine folks in a company
> 25 Of various classes of people who had fallen quite by chance
> Into fellowship, and they were all pilgrims
> Who intended to ride to Canterbury.
> The bedrooms and the stables were spacious,
> And we were very comfortably accommodated.
> 30 To be brief, by the time the sun had gone down,
> I had spoken with every one of them to such effect that
> I was accepted into their group straightway,
> And had agreed to rise early,
> To begin our journey, as I shall tell you.

These lines give the basis for the frame story upon which Chaucer will build towards the end of the *Prologue*. The style is markedly different from the opening eighteen lines with "their high-flown literary conventions modeled on French poetry" (Howard 89):

> Bifil that in that seson on a day,
> In Southwerk at the Tabard as I lay (19-20)

The first sentence did not reveal its subject and verb ('folk long') until line twelve, but here the sentence beings with the main clause ('it befell'). The first word is the verb, the narrator having jettisoned the subject of the sentence to produce the first line in the poem which begins with a hard, short consonant. Contrast the sound of these lines with the first lines of the poem. Here the vowels are short and hard, particularly at the end of each line where three short monosyllables foreshorten the lines and bring them to an abrupt end.

The narrative switches abruptly from third person omniscient to an individualized (ultimately a named) first person narrator. In addition, the reader is personalized and directly addressed as "yow" (34 & 38). The verb tense switches abruptly from the continuous present which ended the first sentence to the simple past tense, and the story, based firmly in contemporary reality, is described in a deliberately unpoetic, conversational narrative style. There is, for example less alliteration in these lines than in the opening sentence (respectively five examples to two) and less personification (respectively five examples to one).

All notions of hierarchy, structure and order are immediately abandoned as the reader is thrust without preparation into a world where life is dominated by chance. The narrator happens to be at the Tabard when a group, which has previously formed by pure happenstance, happens to also be there, "Bifil that ... on a day ... as I lay ... by aventure yfalle / In felaweshipe" (19-26). The laws of cause and effect, which dominated the invocation of spring, quite simply do not seem to be operating here; we are in a world where life is random and where judgments will prove to be subjective rather than authoritative, "so as it semed me" (39).

These lines are, however, deceptively simple. The Pilgrim's being at the Tabard is carefully related to the theme of rebirth established in the first sentence by selective repetition. Just as pilgrims "from every shires ende / Of Engelond ... wende" their way to Canterbury (16-7), so the Pilgrim reports that he is at the Tabard, "Redy to wenden on my pilgrimage" (21), and just as nature rouses the "corages" of the birds (11), so the Pilgrim is impelled to visit Canterbury "with ful devout corage" (22). Note, however, that the adjective "devout" clearly identifies the narrator's motivation as spiritual.

The lines also establish a characteristic of the pilgrim-narrator which is fundamental to understanding the portraits: Pilgrim Chaucer is easily impressed, generous in his praise and given to superlatives. The first example is his evaluation of the accommodation and hospitality which he and his fellows receive at the Tabard, "wel weren we esed ate beste" (28). The paraphrase, "[we were] made very comfortable" (Kirkham and Allen 14) entirely misses the naïve, whole-hearted approval implied by the word "beste."

The overriding significance of these lines, however, is that in them Chaucer does two things of crucial importance. Firstly, he describes the dual rôle of the Pilgrim: at once accepted into the company, yet not an integral part of it. This establishes the Pilgrim's unique perspective as outsider/observer: each of the travelers is new to him and because of this he studies them, meticulously noting everything he sees and hears. The word "felaweshipe" (26 & 32) is given emphasis by repetition. The word implies "community of interest … a company of equals … the state of being comradely" (Merriam-Webster), and the Poet's implication in using it is that, by joining the group, the Pilgrim assumes himself to be amongst like-minded people to whom he feels an obligation of loyalty – two huge errors of judgment that the Pilgrim only comes slowly and imperfectly to understand.

Secondly, with the single word "sondry" (25), Chaucer does something which no writer of a short story collection had ever done before. Certainly writers had previously used a unifying frame narrative, and although we cannot be certain which of these collections Chaucer had actually read, it is perfectly clear that he was aware of the genre. The ancient *One Thousand and One Nights* has a single storyteller, Scheherazade, who must keep her husband in suspense with her stories from day to day to prevent him from having her executed. Boccaccio's *The Decameron* (c. 1353) has one hundred tales told by ten storytellers, all young nobles spending two weeks in the countryside of Fiesole having escaped plague-stricken Florence. In the first example, the voice of the storyteller is obviously the same each time, and in the case of the second the ten storytellers (seven women and three men) are all from the same aristocratic class, so they tell the same kinds of tales in the same kinds of ways.

What Chaucer does in *The Canterbury Tales* is to individualize his storytellers both in terms of their place in society, their temperaments, and the developing relationships between individuals in the course of their journey. To give an example, when the Knight concludes the first tale, the Host nominates the Monk to tell the next story. However, the drunken Miller insists that he has a tale which can top the Knight's story and threatens to leave if he is not allowed to tell it, at which the Host gives in. Now there is a running feud between the Miller and the Reeve, so that when the Miller tells a story which mocks a foolish carpenter, the Reeve, a carpenter by trade, insists that he tells the next tale and proceeds to tell a story about a miller who is tricked. Thus the sequence of the tales is dynamic.

Critics are right to point out that this design is carried out imperfectly, yet the frame story, at the very least, enables Chaucer to include a wide variety of story genres ranging from the comic, bawdy fabliaux of the Miller, Reeve and Merchant to the romances of the Knight, Wife of Bath, Clerk and Franklin, even if the dynamic element of the story telling game is only partially realized. Benson writes of *The Canterbury Tales*:

> The work is energized by unexpected juxtapositions of styles and subject-matter, so that, for example, a long romance of ancient heroism comes before a short, witty tale of local lust and an account of alchemical swindlers follows a story about ancient martyrdom ... No other medieval story collection has a frame that is so lively and dynamic. (In Boitani and Mann 127)

In this variety of tone and subject matter lies the total originality of *The Canterbury Tales*.

Lines 35-42:

1. Read these lines and skip ahead to lines 727-48. What sort of personality does Chaucer give his narrator? How does the Pilgrim understand his task as narrator?

```
35      But nonetheless, whilst I have the time and the opportunity,
        Before I proceed any further with this tale,
        It seems to me rational
        To describe to you the personality
        Of every one of them, so far as I could judge,
40      And what they looked like and what their social status was,
        And also what clothes they were dressed in;
        And I will begin with a knight.
```

The most obvious stylistic feature of these lines is the plethora of personal pronouns: "I" is used three times, "me' once, "yow" once, "hem" once, and "they" twice. The effect is to personalize the narrative. The narrator's close relationship with the reader is established, and through this the reader gains an impression of the reality of his characters. In the portraits themselves, which are of necessity in the third person, the Pilgrim will maintain this conversational relationship by throwing in occasional personal pronouns such as "I gesse" (82, 117) and "I noot" (286). Look out for them. Notice also the Pilgrim's comic pun, "Er that I ferther in this tale pace" (36). To "pace" is to walk; the horses will "pace" to Canterbury. Sharing a joke with the reader helps to establish a relationship.

Now the Pilgrim sets out his approach to describing the pilgrims. The word "resoun" (37) is a medieval term from rhetoric meaning order, the proper sequence of parts in a speech, and the Pilgrim goes on to set out exactly the structure which he will use to describe his companions. As we shall see, having been so firm in establishing the order he will impose on his writing, the Pilgrim pretty much ignores it in the actual portraits, which is an example of the Poet's gentle humor at the Pilgrim's expense. Baldwin states, "Chaucer's innovation in the *descripto* was the inorganic, disordered, and inconsequent piling up of details" (48). There is a clear parallel between Chaucer's deliberately disorganized descriptions of the pilgrims and the irregular ordering of their portraits.

The word "condicioun" (38) is actually a rather wide term meaning 'state of being' including both inner character, or nature, and conduct and external circumstances. It is variously rendered as: character and behavior, disposition, qualities, personal circumstances, state, socio-economic circumstance, and status and wealth within their social group. In opting for the word 'personality,' I have preferred the first three suggestions since the rest are covered by Chaucer's pledge to say "of what degree" each person is (40). In describing the personality and temperament of the pilgrims, Chaucer makes a great deal of use of the Theory of Humors which held that the human body was filled with four basic substances: black bile (earth), yellow bile (fire), phlegm (water), and blood (air). A surplus or imbalance of one fluid, determined by planetary influences at the time of birth, affected the personality, physical appearance, and health of a person. Humorism identified four basic human types: sanguine (blood), physically attractive, extrovert, courageous, joyful and amorous; choleric (yellow bile), easily angered, irascible, highly sexed; melancholic (black bile), introspective, somber, sleepless, irritable, lean but gluttonous; and phlegmatic (phlegm), cold, unemotional, introvert, disinterested in sex. In each case, the excess of one of the four humors determined a person's psychology and physical appearance. Even where Chaucer does not make explicit reference to a pilgrim's humor, this theory underpins most of the descriptions.

The phrase "whiche they weren" is usually rendered as "who they were" which is accurate but pretty meaningless. Since the portraits spend a lot of time describing the physical appearance of the pilgrims, I have opted for the wording "what they looked like" though the term more accurately refers to the essential qualities of each pilgrim as indicated by their physical characteristics. In describing the physical appearance, and particularly the face, Chaucer will draw on the theory of physiognomy (in the Middle Ages *fisnamy* or *visnomy*) which held that a person's outer appearance is a reflection of inner character, morality, and personality.

Finally, unambiguously, Chaucer says he will describe the pilgrims' clothes and accessories, "what array that they were inne" (41). Throughout the fourteenth century, Parliament issued a series of sumptuary laws (1309, 1336, 1337, and 1363) in an attempt to define the type of apparel and diet appropriate to each individual's status in society. The 1363 Statute denounced the disregard for the traditional hierarchy of estates as evidenced by people at all social levels using their greater disposable incomes to dress above their station, "apprentice boys dress like masters, masters like valets, valets like squires, squires like knights, to the great destruction of lords and commons." These attempts to use legislation reflects the concern of the nobility about the growing affluence of the urban and merchant classes who could afford to dress like their social superiors, and also concern about the rising aspirations of laborers who, after the Black Death caused a shortage of manual laborers, were able to charge more for their services and also showed a tendency to dress above their station.

The limitations imposed by the 1363 Statute Concerning Diet and Apparel are summarized below:

Lords with lands worth £1 000 annually and their families: no restrictions.

Knights with land worth 400 marks. ie £266 13s 4d annually and their families: may dress at their will, except they may wear no weasel fur, ermine or clothing of precious stones other than the jewels in women's hair.

Knights with lands worth 200 marks. ie. £133 6s 8d annually and their families: fabric worth no more than 6 marks ie £4 for the whole cloth: no cloth of gold, nor a cloak, mantle or gown lined with pure miniver, sleeves of ermine or any material embroidered with precious stones; women may not wear ermine or weasel-fur, or jewels except those worn in their hair.

Esquires with land worth £200 per year, and merchants with goods to the value of £1 000 and their families: fabric worth no more than 5 marks. ie £3 6s 8d for the whole cloth; they may wear cloth of silk and silver, or anything decorated with silver; women may wear miniver but not ermine or weasel-fur, or jewels except those worn in the hair.

Esquires, gentlemen with £100 per year, and merchants with goods to the value of £500 and their families: fabric worth no more than 4 1/2 marks, £3, for the whole cloth; no cloth of gold, silk, or silver, no embroidery, no precious stones or fur.

Yeoman and their families: fabric worth no more than 40s, ie £2 for the whole cloth, no jewels, no gold, silver, embroidery, enamelware or silk; no fur except lamb, rabbit, cat or fox; women not to wear a silk veil.

Servants and their families: fabric worth not more than 2 marks for the whole cloth; no gold, silver, embroidery, enamel or silk; women not to wear a veil worth more than 12d.

Carters, ploughmen, drivers of ploughs, oxherds, cowherds, swineherds, dairymaids and everyone else working on the land who does not have 40 shillings of goods: no cloth except blanket and russet at 12d per ell, belts of linen (rope). (Gilbert)

This Statute was repealed in the following year, and in 1378-9, a further attempt to introduce sumptuary legislation under Richard II also failed. In fact, sumptuary laws were seldom enforced in the fourteenth century and completely failed in holding back the tide of social flux and mobility because those with a growing disposable income continued to use "array" as a way of expressing their own view of themselves. Nevertheless, Chaucer knows that his readers would be aware of these laws and has them in mind when he describes the pilgrims.

This section ends with the rhetorical flourish of anaphora (the repeating of a word or sequence of words at the beginning of neighboring clauses):

To telle yow al the condicioun
Of ech of hem, so as it semed me,
And whiche they weren, and of what degree,
And eek in what array that they were inne;
And at a knight than wol I first biginne. (38-42)

The effect of the repetition is two-fold. Firstly, it reinforces the sense of the narrator being in firm control of his material and also of the importance of the categories of description (the very ones that the Pilgrim will largely ignore), and secondly it speeds the rhythm of these lines giving the reader a sense of the narrator's impatience to begin.

The decision to begin with the Knight is generally seen to be appropriate given his high status. (The Host also fixes things so that he ends up telling the first tale.) However, in doing so, the *Prologue* does not follow the structure of estates literature in which the ecclesiastical characters are presented first because they are seen as having higher status than lay characters. Thus John Gower's *The Voice of One Crying Out* states, "There are the cleric, the knight, and the peasant, three carrying on three different things. But I intend to write about the prelates first" (Norton Anthology). Some commentators see the Pilgrim's decision as an intentional misstep inserted by the Poet, a point which is particularly apposite if the Knight is intended to be understood as a landless knight fighting for money rather than as an idealized embodiment of Christian chivalry. Interpreted in this way, the error in the ordering of the portraits from the very outset justifies the Pilgrim's later apology for not having "set folk in hir degree" (746), and prepares us for the Poet's intention, which the BookRags author describes thus, *"The Canterbury Tales* are essentially a Chaucerian satire; the author sets out to deliberately upset the social order present at the time and proceeds to mock the faults innate in the characters."

In fact, in the descriptions of his fellow travelers, the Pilgrim will no more follow rigidly the categories outlined in these lines than he will follow the principle of social order which is normally adhered to by writers of estates satire. The phrase "so as it semed me" (39) establishes the subjective nature of the descriptions which will be limited by what the Pilgrim can observe for himself, what he can gather from what the travelers say about themselves, and (most importantly) what he can actually understand. In some ways, the portraits tell us as much about the personality of the narrator as they do about the pilgrim being described. By the time the Pilgrim confides that, "My wit is short, ye may wel understonde" (748), the reader will have had plenty of evidence of that. What these lines cannot tell us (since they are the words of the Pilgrim) is the comedy which the Poet will infuse into the Pilgrim's descriptions and the degree to which he will succeed in "encapsulating … [each] pilgrim, making him vivid and memorable … [and presenting] an inner reality, the reality of each pilgrim's character, frame of mind, place in society – the very realities which will dictate their choice and treatment of tales" (Howard 103).

Chapter Four: The Knight, The Squire and The Yeoman

Breaking with the normal pattern of Estates Satires, the portraits begin with two high-status representatives of the Second, Temporal, Estate followed by a very low-status representative of the Third Estate.

Lines 43-78: The Knight

[A knight] is obliged to be worthy. Therefore he may not ... be mixed up in misdeeds; on the contrary, he must seek prowess of arms in pure honor. But according to what people say nowadays, there are many who observe poorly that which they have covenanted. They often forget that which pertains to a brave man; they seek not their honor in France but rather stay at home and make war on their neighbors. They are unworthy of shield and lance... (John Gower *Vox clamantis* or *The Voice of One Crying Out* Norton Anthology)

Modern readers have a preconception about knights which derives more from Sir Walter Scott and Hollywood movies than it does from historical reality. Just because we tend to look at medieval chivalry through rose-tinted spectacles does not mean that Chaucer's contemporaries so did.

Knights were members of the noble class: the knightly caste was, in theory, closed to all who were not born into it. However, in practice:

villeins did indeed become knights in the twelfth century, and in the thirteenth the process was almost commonplace. The chief reason was the growing wealth of the merchant class ... At the other end of the economic scale, again despite all prohibitions to the contrary, many a poor soldier won knighthood through valor in the service of a lord ... Despite precepts, codes, and admonitions from the Church, the knight's life was normally lived on a lower plane than that embodied by the chivalric ideal. The reason was that the great majority of knights were, horse and armor aside, penniless ... The normal business of a knight was war, and often as a mercenary. (Gies and Gies 89-90)

Fighting could be very lucrative for a knight, even one who was not technically a mercenary. Sources of income began with payment from the knight's lord for his services (the days of feudal obligation were virtually over), and then there was money gained by capturing and ransoming important prisoners, booty taken from the defeated enemy towns and villages, and finally protection money paid by the enemy to buy off an attack. On the other hand, sometimes lords did not pay the wages they promised, if a knight was captured he might have to pay his own ransom, and one third of a knight's gains on campaign would be due to his lord (Prestwich 185). A soldier of fortune might echo the statement which the Knight's contemporary the Bascot de Mauléon made to Froissart in 1388, "I have at times been so miserably poor that I had not a horse to mount, at other times rich enough, just as good fortune befell me" (quoted in Prestwich 183).

When it comes to assessing the moral value of crusading, objectivity fails us, and we must acknowledge two radically different views of crusading knights in the mid-fourteenth century. Writing in 1907, Manly states that though chivalry was, by the time Chaucer wrote, a doomed system "the flame of devotion flared wider and higher and burned for a moment with unwonted intensity and purity' ("A Knight" 90), whilst in complete contrast Hopkins writes that, "The later middle ages saw a new kind of knight who was a professional adventurer, motivated by nothing higher than gain - a mercenary in fact. By the mid-fourteenth century there were large numbers of these men in Europe, with no place in society other than as soldiers of fortune."

It is generally believed that in this portrait Chaucer drew on the crusading experiences of the Scrope family of Yorkshire, "a family represented at all of the episodes described" in the Knight's portrait with the exception of his service in Tlemcen and Turkey (Phillips

282). Sir Richard Waldegrave, a Suffolk knight with whom Chaucer was personally acquainted, served with Peter I of Cyprus in Turkey (1361) and at Alexandria (1365), and in Prussia (1361) (Phillips 282-3).

General:
1. What are the five ideals of knightly behavior?
2. Chaucer lists the Knight's campaigns in a rather disorderly way. Arrange them chronologically. (You will need to do some research beyond the information in the edition we are using.)

Pilgrim:
3. The tone of this portrait is generally taken to be uncritical approval. Make a list of all of the words and phrases that suggest the Pilgrim's admiration for the Knight's life and values.

Poet:
4. Writer Terry Jones has suggested that the tone of this portrait is actually ironic and that the Poet very deliberately describes a medieval mercenary – literally a sword for hire. Can you find anything in the portrait on a first reading that would justify this conclusion?

In this portrait, perhaps more than any other, understanding of the Poet's meaning depends upon the interpretation of ambiguous denotations, connotations, nuances, and levels of meaning. The modernization below aims to be neutral.

> There was a Knight, an outstanding man,
> Who from the first moment that he began
> 45 To go on military expeditions loved cavalry warfare,
> Loyalty and honor, generosity and good conduct.
> He served admirably in his lord's campaigns
> And no man had ridden further than he
> Both in Christian and in Heathen lands,
> 50 And he was always honored for his qualities.
> He was at Alexandria when it was captured.
> He had often sat at the head of the table in the place of honor,
> Above knights from all other countries, when in Prussia.
> He had gone on raids in Lithuania and in Russia
> 55 No Christian man of his rank had done more.
> He was in Granada at the siege
> Of Algezir and had ridden in Benmarin.

42

He was at Ayas and Attalia
When they were taken; and in the Mediterranean
60 He had been part of many noble armies.
He had been in fifteen deadly battles
And had jousted three times as the champion of our faith in Tlemcen
In the lists, and always he had killed his opponent.
This same distinguished Knight had also been
65 Once with the Lord of Palatia
Fighting against another heathen in Turkey
And always he won an outstanding prize.
Although he was so eminent, he was also wise,
And, to speak of his bearing. he was as modest as a young lady:
70 He had never spoken rudely
In all of his life to anybody, no matter what his social class.
He was a true, perfect knight.
But to describe his apparel and accessories
His horses were good, but his clothes were not elaborate;
75 He wore a surcoat of simple fustian cloth
Spotted with rust from the chain mail of his habergeon,
For he had come straight from a military expedition
And set off at once to make his pilgrimage.

The traditional interpretation of the Knight sees Chaucer as describing a figure symbolic of the ideals of chivalry: a devout champion of the Church, a defender of the faith against the heathen, a protector of the weak, and a defender of justice. The BookRags author writes, "He is presented as the glorious, valiant and truthful representation of what a knight should be" (although it is only fair to add that in the very next paragraph the writer argues that the portrait is satirical), and Muriel Bowden argues that the Knight is a representative figure of those men "of great courage and rectitude who have lived as nearly as they could according to their religious and ethical beliefs, and who have been admired and loved by those with whom they have come into contact … Here is someone who is actually and metaphorically a *chevalier sans peur et sans reproche*" (*Guide* 20). This interpretation argues that the Poet intends the reader to understand the Knight as representing the ideal embodiment of militant Christianity in the same way that the Parson undoubtedly represents the ideal embodiment of clerical Christianity and the Ploughman the ideal of the laboring estate. A rather more nuanced view argues that the Poet describes the Knight as a representation of an already anachronistic ideal of militant Christianity, and a still more extreme view sees the portrait as an exposé of the corruption of the ideal of militant Christianity.

The traditional interpretation is exemplified by David Williams:

> The narrator's presentation of the Knight ... seems to correspond to the artistic principles he [Chaucer] has laid down. His description falls into three parts, as do, by and large, all the descriptions: his virtues, his behavior, and his physical appearance. His virtues are presented first and emphasized, for he is, within his limits, truly virtuous ... The Knight is specified as not only a good soldier but as a model of the reasonable man, combining in a proper harmony the male (*vir*) virtues (*virtus*) of courage and wisdom with the female virtues of mercy and prudence. Thus the Knight embodies balance. (Williams 31)

In contrast, Donald Howard argues that the portrait of the Knight is intended to be understood as conveying an image of the decline of chivalry in the context of "a disordered Christian society in a state of obsolescence, decline and uncertainty" (Howard 104). He writes:

> The Knight, of the lesser nobility, is an obsolescent hero, a 'knight of the Cross.' The battles in which he has participated stretch back forty years. The three lists in which he has engaged at Tramissene would have seemed old-fashioned in the 1380s, for proper wartime lists became less frequent as warfare and weaponry became more elaborate ... That he is meant to be viewed as an obsolescent figure is underscored by the portrait of his son the Squire. (Howard 90)

Terry Jones goes much further arguing that the Poet's description of the Knight "instead of conforming to a pattern of Christian chivalry, has more in common with the mercenaries who swarmed across Europe ... and who brought the concept of chivalry into disrepute and eventual disuse" (Jones 2). Jones believes that the modern reader's romantic idealization of knights owes more to writers like Thomas Mallory and later Victorians such as Alfred Lord Tennyson who described the knights of Camelot centuries after knighthood itself had passed into history. Jones claims that it is clear from the study of contemporary sources that in Chaucer's day the decline of the feudal relationship between knight and lord and "the growth of the mercenary soldier represented ... the general erosion of social values" (Jones 13) and specifically "the reduction of a social relationship to a callous money relationship" (Jones 12) were common themes. He argues that "the poor appearance of the Knight ... his dingy tunic and lack of armorial bearing" (Jones 27) would have identified him for Chaucer's readers as a poor knight, that is, one with no (or very small) landholdings who financed himself by hiring out as a mercenary and by the plunder gained in wars. The 'M' brand shown on the Knight's horse in the Ellesmere Manuscript may stand, Jones believes, for 'Milano' which would identify the Knight as a member of the infamous White Company, a vicious mercenary force operating in Italy under the command of Sir John Hawkwood.

As noted earlier, Jones' book produced a backlash of critical reaction; Morgan's "The Worthiness of Chaucer's Worthy Knight" (2009) may stand as an example of the case for the defense. Brewer, writing in 2000, dismisses revisionist critics who find irony in the Knight's portrait commenting rather archly, "they do not appreciate the nature of chivalry. They judge it in terms of modern pacifist, humanitarian, post-Christian ideals, which could not be shared by Chaucer" (Brown ed. 67). Thus, the very first portrait throws the modern reader into a hotly contested debate. Let us see if we can shed some light.

Where was the Knight?

It seems logical to begin with history since there we can hope for some objectivity. The Knight is a Crusader because all of the campaigns with which he is associated are against the infidel and most (if not all) had the specific sanction of the Church. However, as early as 1971 (a decade before the publication of Terry Jones' revisionist theory) John Halverson stated in a note to the text that all of the Knight's campaigns were "far-flung sites of various, often private, wars or campaigns ... under various leaders. The Knight is probably a mercenary soldier" (5).

Two of the three superlatives in the portrait relate to the number of campaigns the Knight has fought and the distance which he has travelled to do so:

> And therto hadde he riden, no man ferre,
> As wel in cristendom as in hethenesse, (48-9)

No Cristen man so ofte of his degree. (55)

Sixteen of the thirty-five lines of the portrait are devoted to a list (which is in neither chronological nor geographical order) of the Knight's campaigns; ten specific places or regions are mentioned where he has campaigned, though it is implied that the list is not complete, "At many a noble armee hadde he be" (60). These details mean that he must be in his early to mid-sixties, but there is little dispute that the length of his career (1342-75) and the sheer number of campaigns in which he has been involved strains credibility. However, whether the Poet intends the reader to regard the Knight as a representative symbolic figure or to read these superlatives as hyperbole undercut by irony (like so many superlatives in the other portraits) is unclear.

Much has been made of the fact that the Knight has fought almost everywhere except in France where, for the entire period of his career, his King (first Edward III and then Richard II) was involved in the Hundred Years' War. He appears not to have been present at the English victories of Crecy (1346), Calais (1347), Poitiers (1356) and Najera (1367). (Pollard argues that the Knight's campaigns not only fall into chronological groups, but also that the gaps between these groups allow the Knight to have taken "his fair share of fighting" in the King's wars in France [32], but this looks like special pleading.) The Knight has certainly been in almost continuous service, which the Pilgrim presents as a guarantee of his piety, but this detail also cuts both ways. The Poet might have expected his reader to have in mind the distinction made by Urban who writes that, "One rule of thumb is: *vassals go home for the holidays, mercenaries fight on*" (emphasis in original 61) and by Gravett, "landless knights had less call on their time at home, and were often willing to stay in the field" (85).

As Manly points out, all of the Knight's campaigns "lay on the borderland between the Christian world and heathendom … [and] fell into three groups: those against the Moors in Spain and northwest Africa, those against the Saracens in Egypt and Asia Minor, and those against Slavic heathendom in Prussia and Lithuania" (*New Light* 255). However, given that Chaucer wrote *The Canterbury Tales* between 1387 and 1400, and that the Seventh Crusade, led by Saint Louis IX of France, ended in his defeat and capture in 1250, and that Acre, the last Crusader stronghold, fell in 1291, it is certainly true to say that the golden age of crusading was well and truly past.

1342-1344: At the Siege of Algezir (Algeciras), fighting for Alfonso of Spain

By the mid-fourteenth century, the Moors in Spain had been pushed back to the southern province of Granada. The town of Algeciras was besieged by King Alphonso XI of Castile for two years before it fell in March, 1344. The gain was temporary, however, since in 1368 the Moors repossessed the town which was destroyed and abandoned on the orders of Muhammed V of Granada.

There is clearly nothing dishonorable in the Knight being associated with the siege of Algezir. He was in good company since William Montacute, Earl of Salisbury, ambassador of King Edward III to the court of Castile, and Henry, Earl of Derby, also fought in the siege along with a significant number of English knights. Nevertheless, by the time Chaucer was writing, what had been achieved in 1344 had already been lost.

1345-1360: Fighting in N. Africa and Turkey for a Turk and in Belmarie and at Tramissene for the Moors

These are the most difficult of the Knight's campaigns to identify and date. "Belmarie" is tentatively identified with Balmarie (Benmarin) in Morocco. Balmarie and Tramissene (Tremezen or Tlencen) in Algeria were Moorish kingdoms in North West Africa constantly at war with each in the early fourteenth century. Tramissene came under domination of Balmarie in 1335 which left the King of Morocco free to attack Spain. However, this date is too early for the Knight to have been involved. Bowden cites the victory of Alphonso XI over the king of "Benermeren" in 1341, but this campaign was in Granada not Africa (*Commentary* 53). In 1366, Pedro the Cruel, King of Castile, faced an invasion led by his bastard brother Henry of Trastamara. Froissart writes:

> Don Pedro did not hesitate following this advice, but sent to the king of Portugal, who was his cousin-german, from whom he had a large body of men; and also to the kings of Granada, Bellemarine, and Tramesames; with whom he entered into alliances, and engaged to support them in their kingdoms, and not to make war against them for the space of thirty years. These kings, on their part, sent him upwards

47

of twenty thousand Moors, to assist him in his war. (*Chronicles*)

Again, the fighting was in Spain. However, this at the least proves that Christians fighting alongside Moslems was not uncommon.

Of course, the whole point of crusading knights was to fight the infidel, but fighting for one Moslem against another Moslem, which is what the Knight appears to have been doing in Balmarie and Tramissene, could be morally and religiously justified on the basis that 'the enemy of my enemy is my friend.' Gies and Gies point out that, "Even The Cid, epic hero of Spanish chivalry, spent considerable time in the employ of the infidels, leading expeditions for the Moorish king of Saragossa against Christian princes. For poor knights dependent on their swords for their livelihood, one employer was as good as another" (92).

The Knight has "foughten for our faith at Tramissene / In listes thries, and ay slain his foo," that is, he has fought three times as the champion of Christianity in formal single combat with Moslem champions and each time he has killed his opponent (62-3). Editors are largely silent on the lists at Tramissene, and it seems possible that they are pure invention by Chaucer, although given the accuracy of the rest of the information this seems odd. Bowden quotes Froissart's account of an expedition in 1390 against "Bellemarine" and "Tramesainnes" in which the Saracens challenged "ten Christian nobles to combat bodily in the lists an equal number of Saracens" (*Commentary* 53). This supports Pollard's idea that the Knight was stepping forward as the champion of a Christian army to meet the champion of a Moslem army (36).

Against this interpretation, it may be argued that for the Knight to have done this three times is improbable. Jones states that the only Christian knights in "Belmarye" at this period were "mercenaries *in the pay* of the Moors" (emphasis in original 65), and that "the only Christian involvement [in "Tramyssene"] was that of the mercenaries habitually employed by either side [the Marinids and the Zayanids]" (79). It appears that once again the knight was in Tramissene fighting for one Moslem lord against another Moslem. However, there is one other possibility: given that within the fiction of the frame story the Pilgrim must have obtained all of his information from the Knight, it is just possible that the Knight talks of fighting for the Christian faith in a Moslem land as cover for the fact that he was fighting on the side of Moslems. In other words, the lists at Tramissene may indeed be an invention, but an invention which the Poet intends his readers to attribute to the Knight.

The Emir of Palatie (modern Balat) was a Seljuk Turk in almost constant conflict with the emirate of Menteshe. In 1365 the Emir signed a treaty with Peter of Cyprus, but it "was in no way a religious pact" (Jones 88). Here, beyond question, the Knight was fighting for an infidel against an infidel. Bowden's attempt to argue that Chaucer's contemporaries "would think it fitting that his own hero should give knightly service to Palatye" during a period of concord between Moslems and Christians, is unconvincing (*Commentary* 58).

1361: Satalye, fighting for Peter of Cyprus

From his accession in 1360, Pierre de Lusignan, King of Cyprus, was concerned about Moslem raids from Asia Minor where the Christian kingdom of Armenia had been reduced to a few fortified towns on the coast. In 1361, Peter sent reinforcements to assist the town of Courico which was being attacked by the Turks. He then assembled all the knights in his service and collected a fleet of one hundred ships in the port of Famagusta for an attack on Adalia (Attalia, Antalya, or Satalie), capital of the sanjak of Tekke-ili and one of the strongest fortresses of the Turks in Asia Minor. Bowden comments of Peter's motivation, "[he] may have had his genuine crusading spirit mixed with a touch of human greed when he set out to regain the wealthy city [of Satalye]" (*Commentary* 55).

The Cypriot forces, which included a contingent of English knights under the Earl of Hereford, disembarked close to Adalia on the 23rd August, and at dawn on the 24th August took by assault the fortress deemed to be impregnable. Hearing of this success, the emir of Lajazzo and the lord of Candalor sent embassies to King Pierre offering to pay an annual tribute and to acknowledge his possession of Courico and Adalia; Peter accepted. He stayed in Antalya until 8th September 1361. An attempt by the Turkish sultan Tacca to retake Adalia was decisively repulsed in the spring of 1362 leading to the additional capture of the Moslem city of Myra.

It was his success in this military expedition, together with his knowledge that the towns he had conquered could not be held against the full might of the Turks, which encouraged Peter to propose a more general crusade against the Moslems in the Middle East. So, on the one hand, this campaign is probably the most successful in which the Knight participated, but, on the other, it was the prologue to a further campaign which ended disastrously.

1365: Alexandria, fighting for Peter of Cyprus

Between 1362 and 1365, Peter I made plans for a Crusade against Alexandria to end its dominance as a port in the Eastern Mediterranean in the hope that Cyprus would then benefit from the redirected trade. He visited the courts of Europe to gather support and financial aid, visiting Pope Urban V in Avignon and also coming to England in November, 1363, where he stayed six weeks during which time Chaucer presumably met him. Despite the support of Urban V, Peter failed to persuade any European monarchs to take part in a crusade, though nobles from England and France did join him. He also employed mercenaries from the infamous White Company who were attracted by the prospect of plunder and the papal promise of indulgences for their sins (Phillips 283-4).

In October 1365, having learned of a planned Egyptian attack against Cyprus, Peter set sail with a fleet of 165 ships reaching Alexandria on October 9th. Alexandria fell to the crusaders on the following day in what was a remarkable feat of arms. In the next two days, Peter's army was responsible for the horrible sack and massacre of the city including its Christian quarter. The French poet Guillaume de Machaut termed it "a massacre unequalled since the time of Pharaoh" (*La Prise d'Alexandrie*). Peter had intended to advance towards Cairo, but seeing the strength of the forces ranged against them the European knights refused to follow him. Philip of Mézières (c.1327-1405) in his *Account of the Alexandria Crusade* reported the Papal Legate as addressing Peter's troops thus, "He showed clearly how God's honour, the good of Christendom, and the acquisition of the city of Jerusalem hung on the retention of Alexandria ... but by the Devil's work, the majority stood in his way ... they had no trust in God" (quoted in Phillips 285).

Peter permanently abandoned Alexandria on October 12th. Andrea Hopkins in her book *Knights* comments on the consequences of Peter's use of mercenaries:

> One of the greatest scandals of the age resulted from the recruitment of such men in the "Crusade" against the city of Alexandria in 1365. The mercenaries sacked the city, slaughtered thousands of its inhabitants (including many

Christians) stole as much loot as they could carry and then went home, with the result that the city fell back into the hands of 'the Infidel' within days of its conquest.

Peter's troops returned home with seventy shiploads of booty, but nothing else was gained; in fact, Moslem hostility to the West was increased with the Sultan of Egypt initiating reprisals against Christian merchants in Syria and Egypt. Finally, after failing to raise support among the European monarchs for a renewed crusade, Pope Urban V advised Peter to make peace with the Sultan. In the technical sense, Peter's attack on Alexandria is a Crusade since a Crusade had been called for by Urban V, but it was motivated largely by economic interests and not by religion. Bowden concludes that his experience at Alexandria taught Peter that "most contemporary crusaders were actuated solely by greed" (*Commentary* 57-8).

By the time Chaucer's pilgrims set out for Canterbury, Peter of Cyprus was dead. His increasing irrationality and violent temper led three of his own knights to murder him in his bed, "The murderers smashed his skull, cut his throat open, dressed him in a tramp's clothes, and left the corpse in the palace hall" (Phillips 285).

It certainly seems that having been at "Alisaundre … when it was wonne" (51) reflects no particular credit on the Knight, yet the Poet places it as the first, keynote, detail of his campaigns.

1366: Lyeys (Lyas, Ayas in modern Turkey), fighting for Peter of Cyprus

Following the withdrawal from Alexandria, most of the English knights in Peter's army seem to have returned home, but this Knight appears to have stayed on and been present at the capture of Lyeys in Armenia, in October, 1367. Pollard comments, "The town was 'won' easily enough, but the citadel resisted all the efforts of Pierre's small force, and after burning the town he retired" (36).

1368-75: Fighting in Pruce (Prussia) and Lettow (Lithuania) and raiding into Ruce with the Teutonic Knights

The Northern Crusades were undertaken against the pagan states of Northern Europe around the southern and eastern shores of the Baltic Sea including Prussia and Lithuania. The Teutonic Knights completed their conquest and conversion of Prussia by the 1280s, but would continue to be engaged for a further century in a struggle with the Grand Duchy of Lithuania then the last stronghold of paganism in

Europe. Phillips reports that, "The Teutonic Knights, based at Marienberg in Poland, had responsibility for the conversion and defeat of these pagans, although the morality of using warfare as a means of conversion provoked fierce debate in ecclesiastical circles" (286).

The Knights launched annual attacks against the Lithuanians called 'reisen' (journeys); the fighting was particularly brutal reducing much of the land to uninhabited wilderness. Austrian poet Peter Suchenwirt (c.1320-1395) provides a contemporary account of the treatment he witnessed of pagan Lithuanians by the Teutonic Knights:

> Women and children were taken captive; What a jolly medley could be seen: Many a woman could be seen, Two children tied to her body, One behind and one in front; On a horse without spurs Barefoot had they ridden here; The heathens were made to suffer: Many were captured and in every case, Were their hands tied together They were led off, all tied up - Just like hunting dogs. (Quoted in Saity)

The use of the word "jolly" here suggests that those who went on these raids (including our Knight) did not have modern moral sensibilities. The Teutonic Knights ultimately failed to subdue pagan Lithuania.

Russia was, of course, a Christian country, but one which followed the Orthodox Church. In 1378, Pope Urban authorized a crusade against these schismatics.

Conclusion:

The Knight appears to be connected with campaigns whose gains, if any, had been lost by the mid-1380s when the *Tales* were begun. In the case of Alexandria, we can go further and say that he is associated with a Pyrrhic victory ultimately very costly to the Christian cause. Although we can never know Chaucer's intention or the interpretation which contemporary audiences would have placed on the Knight's portrait, these facts would have been better known to Chaucer's readers/listeners than they are to the modern reader.

The Portrait

However the reader comes to interpret the portrait of the Knight, all will agree that this is a description of a type rather than of an individual. Not one detail of his physical characteristics ("whiche they weren" [40]) is given. As Baldwin puts it, "The career projects the person, and we do not know *the* knight directly, but only *a* knight through the composite of the battlestained campaigner and the Christian military-apologist" (emphasis in original 44-5).

The description of the Knight opens with his "condicioun." The first adjective is "worthy" a word which signifies value; however, value can be judged either in terms of moral qualities or of worldly goods, and as a result the word is ambiguous. Its precise meaning depends upon its context. The Old English word *weorth* meant 'of a specified value,' giving the Middle English meaning 'having monetary or material value.' However, the word also meant 'estimable' (Merriam-Webster). Jones argues that Chaucer "almost invariably used it to mean 'well-to-do' or 'of high social standing,'" and that he "applied it most frequently to characters he was satirizing" (32). Similarly, the BookRags author notes that, "Chaucer uses the word 'worthy' five times in the Knight's prologue, each time it becomes more soured with sarcasm and ridicule." In contrast, Morgan quotes the oldest meaning of "worth" recorded in the Oxford English Dictionary, "distinguished by good qualities; entitled to honour or respect on this account; estimable." Critics who understand the five uses of the word in this sense must acknowledge that these are the only times that the word is used in the *Prologue* without ironic intention.

The Poet's irony usually works by following an apparent praise-line with a disparate detail that undermines its positivity, so it is appropriate to ask what detail immediately follows each use of the word "worthy." Immediately after the Pilgrim's first use of the word, we are told that "fro the time that he first bigan / To riden out, he loved chivalrie" (44-5). These lines encapsulate the whole debate over the Poet's intentions since the term "chivalrie" might indicate either fascination with the theory and practice of cavalry warfare, or devotion to the ideals of knighthood, or both. If we take it to mean the former, then the word "worthy" must be balanced against this statement by Count Konrad of Landau, leader of the mercenary Ventura Company in Italy, who wrote of campaigning, "It is our custom to rob, sack and kill he who resists. Our income is derived from the funds of the provinces we invade: he who values his life pays for peace and quiet from us a very steep price" (quoted in

Prestwich 124). Clearly Count Konrad is estimating worth in monetary terms.

The second use of the word, "Ful worthy was he in his lordes werre" (47) is also ambiguous. Since the Knight has clearly served a number of lords throughout Europe, he has not served his feudal lord. Of course, his ultimate feudal lord is the King of England who he has not served because he has taken no part in the French wars. On the other hand, the line can be taken to mean that he loyally follows his commander, whoever that may be. Even more positively, the line could be taken to imply that he has served God throughout his life. This is followed by the implausible superlative that no man has ridden further that the Knight in the service of God on which Kirkham and Allen comment, "a single person can hardly have been at all of [these campaigns]" (17). As we have already seen, this hyperbole too can either be interpreted positively or negatively.

The third example, "worthiness" (50), is immediately followed by the detail that the Knight was at Alexandria when it was captured. Given what we know of this campaign, this detail seems unambiguously negative. The fourth "worthy" (64) is followed by the details of the Knight's service for Moslems against Moslems which must be seen as somewhat negative despite the various ways in which it was defended at the time. The final use of "worthy" (68) is followed by the detail that the Knight has maiden-like humility and does not use profanity, both of which are very admirable but rather odd as an illustration of "worthiness." On balance, this analysis of the text appears to support the conclusion of the BookRags author.

The portrait has thirty-six lines: twenty-one are devoted to the Knight's military campaigns (lines 47-67), four to describing his dress (lines 73-76), four to his non-military conduct as a knight (lines 70-1 and 77-8), and six to his personality or temperament (lines 43-6, 68 and 72). What is highly significant is what is not included in the portrait. Firstly, as Brewer (who dismisses any ironical intention in the portrait) concedes, "Chaucer makes no mention of what may be called the 'administrative' side of a knight's duty, the maintenance of justice within the realm and defence against enemies" (Brown ed. 63). Secondly, for a description which is replete with geographical names (thirteen in all), it is surprising that we are given no indication of where the Knight is from – information which we are given for the Prioress, Clerk, Shipman, Wife, Reeve, and Pardoner. This detail would help us to locate the Knight's position on the feudal pyramid since, "Every village had a lord … [and a] resident lord was usually a petty knight who held only one manor" (Gies and Gies 141), and "everyone who possessed land worth £40 a year is supposed to become a knight" (Prestwich 24). The unmistakable implication of this omission is that this Knight holds no manor(s). Whether this Knight is landless because he was originally a villein knighted in the field or because he is the younger son of a nobleman who received no inheritance, it would follow that he is totally dependent on what he can earn in war either in fees for his services, or in booty and ransom. This was very common and not, in itself, dishonorable: the difference between a loyal knight and a mercenary was more apparent than real.

Prestwich lists the chivalric ideals as: "*largesse*, or generosity; *courtoiseie*, or courtesy; *prouesse*, or prowess; *loyauté*, or loyalty" (33). The Pilgrim notes the Knight's qualities as, "Trouthe and honour, fredom and curteisie" (46). Except that the order is different, they are the same, although as Wetherbee points out "Chaucer … says nothing of the traditional knightly obligation to keep the peace and defend the weak" (23). The list of personal qualities is expanded upon later:

> And though that he were worthy, he was wys,
> And of his port as meeke as is a maide.
> He nevere yet no vileynie ne saide,
> In al his lif, unto no maner wight.
> He was a verray, parfit gentil knight. (68-72)

These details of his good manners significantly refer to the Knight's chivalric deportment when not at war; they contain the only simile or metaphor in the entire portrait comparing the Knight to a "mayde" (69). He is a modest man who never uses oaths or foul language - notice the strong quadruple negative in the quotation above which certainly adds emphasis. However, it also reminds us that the Knight is being praised solely by using negatives which may be regarded as somewhat less of a glowing endorsement than we would expect. In contrast, the idealized portrait of the Parson has a balance of negatives and positives.

The most positive phrases used in the portrait are those which describe the honor which the Knight wins in battle. The first example concerns his participation in the Northern Crusades:

> Ful ofte time he hadde the bord bigonne
> Aboven alle nacions in Pruce; (52-3)

The Table of Honor, or Ehrentisch, was a feast usually held at Königsberg, at which the Teutonic Knights awarded to those so elevated badges which read, "Honor conquers all." Phillips comments, "Such a highly esteemed aware reflected immense prestige on the recipient and was borne with great pride at public events back home ... Such occasions added greatly to the allure of the Reisen" (288). For the Knight so frequently to have been given the place of honor at the table, above knights from other nations, is certainly impressive.

The second example records that whilst in the service of the Moslem Lord of Palatia, "everemoore he hadde a sovereyn prys" (67). This is frequently explained as his having won some abstract honor: a great reputation, the prize of fame, or high esteem. But if the words actually mean what they appear to mean, then the Knight invariably won a 'kingly' reward from his employer or got the biggest share of the loot, which is not abstract at all. The phrase "sovereyn prys" might even indicate the Knight's pride in taking the prize due to, or fit for, the king.

The most negative phrase used to describe the Knight's campaigning relates to campaigning in Lithuania:

> In Lettow hadde he reysed and in Ruce, (54)

The terms "reysed" is variously rendered as raids, seasonal campaigns, or the neutral military expeditions, but it seems to refer to the annual 'reisen' made by the Teutonic Knights against the pagans which, we have already seen, were notoriously brutal. Mann aptly summarizes the Knight's rôle as described in the portrait as being "merely to fight, win, and move on" (quoted by Calabrese in Lambdin and Lambdin 10). For the Knight, campaigning appears to be an end in itself.

The poor state of the Knight's clothes is traditionally interpreted to indicate his pious anxiety to fulfill his religious duty of pilgrimage as soon as he returns from campaign, even before he has had a chance to change his clothes. This would certainly make him virtually unique amongst the pilgrims since almost all of the others (the Reeve, Clerk, Wife of Bath and Man of Law are exceptions) are wearing their very best clothes to make a positive statement about their status, or about the status to which they aspire. At least the

Knight's dress means that he is in no danger of infringing sumptuary laws:

> He was a verray, parfit gentil knight.
> But, for to tellen yow of his array,
> His hors were goode; but he was nat gay.
> Of fustian he wered a gipon
> Al bismotered with his habergeon,
> For he was late ycome from his viage,
> And wente for to doon his pilgrimage. (72-8)

Once again, notice how the praise-line (which is the third and last superlative in the portrait) is immediately followed by details which, to say the least, tend to qualify the praise. In this case, the Poet signposts the incongruity by using the qualifier "But," a word frequently used at the beginning of lines near the end of a portrait to signal the introduction of negative details which will cause the reader completely to re-evaluate the character being described. (Look at other examples of this structural device in the portraits of: the Merchant, line 286; the Cook, line 387; the Summoner, line 661; and the Pardoner, line 703.)

Bowden sees no qualification implied in the details of the Knight's dress. On the contrary, she stresses that the Knight avoids the excesses of medieval homilists such as the Parson who denounces pride as shown in "in outrageous array of clothing" and "the sinful costlewe array of clothinge" ("The Parson's Tale"). The Knight wears a gypon of "fustian," a course wollen cloth, which Bowden takes to show "the honourable stains of long-service" (*Commentary* 51).

That the reader does not immediately suspect naïveté in the justification of the Knight's dress offered by the Pilgrim is explained by the fact that the reader's ear has not yet become sensitized to the Poet's irony. Imagine if this portrait had come towards the end of the *Prologue*. Would we believe this explanation after understanding how the Merchant's fine clothes hide his near-bankruptcy, or that the Prioress' wimple actually accentuates her sex-appeal? However, when we re-read the Knight's portrait having understood the way in which the Poet uses the Pilgrim-narrator, we must at least suspect that, as so often, the Pilgrim accepts the Knight at the Knight's own valuation of himself and so repeats a self-justification which the Poet expects the perceptive reader to view with some skepticism. Jones concludes, "He has no livery, no coat-of-arms, no shield, no belt and only a miniscule retinue. He has no name, no family, no manor house, no lands" (122).

The illustration of the Knight in the Ellesmere Manuscript makes him look dignified and well dressed. It is one of the least accurate of the Ellesmere illustrations – perhaps the artist drew his own conception of a knight rather than following the Pilgrim's description of this Knight. The Poet appears to offer a contrast between the quality of the Knight's horses and the state of his dress. However, given the crucial rôle of horses in chivalry, what is significant is how little is said of his horses. In the *Prologue*, the Poet specifies the mounts of five pilgrims: the Monk rides a palfrey, the Shipman a rouncy, the Wife of Bath an ambler, the Ploughman a mare, and the Reeve a stot. One would expect an idealized knight to ride a destrier, the elite war-horse of the fourteenth century, or at least a courser. The Poet goes against all literary precedent in showing the Knight in soiled clothes: only villainous knights or righteous knights in disguise were so described:

> Cleanliness is central to the interpretation of Chaucer's costume rhetoric in the Knight's portrait, for on the spiritual level his 'bismotered' condition announces his lack of perfection, and on the literal level illustrates his failure to meet the social demands of ideal noble dress ... Chaucer has given us a knight whose armor is improperly cleaned or polished, being either rusty or oily, and such armor represents reality instead of a romantic depiction of a knight's life. (*Chaucer's Pilgrims and Their Clothing*)

That the Poet intends the stained gipon to be symbolic is suggested both by the fact that no mention is made of that garment bearing any heraldic device or family coat of arms, which would serve to link the Knight to the nobility, and by the forceful verb "bismothered" which is only weakly rendered by the word 'stained' (76). The following is pure speculation (by which I mean that I am not aware than any other critic has ever suggested it): if the "gipon" represents the cultural ideals of knighthood and the chain mail "habergeon" the military component (not, on the face of it, a particularly strained reading), then the rust-soiled gipon is symbolic of how the ideals of chivalry are, inevitably, compromised by the harsh realities of warfare.

Certainly, that is not an idea which would have been alien to Chaucer's time.

To sum up, Gravett writes, "[E]ven if not technically a mercenary, Chaucer's dowdy knight is a far tougher character than a first reading would imply, and almost certainly, a contracted knight" (130). He is not a knight out of the tales of Courtly Love but an actual knight of his time, a man whose chivalric ideals are inevitably compromised by the reality of medieval warfare. The Knight may not be a mercenary in the technical sense of the term, but he is not the "verray, parfit gentil knight" of the Pilgrim either (72).

The traditional view is that the first portrait sets the moral 'gold standard' by which the other pilgrims are judged. However, it is hard to disagree with the BookRags author that, "Chaucer's dismantling of the Knight's character sets the tone for the [remaining portraits and] Chaucer's unraveling of their [the pilgrims'] moral facades and noble status."

Lines 79-100: The Squire

> One part of the knightly estate seeks after woman's love ...
> if a knight chooses a woman's love for himself, then he will
> pay for it more dearly ... He will give up so many good
> things for it – his body, his soul, his property, everything
> that Nature or God has imparted to him. (John Gower *Vox*
> *clamantis* or *The Voice of One Crying Out*
> quoted in Miller 199-200)

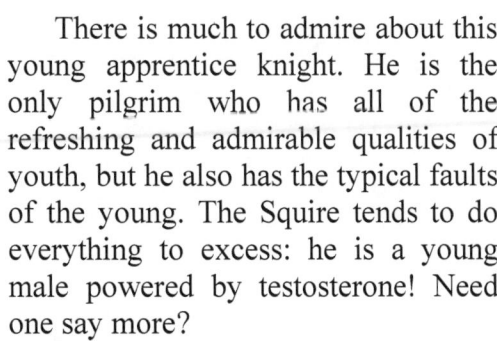

There is much to admire about this young apprentice knight. He is the only pilgrim who has all of the refreshing and admirable qualities of youth, but he also has the typical faults of the young. The Squire tends to do everything to excess: he is a young male powered by testosterone! Need one say more?

The Ellesmere illustration depicts him riding a spirited horse.

Pilgrim:

1. What entirely appropriate skills and achievements suggest that the Squire will eventually make an outstanding knight?

2. What features of the Squire's clothing makes him stand out in pleasant contrast to the rather drab appearance of some of the other pilgrims (including his father).

Poet:

3. The Squire's meticulous attention to personal grooming and his desire to be in the latest fashion is gently mocked by the Poet. How?

4. What evidence is given that the Squire is motivated in almost everything he does by the values of Courtly Love? Explain the implicit criticism which the Poet intends the reader to understand.

	With him there was his son, a young Squire,
80	A lover and a lively apprentice knight,
	With his hair curled as if he'd used curling tongs.
	He was twenty years of age, I guess.
	Of stature he was of average height,
	And wonderfully agile, and of great strength.
85	And he had been once on campaign
	In Flanders, in Artois, and Picardy,
	And conducted himself well, in such a little space of time,
	Hoping to win his lady's favor.
	His clothes were embroidered like a meadow
90	All full of fresh flowers, white and red.
	Singing he was, or playing the flute, all day long;
	He was as fresh as the month of May.
	His gown was short, with long, wide sleeves.
	On his horse, he had an excellent seat and was a skillful rider.
95	He knew how to compose songs and write beautiful verses,
	Joust and also dance, and vividly imagine and write.
	He loved so passionately that at night
	He slept no more than does a nightingale.
	Courteous he was, humble, and willing to serve,
100	And carved his father's meat at the table.

The Squire appears to embody the colors, youthful vitality and life force of the spring itself, and as such he is not only a contrast with his father but also "many of the more worn and cynical pilgrims whose descriptions follow"(Kirkham and Allen 21). The alliteration of short, hard consonant sounds is used to suggest the Squire's energy:

> A lovyere and a lusty bacheler
> With lokkes crulle as they were leyd in presse. (80-1)

and again:

> Al ful of fresshe floures ... (90)

Another device to convey the young man's animation is the use of the conjunction "and." The word occurs eight times in the portrait, six times connecting skills and qualities (lover and lusty apprentice, agile and strong, sits and rides well, writes music and verse, jousts and dances, conceives and writes) and twice connecting adjectives (white and red, long and wide). The effect of a multitude of details all coming at once is to impress upon us how vital and multi-talented this young man is. A similar effect is achieved by the repetition of active verbs in the last seven lines of the portrait: eight strong verbs are crowded into these lines suggesting almost frenetic activity, "[He could] songes make and wel endite, / Juste and eek daunce, and weel purtreye and write. / ... he lovede ... / And carf biforn his fader at the table" (94-100). Some commentators suspect a comic sexual double entendre in the line, "Wel koude he sitte on hors and faire ride" (94), but this may being going too far. What each of these details does is to humorously associate the Squire with animal sexual energy without actually going into the physical aspects of sexual intercourse, such as the pregnancies which result from the Friar's seduction of young women (see lines 212-3).

However the reader finally interprets it, the portrait of the Knight undoubtedly stresses the military aspects of chivalry whereas that of the Squire represents the cultural aspects which have come to be defined by the term Courtly Love ("Late-medieval code that prescribed the highly conventionalized behavior and emotions of aristocratic ladies and their lovers. It was the theme of an extensive literature that began with late 11th-century troubadour poetry in France and swiftly pervaded Europe. The courtly lover, who saw himself as enslaved by passion but fired by respect, faithfully served and worshiped his lady-saint. Courtly love was invariably adulterous, largely because upper-class marriage at the time was usually the result of economic interest or the seal of a power alliance." [Mirriam-Webster *Concise Encyclopedia*]). Howard, however, suggests that the two portraits are deliberately complementary having the same tone and intention:

> That [the Knight] … is meant to be viewed as an obsolescent figure is underscored by the portrait of his son the Squire. While the father is a warrior for old causes, the son exemplifies the fads of courtly life … The Squire must not be thought foppish or degenerate; but the knighthood and chivalry to which he has been bred is shown in decline."
> (Howard 90-91).

In contrast to the portrait of the Knight, very few details are given of the Squire's campaigns. We learn only that:

> … he hadde been somtime in chivachie
> In Flaundres, in Artois, and Picardie,
> And born him weel, as of so litel space,
> In hope to stonden in his lady grace. (85-88)

Notice that the Poet draws attention to the very limited nature of his actual military experience by the phrase "of so litel space." Unlike his father, whose motivation is, at least ostensibly, to win favor in the eyes of the Lord, the Squire follows the values of Courtly Love poetry by going into battle to win his lady's regard. This is also his motivation for taking part in jousts since they were a way of displaying courage. The tournaments of the fourteenth century were conducted with blunted weapons, and that the whole idea was not to kill one's opponent:

> And much with ladies 'twill advance
> Thy suit, if well thou break'st a lance,
> (Romance of the Rose quoted in Bowden Commentary 76)

Lances were designed to splinter when they came into contact with the opponent's shield. Of course, jousting was still very dangerous, and accidents did happen: in 1382, William Montague, Earl of Salisbury, killed his own son in a tournament.

The nature of the Squire's only campaign is, however, significant. William Urban identifies it as the campaign of Henry Despenser, Bishop of Norwich, who, in the name of Pope Clement, raised an army composed of mercenaries and volunteers which landed in April 1383 at Calais intending to march through France to Avignon to depose the rival Pope Urban. That plan being abandoned, however, Despenser decided to use his army to invade Flanders despite the fact that Flanders also supported Pope Clement. Thus "a questionable crusade [shifted easily] to a questionable act of English policy ... The Westminster Chronicle denounced the whole affair as infamous and an 'everlasting humiliation to Englishmen'" (66). Howard makes the same point, "As a fledgling warrior he has 'borne him well' on one campaign, the disreputable 'crusade' waged in 1382-1383 against the French in Flanders, a scandal, as it actually was, on which unruly captains plundered the land" (91). Once again, a praise-line, "In hope to stonden in his lady grace" is juxtaposed with a detail which ironically undercuts it. This is how the Poet's irony works. Bowden, who is firm in concluding that the Knight's many campaigns are all officially sanctioned crusades (*Guide* 21), concludes that "Chaucer could never have depicted a 'parfit gentil knyght' as having a share in the so-called 'crusade in Flanders,' for that expedition was backed entirely by political and commercial interests, not by any pious zeal," though she finds the young man's desire to "show his current lady his prowess in battle" to be "an instant and valid excuse" for his presence on this campaign (*Guide* 43), a conclusion with which it is hard to agree.

The Squire is expensively dressed for the manor hall whilst his father wears at least some of the same clothes he wears on campaign. According to the Sumptuary Statute of 1363, esquires worth over one hundred but less than two hundred pounds a year were allowed no embroidered clothing, so the Squire is asserting by his apparel that he is worth over two hundred pounds a year - which may or may not be the case. The Squire's clothes are colorful and elegant. He wears an elaborately embroidered, fashionable demi-gown, reaching only to the knees, with wide, long, rather impractical sleeves. The illustration in the Ellesmere Manuscript, which follows the text closely, also shows him wearing shoes with long points, a crucial detail since he is clearly in contravention of the Sumptuary Law of 1336 stated that "'no knight under the estate of a lord, esquire or gentleman, nor any other person, shall wear any shoes or boots having spikes or points which exceed the length of two inches, under the forfeiture of forty pence." These rather impractical garments are indicators of wealth; the Squire is one of several pilgrims who attempt to elevate (or at the least to assert) their social status by their clothes.

The Squire, however, appears to be presented by the Poet as the medieval equivalent of a fashion victim (i.e. a person unable to identify commonly recognized boundaries of style). There can be no doubt that the Squire illustrates that extravagance in dress which medieval homilists consistently denounced. The Parson will object to "inordinat scantnesse" in clothes (the Squire's short gown which shows altogether too much leg) and "superfluitee / of clothynge, which that maketh it so deere, / To harm of the peple; / ...the cost of / Embrowdynge" ("The Parson's Tale"):

> Embrouded was he, as it were a meede
> Al ful of fresshe floures white and reede (89-90)

In describing the Squire's clothes, the Poet makes it appear that it is the Squire himself who has been embroidered, and he obviously intends the simile which follows to suggest effeminacy: our trainee warrior is like a meadow full of flowers. The suggestion of effeminacy is reinforced by the description of the Squire's carefully dressed, long hair, "With lokkes crulle as they were leyed in press" (80-1). The other pilgrim who has long hair, and who takes excessive care over how he wears it, is the sexually ambiguous Pardoner, and the only other use of the term "lokkes" in the *Prologue* comes in his portrait, "smothe it heenge his lokkes that he hadde" (678). It is only fair to add, that "lokkes' clearly did not always have a feminine connotation; it is used in "The Cook's Tale" to describe the apprentice Perkyn, "With lokkes blake, ykembd ful fetisly" and in "The Miller's Tale" to describe the poor scholar Nicholas "He kembeth his lokkes brode, and made hym gay" – both handsome young men and decidedly heterosexual! However, the reference to his possible use of curling irons is surely a comic detail.

The Squire also shares with the Pardoner the desire to dress fashionably, though the effects are different: the Squire appears elegant but the Pardoner is absurd. McAlpine comments, "The *Middle English Dictionary* records only two uses of the word 'effeminate,' both in the sense of 'self-indulgent' or 'unreasonable.' Satires of the fop, often described as long-haired and beardless, reflect a perception of feminization of behavior and appearance without any necessary suggestion of homosexuality'" (in George 128). This seems to be an entirely appropriate description of the Squire as he appears in the portrait: he comes close to the line which separates the dandy from the fop, but in the end he stays on the right side of that line. This is the source of the Poet's gentle mockery.

It is often said that the Squire is presented as "an admirable example of his kind" (Kirkham and Allen 21), and some critics even place this amongst the ideal portraits (though without much conviction), but this is to take the Pilgrim's view at face value. The Squire is an embodiment of the ideals of Courtly Love, and to be sure, the Poet finds nothing to morally censure in the young man, but he does find much that is comic. Everything about the Squire is excessive, particularly his devotion to ladies. However, it is noticeable that, as compared to the presentation of the sexually active pilgrims (the Monk, Friar, Wife of Bath, and Summoner), the Squire's sexual exploits are described euphemistically, almost coyly:

> So hoote he lovede that by nightertale.
> He sleep namoore than dooth a nightingale. (107-8)

These lines link the Squire with the birds in the first sentence that "slepen al the night with open ye" which makes his hypersexuality appear appropriate to his age, the spring of his life (10). Moreover, these lines imply that he is awake not because he is having sex but because he is pining away composing poetry on the love of his lady. In the literature of Courtly Love, the lady beloved of the knight/squire is pure, noble, virtuous and unattainable, and this very futility makes the lover more ardent and long-suffering. This seems to be the Squire's fate.

It is only at the end of the portrait that an attempt is made to link the worlds of the Squire and of his father:

> Curteis he was, lowely, and servisable,
> And carf biforn his fader at the table (99-100)

These words at least suggest that the Squire is being inducted into the wider values of chivalry, though the emphasis is still on the same courtly manners which the Prioress strives so hard to counterfeit rather than on the moral and religious idealism of chivalry.

Lines 101-117: The Yeoman

With the possible exception of the Ploughman, the Yeoman is the lowest member of society amongst the pilgrims, a paid servant though a free man and probably a small landowner. His short hair and suntanned face indicate low status. The position of this portrait is an example of the Pilgrim having not "set folk in hir degree" (746), for had he done so then the Yeoman would have been one of the last portraits. The Pilgrim, however, places him as part of the social group of which he is a part, the Knight's retinue, a group which also symbolizes the tripartite structure of English armies during the Hundred Years' War.

1. Chaucer's inclusion of a Yeoman in his portraits is unique amongst the writings of his time. Can you suggest why?

2. In what ways is the Yeoman's dress a marked contrast from that of the Knight on the one hand and the Squire on the other?

> The Knight had a yeoman and no other servants
> At that time, for he chose to travel so;
> And this yeoman was clad in a cloak and hood of green.
> A sheaf of arrows with peacock feathers bright and sharp
> 105 He carried very carefully under his belt
> (He really knew how to keep his equipment like a true yeoman:
> His arrows did not fall short because of damaged feathers),
> And in his hand he carried a mighty bow.
> A close-cropped head he had and a sun-browned face.
> 110 Of woodcraft knew he all the practices.
> Upon his arm he wore an elegant wrist-guard,
> And on one side carried a sword and a small, round shield,
> And on the other side a bright dagger,
> Well mounted and as sharp as a spear point;
> On his chest he had a St. Christopher medal of shining silver.
> 115 He had a horn on a green shoulder strap;
> A forester he truly was, I guess.

Most commentators find little to say about the Yeoman (the Ellesmere Manuscript does not even provide an illustration) because his portrait does not seem to fit: it is composed entirely physical description and appears to break the pattern of irony which the Poet has established. Those critics who have attempted to fit the portrait of the Yeoman into some pattern have done so in radically different ways. Some insist that this is one of the idealized portraits, which they generally expand to include the Knight, Squire, Clerk, Parson and Plowman. Thus, Kirkham and Allen call him, "an anonymous and idealized type" (23). Others have placed this amongst the ironic portraits on the grounds that a portrait in which the Pilgrim tells us in such detail about how well the Yeoman prepares himself for action, but says nothing at all about how the man acts, must be intended by the Poet to be ironic. Rather than explaining the intention of the text, both interpretations seem to impose a meaning onto the text.

Two features of the style of the portrait are significant. First is the predominance of monosyllabic words. There are one hundred and twenty-three words used to describe the Yeoman, and I count only twenty-one words having more than one syllable which is unusually low. Second is the frequency of the conjunction "and" which is used eight times in seventeen lines each time linking items of clothing or equipment. (Contrast the use in the Squire's portrait mainly to link active verbs). Both of these features of style are particularly fitting for a description of a simple man who is defined by his occupation. The Poet ends the portrait with a joke against the Pilgrim who, having given a definitive description, draws a comically tentative conclusion, "A forster was he, smoothly, as I gesse" (117). The Poet's joke, of course, is that the narrator is serious and totally unconscious that he has said anything amusing.

The Yeoman has no individual identity or personality. Only one line is given to physical description, "A not heed hadde he, with a broun visage" (109). His short hair is in stark contrast to the Squire's "lokkes" emphasizing the gulf in status between the two, a point which is reinforced by his sun-browned face. The Yeoman is entirely defined by what he wears and carries (ten lines) and by his skill in his vocation (four lines), which is to say that he is entirely defined by his lowly place in society. In purely realistic terms, the Yeoman carries rather too much equipment, just as the Knight seems to have been on too many campaigns. However, the number and range of his accessories symbolically suggests his dual rôles as warrior and forester. The latter should be understood as meaning gamekeeper, someone familiar with the ways of forest creatures and able to use his knowledge effectively in hunting. Some critics have argued that this means that the Yeoman is in charge of his lord's (i.e. the Knight's) hunting lands, suggesting that the Knight is a substantial landowner. It is a perfectly reasonable argument, but it is inconsistent with much in the Knight's portrait. Probably, Chaucer's desire to show a typical Yeoman overcomes his desire for consistency. After all, the same is true of the portrait of the Squire: Chaucer presents a typical squire, but it is hard to see the young man he portrays as actually being the Knight's son.

As a fighting man, the status of a yeoman is below the knights and squires, but above the ordinary foot soldiers. His main weapon is the English longbow (which, given its effectiveness in the Hundred Year's War, was a highly respected weapon), but he also carries a sword, dagger and shield. The simile which rates his dagger "sharp as point of spere" (114) further emphasizes the Yeoman's function in warfare. In peacetime, the Yeoman's rôle is to be part of his lord's household. His bow also serves for hunting and the portrait stresses his skill – his arrows do not miss their mark.

The Yeoman's accessories infringe the 1363 Sumptuary Statute which specified that a yeoman wear no girdle, no harnessed knife, and no gold or silver. Firstly, he wears a "gay bracer" (111) which is obviously more than simply a functional wrist guard, and secondly his horn is attached to a "bawdrik" (116) which was a decorated belt. More significantly, he carries a "gay daggere / Harneised wel" (113-4), that is, an ornamented dagger in a sheath decorated by polished metal, which conflicts with the rule against wearing any harnessed knife. These details stand in contrast to the Knight whose "array ... was not gay" (73-4). That the Yeoman wears a St. Christopher suggests at the least conventional piety, St. Christopher being both the patron saint of foresters and of travelers in general, but that the medal is of "silver sheene" (115) would be inappropriate for someone of his status. A yeoman is not allowed to wear chains of gold or silver, but he is only the first of several pilgrims who will turn a religious symbol into an item of jewelry. Some critics have found this dressiness on the part of the Yeoman to be significant, as it certainly is, for example, in the case of the Guildsmen, and although the portrait associates it with no moral lapse a certain vanity is ironically implied. This is, presumably, why the Poet specifies that he carries, "A sheef of pecok arwes" (104), peacocks being traditionally associated with vanity (compare Langland's "Lady Peacock Proud heart" in *The Vision of Piers Plowman).* Beyond this, the inner life of this character is a complete mystery to us.

There is, in fact, further irony in the portrait, but it refers back to the status of the Knight:

A Yeman hadde he and servantz namo
At that time, for him liste ride so, (101-2)

A knight would normally have a retinue of followers, and indeed the size of the retinue would be a good indication of the knight's status. Landholders have a natural retinue of their household, but ours is a landless knight, and so he would have to employ men. Conlee makes the point that "the Knight is maintaining only the minimum number of attendants required to uphold the honor of his rank" and quotes from Lull's *Ordre of Chyvalry,* "it behoveth [a knight] that there be given to hym a squyre & a servaunt that may take hede to his horse"

(Conlee in Lambdin and Lambdin 29). The Pilgrim blithely passes off the paucity of the Knight's retinue as a matter of personal choice; however, the Poet expects the reader to interpret the decision as enforced.

Chapter Five: The Prioress, the Monk and the Friar

The Pilgrim now moves on to the first of a number of portraits of clerics. Hirsh points out that this second sub-set of pilgrims "is the only group among the pilgrims all of whose members have taken religious vows" (86). The Prioress, the Second Nun (a shadowy figure in the *Prologue* though she is one of only three women who tell tales), the Nun's Priest (not described but also allocated a tale), the Monk, and the Friar are members of the First Estate about whom Chaucer's readers would have a clear set of expectations. That all three of the figures described falls well short of these expectations allows Chaucer further to develop the dynamic relationship between the voices of the Pilgrim and the Poet. Nevertheless, it is important to note that Chaucer follows the tradition of medieval estates satire in attacking not the office but the abuse of the office.

These three clerics each belong to a holy order: the Prioress and the Monk are Benedictines, and the Friar is a Franciscan:

> Religious orders were so called because they were "ordered" or "regulated" by a *regula*, i.e., a "rule" (the latter noun comes into English from Old French *reule* via Latin *regula*), and a division was recognized between *regular* clergy, those subject to the rule of a monastic order, who lived in a religious community, and secular clergy, those subject to the bishop of a diocese, who lived in the world. Both regulars and seculars were ultimately subject to the pope. The oldest religious rule in this sense is the *Rule of Saint Benedict* devised in the sixth century by the founder of the Benedictine order, who has been called the "Father of Western Monasticism." ("Medieval Estates and Orders")

Donald Howard identifies the theme which unites the three portraits:

> [The Prioress, the Monk and the Friar] reveal what was throughout the Middle Ages the fundamental flaw in the practice of the religious life, that its values and ideals were contaminated by secular – and chiefly aristocratic – ones. Laymen put a high value on social status, upon the acquisition of property and wealth, upon sexual relations, love, and family. Members of religious orders were, by ancient tradition, expected to renounce these preoccupations – to renounce 'the world' – in vows of obedience, poverty, and chastity. Yet the Prioress, the Monk and the Friar are all

class conscious … The abuses of the three mount in intensity – the Prioress's are peccadilloes which have a certain charm, the Monk's are bold offenses against the heart of the tradition (he apparently violates all three of his vows), and the Friar's make a veritable compendium of the wrongs ascribed to friars in fourteenth-century attacks. (Howard 92)

Each of the clerics strives after gentility and in doing so betrays the values of her/his order. It is the thematic progression of immorality that Howard identifies above which accounts for the ordering of the three portraits, for in terms of status men should always outrank women.

In all of the portraits of clerics in the *Prologue*, what critics call Chaucer's 'costume rhetoric' is particularly important for, whilst lay people could only be judged against unenforced sumptuary laws, those in holy orders had to conform to a stricter code of dress. The fact that costume is not simply a matter of literary convention is clear from this statement made in 1342 by John Stratford, Archbishop of Canterbury:

> The external costume often shows the internal character and condition of persons … [T]he behavior of clerks [in the manner of their dress] ought to be an example and a pattern of [i.e. for] the laity" (quoted in Hodges 3)

Both virtues and vices can be symbolized by dress.

Lines 118-164: The Prioress

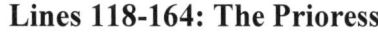

Neither learning not understanding, neither constancy nor virtue such as men have flourished in women [in holy orders] … They think the Scriptures permit them to do as they do … Woman strives for what is forbidden … Therefore on Venus days they eat meat because of their weak stomach. (John Gower *Vox clamantis* or *The Voice of One Crying Out* in Miller 226)

A prioress held a high status position in the Church being the head of a religious house and being responsible for both the spiritual and managerial aspects of leading a priory, which immediately suggests a potential conflict between the world of the spirit and the world of man. Since like all religious houses a priory had a duty of hospitality to travelers, the Prioress would have had plenty of opportunity to interact with members of the nobility. This Prioress has been identified with the Benedictine priory of St. Leonard's at Stratford-at-Bow which is referred to in relation to her speaking French.

Pilgrim:
I do not think it is an exaggeration to say that the Pilgrim is smitten with the Prioress (i.e. he falls in love with her a bit despite the fact that she is a nun!)
1. The Prioress is an attractive woman. What physical features does the Pilgrim mention with obvious admiration?
2. The Prioress has mastered the social graces. What details are given of: a) the way she socializes with others; b) her education; c) her table manners?
3. The Pilgrim praises her moral nature. What supporting examples are given to illustrate the Prioress' charity and pity?

Poet:
Put simply, this lady is just not cut out to be a nun: she has no avocation for her vocation! In fact, everything about her is inappropriate to her religious calling, which gives the Poet plenty of scope for irony.
4. Explore this inappropriateness by considering the following: a) the true form and function of a nun's habit at this time; b) the influence which courtly manners have had on this lady; c) the true meaning of "conscience," charity and pity for a nun [Think Mother Theresa here!]; d) the influences of the romances of Courtly Love on the world-view of the Prioress (focus on "'Amor vincit omnia'" [162]).
5. Do some historical research. Explain why the Prioress may have been representative of many young women in Chaucer's day who were caught between two codes – the world of courtly romance and the world of religious devotion.

> There was also a nun, a Prioress,
> Who had a natural and modest way of smiling;
> 120 Her biggest oath was only to swear by Saint Loy;

And she was called Madame Eglentyne [Sweet-briar or Wild Rose].
She sang the divine service beautifully
Singing with a very attractive nasal tone,
And she spoke French very gracefully and elegantly
125   In the way taught at in her convent at Stratford-Bow,
For the French spoken in Paris was unknown to her.
Her table manners were excellent:
She never let any bits of food fall from her lips,
Nor did she dip her fingers in the sauce too deep;
130   She carried her food to her mouth daintily and took good care
That no drop fell onto her breast.
She took the greatest pleasure in polite manners.
Her top lip she wiped so clean
That when she raised her wine cup, she left no drop
135   Of grease, when she had taken a drink.
Very politely she reached after her food
And certainly she was very entertaining
Very pleasant and friendly in her bearing
And she tried hard to imitate
140   Courtly behavior and to be proper in her manner,
And to be seen as being worthy of respect.
But to speak of her tender heart
She was so full of compassion and pity
That she would cry if she saw a mouse
145   Caught in a trap, if it was dead or bleeding.
She had with her some small dogs that she fed
With roasted meat, or milk or fine bread.
But she cried bitterly if one of them died,
Or if a man hit one of them sharply with a stick;
150   She was all feeling and tender heart.
Her wimple was pleated in a very attractive way
Her nose was well shaped, her eyes gray as glass,
Her mouth small and delicate and soft and red;
But certainly she had a beautiful forehead,
155   I think it was almost a hand-span broad;
For she was certainly not a small woman.
I noticed that her cloak was well tailored.
Around her wrist she wore, made out of small coral,
A double rosary, with large green beads for counting the Lord's Prayer,
160   And from this hung a broach of shining gold

On which was first engraved a capital A
And after that 'Love overcomes everything'.
Another nun she in her retinue,
Who was her secretary; and a priest made three.

Nuns took three vows: Poverty, Chastity and Obedience. Of these, the Prioress breaks the first and the last in fact, and compromises the second by her devotion to the cult of Courtly Love. She breaks her vows simply by being on pilgrimage. Archbishop Melton (writing before 1340) strictly forbade nuns to leave their cloisters "by reason of any vow of pilgrimage which they might have taken" (Bowden *Commentary* 93).

This Prioress is clearly the daughter of a rich family and has been well educated for a woman of her time. Donald Howard argues that comic irony is added to the Poet's portrait if the reader assumes that the good manners which the Prioress strives so hard to exemplify are actually an indication of her status as a member of the nouveaux riche rather than a member of the traditional (even minor) nobility:

It is not clear whether the Prioress is the daughter of a noble
house or, as seems more likely, from the *haute bourgeoisie*
or the 'gentry': one rather assumes that in the circles where
high social rank was taken for granted such manners and
bearing were second nature – a lady of such a background
wouldn't need to 'counterfete' them. (Howard 92)

Whatever the truth about the social status of her family, it is clearly this lady should never have become a nun, but then she probably had little real choice in the matter. Women in Chaucer's day were in law very much under the control first of their fathers and then, if they married, of their husbands. At this time, it was inconceivable for a woman to remain unmarried and live independently; she would have had to live in the household of a male relative. Thus, a father with a daughter who could not find a husband would regard placing the young woman in a convent as the most obvious alternative to marriage – the daughter might or might not agree. Since she totally lacks any religious calling, this was undoubtedly the fate of this Prioress, but since she is not unattractive the family was probably unable to arrange a suitable marriage for financial reasons (e.g., the family could not afford a dowry). Understanding this context somewhat softens the impact of the Poet's double irony: this lady fails to conform to the high moral standards expected of a nun, but she also falls short in her attempt to behave like a court lady.

The priory of St. Leonard, Stratford-at-Bow, London, was a house for Benedictine nuns which became fashionable in the mid-fourteenth century due to its association with Elizabeth of Hainault. Such an association with a lady of the court would indeed have appealed to this Prioress. The evident mismatch between this lady's vocation and her avocation leads David Williams to identify this as the first portrait in which the reader begins to detect the difference in perspective between the Pilgrim and the Poet, "It is in this description that the audience might begin to question the judgment of Pilgrim Chaucer" (Williams 34). However, this view requires us to be tone deaf to the irony in the portraits of the Knight, his son, and the Yeoman. The truth is that in the portrait of the Prioress the reader will find the same ironic devices which have already been identified in the first three portraits.

The Prioress is the first of the pilgrims to be given a name, Madam Eglentyne, suggesting that the Poet intends the reader to see her as an individual rather than a type. However, the name carries multiple connotations. The eglantine, a flower, was a common symbol for Mary the mother of Jesus, who was, of course, a virgin and who embodies love in its purest spiritual form. However, the name, which means Wild Rose, also links this portrait to the poem *The Romance of the Rose* begun by Guillaume de Lorris (c.1230) but completed later in the century by Jean de Meun (c.1375). Colin Wilcockson explains:

> In one passage in de Meun's part of Le Roman de la rose, a character called La Vieille (the Old Woman) recounts the advice she gives to young women on how to catch their men ... [A] young woman ... should have attractive table manners ... she should learn to sing, she should weep to gain sympathy ... she should expose [her] good features in the way she wears her clothes. All these are found in the sketch of the Prioress ... To the audience, acquainted as they would have been with the French poem, there would have been a strong implication that the Prioress's delicate and sensitive behavior is, at least in part, inspired by an attempt to appear sexually attractive. (xvi-ii).

Wilcockson ends his argument by pointing out that the Prioress is the only pilgrim about whom we are given a description of the texture of her lips! Every detail of the description implies the influence of Venus on the Prioress at birth making her of the sanguine temperament.

This is one of the few portraits containing no extravagant superlatives: the Pilgrim does not claim that Madam Eglentyne is the best Prioress in England. There is, however, plenty of praise in the Pilgrim's description. David Williams accurately points to a change in the Poet's approach in this portrait:

> When he gets to the Prioress … (Chaucer's) method of description subtly changes. Her depiction begins not with any reference to virtues, as in the presentation of the Knight, but rather a combination of physical characteristics and petty mannerisms … The narrator has almost forgotten to tell us of her virtues, and that, of course, tells all: the Prioress's moral life is meager and limited. (Williams 33)

The first twenty-four lines of the portrait deal with the Prioress' social accomplishments, that is, those skills which she has deliberately cultivated. Not one of them is directly related to her religious vocation. First is her restraint:

> That of hir smiling was full simple and coy;
> Hire gretteste ooth was but by Seinte Loy; (119-120)

Bowden draws attention to the fact that the words "simple and coy" "belong to the medieval romance … employed either separately or in conjunction with each other to describe a fair heroine's charms," an impression reinforced by the Poet's description of the Prioress' straight nose, broad forehead, grey eyes and small mouth, all conventional attributes of beautiful ladies in medieval romances (*Commentary* 93-5). Manly makes the point that swearing, even by women, and even by clerics, was quite common in Chaucer's time (*New Light* 214-5); nevertheless, it is perhaps surprising that the first thing that the Pilgrim finds to say about a nun is that she does not smile too openly nor curse in a vulgar way: this sounds somewhat like damning with faint praise. However, the Poet is more subtle than this. If the Prioress's smiling is "simple and coy" (119) then, while the Pilgrim means us to see her as appropriately shrinking and modest, the Poet is aware that "coy" carries the implication of being "marked by cute, coquettish, or artful playfulness" (Merriam-Webster). Certainly, the later emphasis on this lady's obsession with romantic love calls the complementary denotation of the word "coy" into question and establishes immediately that artifice is the keystone of her character. Put simply: "her smiling was ful simple and coy" is an oxymoron.

The detail given to illustrate the Prioress's self-restraint contains a joke which commentators have been strangely reluctant to see. It does not help much to know that St. Eloi (Eloy or Eligius) was the patron saint of goldsmiths and of carters, although the Prioress' inappropriate love of jewelry, "theron heng a brooch of gold ful sheene" (160), might suggest her personal reasons for favoring this saint. More significant, however, is that St. Eloi was noted for both his good manners and for the fact that he never swore – in fact, he famously refused to take an oath which King Dagobert demanded of him. Taking a charitable view, Pollard draws the conclusion that "perhaps this means that the Prioress did not swear at all," which misses the Poet's point entirely: nuns should not swear at all, and this one obviously does! Ironically, when an expletive does escape her lips, it is the name of the saint who was noted for the good manners and courtesy which the Prioress tries so hard to cultivate, and, even worse, it is the name of a saint who placed his life at risk by defying a king rather than speak an oath. The critical tone of the portrait has been set within the first three lines.

The Pilgrim continues to describe the kind of accomplishments appropriate to a court lady but inappropriate to a religious woman, yet he seems unaware of any conflict; he is simply dazzled by what he hears and sees. The description of her beautiful chanting of the liturgy carries a clear implication of affectation:

> Ful weel she soong the service divine,
> Entuned in his nose ful semely, (122-3)

In fact, singing through the nose does not produce a pleasing sound; some singing coaches go so far as to have a singer pinch his nostrils shut in an effort to curb this error! Thus, the approving adverbial phrases "Ful weel" and "ful seemly" are meant to be ironic. The same technique is used by the Poet when the Pilgrim comments on the skill which the Prioress has in speaking French:

> And Frenssh she spake ful faire and fetisly,
> After the scole of Stratford atte Bowe,
> For Frenssh of Paris was to hire unknowe. (124-127)

The effusion of the Pilgrim is evident in the hard alliteration of the 'f' sound in "ful faire and fetisly," but the Poet expects us to pick up on multiple ironies in these lines. French was at that time the language of the court; Latin was the language of the Church, and no mention is made of the Prioress speaking Latin. Also, though her French may sound graceful and elegant to the Pilgrim, the Prioress would not even be understood in Paris, which rather defeats the supposed purpose of learning a foreign language and suggests that, in the Prioress, French is a mere affectation rather than a useful skill. Manly suggests that since Elizabeth of Hainaut, the sister of Queen Philippa was a member of the convent at St. Leonard, Stratford-at-Bow for many years then "Frenssh … /After the scole of Stratford atte Bowe" might well have been French as it was spoken in Hainaut, regional variations in accent being much greater in the Middle Ages than they are now (*New Light* 219-20). If Manly is correct, then the Poet's jibe further associates the Prioress with counterfeiting courtly manners. I have one further speculation: the Priory of St. Leonard, Stratford-at-Bow, was located to the east of London on the side of the River Lea. This is the region which was to become famous in later centuries for the Cockney accent, and it would add another level of irony if Chaucer's readers already associated that part of London with the coarse accent of the lowest class of Londoners.

The Prioress, like the Squire, is an embodiment of the ideals of Courtly Love, at least in her own imagination. Her portrait is a list of minor superlatives: the adjective "ful" is used ten times in all (seven times in the first twenty lines) - a not so subtle hint by the Poet that everything is a little over-done! Ten lines are devoted to the Prioress' exquisite table manners: she does not let any food fall from her mouth while she is eating; she does not drop food on her breast as she takes it from the table to put it into her mouth; she does not let her fingers go into the sauce when she dips her food; before she drinks, she wipes her upper lip to ensure that not a speck of grease remains floating in her wine goblet (an important point of etiquette since at this date a wine cup would be shared by two people); and finally she reaches politely to get food from the table. Most of this is taken directly from the advice to young court ladies in *The Romance of the Rose*:

> She ought also to behave properly at table. ... She must be very careful not to dip her fingers in the sauce up to the knuckles, nor to smear her lips with soup or garlic or fat meat, nor to take too many pieces or too large a piece and

put them in her mouth. She must hold the morsel with the tips of her fingers and dip it into the sauce, whether it be thick, thin, or clear, then convey the mouthful with care, so that no drop of soup or sauce or pepper falls on to her chest. When drinking, she should exercise such care that not a drop is spilled upon her, for anyone who saw that happen might think her very rude and coarse. And she must be sure never to touch her goblet when there is anything in her mouth. Let her wipe her mouth so clean that no grease is allowed to remain upon it, at least not upon her upper lip, for when grease is left on the upper lip, globules appear in the wine, which is neither pretty nor nice. (*Norton Anthology*)

The Poet, however, is less impressed than is the Pilgrim. This is how her drinking of wine is described:

> Hir over-lippe wiped she so clene,
> That in hir coppe ther was no ferthing sene
> Of grece, whan she dronken hadde hir draughte. (133-5)

The Poet inserts multiple ironies here. To begin with the obvious, the word "draughte" suggests that there is nothing dainty about the quantity she drinks which can be seen by comparing Chaucer's other uses of the word in *The Canterbury Tales*. In the link to "The Pardoner's Prologue," the Host talks of wanting, "a draughte of moiste and corny ale," and the Pardoner goes on to talk of sheep and a herdsman drinking "of this welle a draughte" and of himself having "dronke a draughte of corny ale"; of the Cook it is said, "Wel koude he knowe a draughte of London ale" (384); and of the Shipman that he "Ful many a draughte of wyn had he ydrawe" (398). None of these examples suggests anything delicate about the quantity drunk or the manner of drinking. In addition, the very act of a nun drinking wine must suggest to the reader the taking of Holy Communion which is precisely what she is not doing. In this context, the comment that there is no "grece" in her drinking is seen to be a pun on the religious term 'grace' meaning the favor bestowed by God: there is not a farthing's worth of grace in her courtly table manners.

The phrase "ful seemly" is repeated to describe three actions of very different significance:

> Ful weel she soong the service divine,
> Entuned in hir nose ful semely, (122-3)

and:

> Ful semely after hir mete she raughte. (136)

and:

> Ful semely hir wimpul pinched was; (151)

The implication of this repetition is that, to the Prioress, the singing of hymns is of equal moral value to the passing of food at supper or the tailoring of garments, and indeed this is so because they are equally opportunities for her to show her cultured refinement. The description stresses that her excellent table manners have been learned, "At mete wel ytaught was she with alle" (127), and later states that, "In curteisie was set ful muchel her lest" (132) leaving the reader with the clear implication that there is not much of her "lest" (pleasure, interest) left for religion.

Whilst the Pilgrim is lost in admiration of the Prioress's sociability, deportment and pleasant demeanor, these lines contain the Poet's most damning comment:

> In curteisie was set ful muchel hir lest... (132)
> And peyned hire to counterfete cheere
> Of court, and to been estatlich of manere,
> And to ben holden digne of reverence. (139-41)

This is the third reference to "curteisie" in the *Prologue*. The Knight is said to love, "Trouthe and honour, freedom and curteisie" (46), and here the word means the devotion of a man's whole life to the absolute value of serving others (and it means this whether or not the reader considers that the Knight actually exemplifies this ideal). The Squire is said to be, "Curteis ... lowely, and servisable" (99), and here the word refers to the same ideal of knightly conduct, symbolized by carving for his father at the table, but the Squire's version is less austere than is his father's, and he clearly extends the concept to include the conventions and mores of Courtly Love. However, when the word is used to describe the ideal to which the Prioress devotes her life, the context makes it clear that "curteisie" refers only to courtly manners. In other words, the word has been progressively degraded until in the quotation above it represents simply a worldly aspiration, in marked contrast to the spiritual aspiration to which the Prioress should devote herself.

In the same quotation, the active verb "peyned" describes a woman who is painstakingly learning the manners of the court rather than a woman who was actually brought up in the court, and the word "counterfete" implies that the Prioress is essentially a fake.

Later, in his "Prologue," the Pardoner will use the same word: in his arrogantly honest boast that he preaches solely for money; he says that he "wol non of the apostles counterfete." In the harsh alliteration of the 'c' sound of "counterfete cheere / Of court," the reader actually hears the Poet's contempt. Contempt is appropriate since all of this effort of learning and self-control is to the end of making the Prioress the center of attention. She longs to "ben holden digne of reverence," that is, she wants to be thought 'worthy' not in the moral sense but in the social sense: she wants to be taken for and treated like a lady of the court. The word "reverence" is particularly well chosen by the Poet because it carries religious connotations of honor and respect: the Prioress wants from others the kind of honor and respect which she should, by the nature of her vocation, give exclusively to God, and this explains why she travels (like a noble lady) with a retinue. Her ambition to "ben holden digne of reverence" is simply a higher class version of the desire of the Guildsmen's wives "to been ycleped 'madame' / … And have a mantel roialliche ybore" (379-80).

Only later (lines 142-50), does the Pilgrim turn to enumerating the Prioress' virtues by describing her moral sensitivity: nine lines in a portrait of forty-five lines. The Poet uses the structural device of the conjunction "But" at the beginning of 142 to signpost the radical change in topic from skills which are unrelated to her religious vocation to a virtue which should be central to it - the Prioress is easily moved to pity:

> But for to speken of hire conscience,
> She was so charitable and so pitous
> She woulde wepe, if that she saugh a mous
> Kaught in a trappe, if it were deed or bledde.
> Of smale houndes hadde she…
> But soore wepte whe if oon of hem were deed,
> Or if men smoot it with a yerde smerte; (142-8)

Notice the contrast in the sound of the lines describing the Prioress' compassion (lines 142-4 and 147) which are full of soft consonants and long vowels, and those describing incidents that would move her (lines 145 and 148) which are dominated by hard, short consonant and vowel sounds. So that the reader does not miss it, her propensity to cry is emphasized by repetition, "wepe … wepte." The Poet assumes that the reader will recall the advice of the Old Woman in

The Romance of the Rose that women should use weeping to attract and manipulate men:

> There is also a proper way to weep, but every woman has the skill to weep properly wherever she may be. Even when no one has caused them any trouble or shame or annoyance, they still have tears at the ready: they all weep in whatever they like, and make a habit of it. But no man should be moved by it, not if he sees the tears flowing as fast as rain, for a woman only sheds such tears and suffers such sorrow and affliction in order to make a fool of him. (*Norton Anthology*)

The Pilgrim intends that we should draw the conclusion that, if this lady's compassion is roused even by the smallest of animals, then her compassion for humans must be boundless. The problem is that there is no evidence to support such an assumption – as is so often the case, what is missing from the portrait is as important as what is there. The Poet means us to understand that the Prioress' moral sensitivity stops with small, cute, furry animals, not that it begins with them, a point which is confirmed by her tale which is full of viciously anti-Semitic attitudes.

Self-restraint and compassion mark the limits of the Prioress' virtues, but her love of animals is further exemplified by her keeping "smale houndes" (146) as pets despite the fact that owning pets is, in itself, inconsistent with the Prioress's vow of poverty. The Prioress is imitating the fashion amongst noble ladies for keeping lap dogs, and, to make things worse, she feeds them with dainties from the table, "rosted flessh, or milk, or wastel-breed" (147). In doing these things, the Prioress breaks a number of the rules of her Benedictine order according to which: she should not allow pets into monastic buildings; she should not be eating meat herself; and she has a duty to perform works to relieve the sufferings of the poor rather than those of her lap-dogs. Manly draws attention to "a prohibition addressed to the nuns of Chatteras in Cambridgeshire in 1345, 'We enjoin also that neither dogs nor little birds be kept by the abbess or by any nun within the limits of the convent...'" (*New Light* 216). Bowden describes "wastel-breed" as the second grade of bread in Chaucer's day (behind *demeine*, the Lord's bread, which even the Prioress would not feed to her dogs), "a fine white bread, probably white … We cannot imagine that it was found on any tables other than those of the well-to-do" (*Commentary* 99).

The last twelve lines of the portrait (151-62) are devoted to the Pilgrim's description of the Prioress herself and of her clothing. The Ellesmere Manuscript clearly shows the Prioress riding sidesaddle (in contrast to the Wife of Bath who just as clearly is portrayed riding astride) a style which had only recently been introduced to England by Anne of Bohemia, wife of King Richard II. In fact, in Chaucer's day, only noble women used the sidesaddle, and then only when they were wearing long gowns, so this is another sign of the Prioress' social aspirations. She wears the nun's habit, but she does so with her own personal style and with attractive accessories essentially subverting the entire intention of the habit.

In the Middle Ages, unmarried women tended to pluck most or all of their eyebrows and their hairline to give themselves a higher forehead. Foreheads were considered sexy! This is why it was customary for a married woman to wear a wimple covering her forehead, hair, and neck as a sign of modesty. Similarly, a nun's wimple is worn to signify that she is married to Christ. The Prioress, however, turns the wimple into a fashion-statement:

> Ful seemly hir wimpul pinched was
> …sikerly she hadde a fair forheed;
> It was almoost a spanne brood, I trowe (151-5).

The hyperbole which ends this description conveys the Pilgrim's typical enthusiasm for excess amongst his companions. Rather than hiding the forehead, the wimple that the Prioress wears actually frames it and calls attention to it, whilst the pleats in the material (presumably to show the line of the neck) add to the inappropriate elegance which is further exemplified in her neat and well-fitting cloak. The cloak of a nun should hide her figure, but this one actually accentuates it, so that the Pilgrim admires her curves, "hardily, she was nat undergrowe" (155). The Poet, however, seems to be implying that this refined lady for whom delicacy seems to be the ultimate value, is actually overweight; like the Monk and the Friar, she eats too well.

Further adornment is provided by the rosary worn around her wrist which ought to be composed of plain wooden beads:

> Of small coral aboute hire arm she bar
> A peire of bedes, gauded al with grene,

>And theron heng a brooch of gold ful sheene. (158-60)

Nuns were supposed to avoid jewelry. In 1227, the Synod of Trier forbade nuns to wear jewels or brooches, gold or silver rings, and gold braids or silk girdles, and in 1263, the statutes of the Hôtel-Dieu of Troyes, forbade the wearing of precious stones except as charms for medicinal purposes.

In the quotation above, everything suggests excess. Firstly, she wears not one but two rosaries as bracelets. Secondly, wood is replaced by exotic coral. Thirdly, the gaudies (the large beads at which the Lord's Prayer is recited) are of green, the harsh alliteration of the 'g' sound suggesting a lack of subtlety (to say the least) in the effect. Finally, from the rosary hangs a broach of "gold ful sheene" plainly breaking the ban on nuns wearing jewelry in a highly visible, unsubtle way. Once again, what is not mentioned in the portrait is as significant as what is described. We have seen that the consecration of nuns was symbolically a wedding in which a nun would be seen as married to God, and to signify this vow of devotion and obedience, a simple ring was placed on the nun's finger. No mention is made of the Prioress wearing her ring.

Much ink has been expended on the words engraved on the Prioress' brooch:

>On which ther was first write a crowned A,
>And after *Amor vincit omnia*. (161-2)

'Love conquers all,' but does the Prioress mean love of God or romantic love? Undoubtedly, she intends the words to refer to sacred love: the Prioress, a virgin, sees herself following the example of Mary the mother of Christ. However, the Poet's entire point is in the ambiguity which the portrait has introduced.

Note: In *Chaucer And Clothing: Clerical And Academic Costume In The General Prologue To The Canterbury Tales*, Chapter 2, Laura Hodges argues strongly that the commonly held view (taken in my analysis) that the Prioress is dressed inappropriately is not supported by contemporary documents.

Lines 165-207: The Monk

> Just as fishes in a flood when they
> are cast out of the water
> Die for drought when they dry
> lying on the earth
> Just so religion rots and dies
> When it abandons the convent and
> cloister to live in the world
> (Langland. *The Vision of Piers
> Plowman* author's modernization)

> Men's thinking frequently turns
> toward new fashions, and the
> altered rule for monks will be
> witness for me on this point. The
> original rule for monks has now
> become curtailed ... The sea is the proper habitat of a live
> fish, and the monastery is the right home for a monk ... A
> fish ought not to be out of the water, nor ought a monk to be
> away from his cloisters... (John Gower *Vox clamantis* or
> *The Voice of One Crying Out* Norton Anthology)

> The monk who has been made guardian or steward of any
> outside property is not a good cloisterer, for then he needs a
> horse and a saddle to get around the countryside, and he
> spends lavishly ... our monk of today regularly seeks fancy
> adornment for his body and disfigures his soul ... [he has] a
> coat adorned with fur ... gray squirrel fur ... Nor does he
> forget a silver pendant but gaily displays it hanging from his
> hood on his breast ... [He] goes along the river with ... swift
> greyhounds as well, and fine spirited horses ... I have heard
> about the children that our monk accumulated while he was
> running around..." (John Gower *The Mirror of Mankind*
> quoted in Patterson 10-1)

The Monk, identified later in *The Canterbury Tales* as Daun
Piers, is an "outridere," one who is officially authorized to leave the
monastery in order to supervise the management of its estates, so
there is nothing inherently inappropriate in his going out into the
world. He is not required, as are most monks, to live secluded within
a single monastery. The problem is not that he goes into the outside

world, but what he does there! This is the first of many portraits which directly address an idea central to the Poet's intentions. Ian Johnston explains it this way:

> [T]he emphasis [is always] on the social basis for virtue. What makes people good or bad Christians, in the world of this poem, is how they treat each other. Virtue is not an abstract matter of doctrine, a purification ritual carried out in contemplative isolation, or a challenge to the individual will. It is thoroughly social, a matter of one's obligations to help others and to refrain from mistreating them.

Pollard draws attention to the *Visitation of Selborne Abbey* written by William Wykeham, Bishop of Winchester, in 1387, exactly contemporary with the *Prologue*. Wykeham found many of the monks at the abbey to be self-professed hunters, and specifically forbade them in future from attending public huntings and from keeping hounds; the penalty for each offence he set at two days fasting on bread and beer. Amongst Wykeham's other complaints against the monks were: that they were ignorant and illiterate (he enjoined them to sit in the cloister and read the Scriptures); that they wore garments edged with fur and silk girdles trimmed with gold; and that they wore expensive boots and gold and silver ornaments. Wykeham noted particularly the abuses of outriders who used riding out to inspect the abbey's manors and farms as an excuse to be absent from the monastery on their own business without the permission of the prior and for as long as they wanted (46-8). Pollard does not say whether Chaucer might have been aware of Wykeham's report, or whether the remarkable parallels with the content of the portrait simply show how common these abuses were.

Pilgrim:

1. The narrator immediately admires the Monk's manliness. What manly activities does the Monk enthusiastically pursue?

2. What are the Monk's arguments to justify why he does not adhere to the rules of his order? The Pilgrim is totally convinced by these arguments. How do we know this? What further points does the Pilgrim make in support of the Monk's position?

3. The Pilgrim is impressed by the Monk's clothes, his physical appearance, and his horses. Give details and explain.

Poet:

4. Comment on the symbolic significance of the "Ginglen" bridle bell. How does the Poet use this extended metaphor to criticize the Monk?

5. In regard to his pursuit of hunting, the Poet comments "no cost wolde he spare" (192). Make a list of all of the things on which he spares no cost, and then remember that monks take a vow of poverty!

6. There are at least three hints in the portrait that the Monk is not celibate – which as a monk he certainly should be. Can you find the hints?

7. The Pilgrim describes the Monk's face as looking "as he hadde been enoint" (199). Whilst he is simply expressing admiring approval of the man's glowing complexion, the Poet is making a joke at the Monk's expense. Explain.

8. The portrait begins with the assertion that this Monk has the qualities "to been an abbot able" (167). That is clearly intended by the Poet as comic hyperbole, but critics disagree on the interpretation of this portrait. Some find it a basically friendly with only gentle irony whilst others see it as bitterly satiric. Which view would you support? Why?

165	A Monk there was, an outstanding man,
	Who rode out of the monastery to look after the estates and loved hunting,
	A man's man, fit to be an abbot.
	He had many exquisite horses in the stable,
	And when he rode, you could hear the bells on his bridle
170	Jingling in the wind quite as clear
	And as loud as the chapel bell does
	Where this Monk was head of a monastery cell.
	The rule of St. Maurus and of St. Benedict,
	Because they were old and a bit strict,
175	This same Monk let anachronistic things slide
	And followed the way of more modern fashions.
	He did not give a plucked chicken for that text
	That says that hunters cannot be holy men,
	Nor that a monk who is a bit careless of his vows
180	Is like a fish out of water -
	That is to say, a monk out of his cloister.
	For that text, he did not give an oyster.
	And I affirm that he was right.

Why should a man study and make himself mad
185   Always reading over a book in the cloister,
Or working with his hands and laboring
As St Augustine said? How does that help a monk serve the world?
Let St Augustine do his manual labor himself!
Therefore this Monk was a hunter,
190   He had greyhounds as swift as birds flying.
Tracking and hunting the hare
Was his chief pleasure, and he spared no expense to pursue it.
I saw his sleeves trimmed at the cuff with costly
Gray fur, the very finest in the land;
195   And to fasten his hood under his chin
He had an elaborate gold pin;
There was a true-love knot at the larger end.
His head was bald, and shone like a mirror,
His face as well, as if it had been anointed with oil.
200   He was a well-built man in good condition;
His eyes glaring and rolling in his head
That shone like the fire under a cooking pot;
His boots were supple, his horse very fine.
Certainly, he was a fine churchman;
205   He was not pale like a suffering ghost.
A fat swan he loved the best of any roast meat.
His horse was as brown as a berry.

The Monk is the male equivalent of the Prioress: whilst she fantasizes about being a court lady, he actually lives the life of a country gentleman. The entire point of becoming a monk was (and still is) to renounce the world of the flesh by entering a monastery in order to concentrate on achieving spiritual purity through meditation, work, study and prayer. Paradoxically, however, the more devout monasteries were perceived to be, the more they attracted legacies from the rich, and so by Chaucer's time many were significant landowners. This Benedictine Monk is an "outridere" (166), that is, a monk whose rôle was to inspect and manage a monastery's outlying lands. This places the Monk in a potentially ambiguous position since he has in theory renounced the very secular world in which he spends most of his time. This Monk resolves the conflict by simply rejecting the rules of his order. His argument in support of this position occupies the central portion of the portrait: sixteen consecutive lines of a portrait of forty-two lines:

> The reule of Seint Maure or of Seint Beneit,
> By cause that it was old and somdel streit
> This ilke Monk leet olde thinges pace,
> And heeld after the newe world the space.
> He yaf nat of that text a pulled hen,
> That seith that hunters be nat hooly men,
> Ne that a monk, whan he is recchelees,
> Is likned til a fissh that is waterlees,-
> This is to seyn, a monk out of his cloistre
> But thilke text heeld he nat worth an oystre. (173-182)

These lines are the Pilgrim's, but they do more than paraphrase the Monk's justification for ignoring the rules of his order. For the first time in the portraits, the reader distinctly hears the actual words of the pilgrim, for example in the references to hens, fish, and oysters. The implicit criticisms of the behavior of monks are derived from estates satire stereotypes, but the idea of putting them into the form of the Monk's own defense of his lifestyle is original to Chaucer.

The Monk's argument rests on a contrast between the "olde" world in which Benedict wrote the original rules and the "newe world" in which monasteries are rich institutions: it is an appeal to realism. The Monk begins with a very modest criticism of the rule of his order: it is somewhat strict. However, he soon expresses himself in stronger terms. The rule that says that hunters cannot be holy men is not worth a plucked chicken; the rule that says that a monk who is disobeying the rule by not staying in the cloister is like a fish out of water is itself not worth an oyster. The Monk intends his food references to be dismissive, since chickens and oysters were plentiful and cheap, but it says a lot about this bon vivant that he naturally draws his imagery from food.

Of course, the Pilgrim, who in the first three lines of the portrait has two superlatives declaring (with emphatic alliteration) the Monk to be "a fair for the maistrie ... / A manly man, to been an abbot able" (165-167), enthusiastically supports the Monk's logic:

> And I seyde his opinion was good.
> What sholde he studie, and make himselven wood,
> Upon a book in cloistre alwey to poure,
> Or swinken with his handes and laboure,
> As Austin bit? How shal the world be served?
> Lat Austin have his swink to him reserved! (183-188)

The Pilgrim becomes quite animated. Listen to those spitted 's' sounds, each one falling on a stressed syllable of the lines' iambic pentameter, and note the exclamation mark. The Pilgrim ends triumphantly with two rhetorical questions obviously borrowed from the Monk, and the emphatic assertion that St. Augustine can work hard if he wants to. Unfortunately, as the Poet is well aware, the argument is patently absurd; far from being unanswerable the two rhetorical questions lead the reader to an obvious reply. Why should the Monk do these absurd things? Because he has freely chosen to be a monk and they are the things monks do. How shall the world be served? It is precisely not the function of monks to serve the world; their focus is (or should be) exclusively on the spiritual world.

The remainder of the portrait describes the appearance of the Monk and his activities. The Pilgrim's tone is impressed and approving, leading to the final comment:

> Now certeinly he was a fair prelaat;
> He was nat pale as a forpined goost. (204-5)

Except, of course, that this man is not a prelate (that is, a high ranking churchman) at all: he is merely an outrider. Similarly, although the Pilgrim enthusiastically asserts him to be, "A manly man, to been an abbot able" (167) we learn five lines later that he is, in fact, merely the "kepere of the celle" (172), that is a small community of monks living at some distance from the main monastery where "conduct could be a good deal more lax than in the mother-house" (Hussey et al. 63).

It is in the Pilgrim's physical description of the Monk that the Poet has most scope for irony. The first observation which the Pilgrim records is the delightful jingling of the bells on the Monk's bridle:

> And whan he rood, men mighte his bridel here
> Ginglen in a whistlinge wind als cleere
> And eek as loude, as dooth the chapel belle.
> Ther as this lord was kepere of the celle. (169-173)

Even the modern reader can see that the Pilgrim's love of superlatives ("als cleere") carries the unintended critical implication that this Monk's devotion to the secular world, metaphorically represented by the bells on his bridle, is to him a call which blocks out the call of the spiritual life, metaphorically represented by the chapel bells. However, this is where research reveals that the Poet intended medieval readers to understand an even more trenchant criticism. David Williams explains how these lines show that the Monk's way of life is an affront to the entire concept of reason which is the basis of the social order:

> The bells on the Monk's bridle are described as ringing every bit as loudly as the bells of the chapel, and this contrast of the two kinds of bells refers the audience back to a well-known symbolic tradition. Medieval art often depicted a crowned figure playing a set of bells graduated in size. The figure represented the harmony of reason, since these bells struck according to a mathematical formula, produced harmonious sound ... The competing bells of the Monk's bridle are not graduated but are all the same size, like sleigh bells. They cannot produce harmony, but rather jangle with a cacophonous sound. It is to this irrational jangling rather than to the sound of harmonious reason that the Monk gallops on his "venerial" ride. (34-35)

The Monk's clothes are inappropriately luxurious. His sleeves are trimmed at the wrist with the most expensive fur and to fasten his hood under his chin he has an elaborate gold pin with a love-knot (a clear parallel to the Prioress' broach with the crowned A), both expressly against the Rule of Saint Benedict, and his boots are made of the finest supple leather. Physically, the Monk appears, despite the approving tone of the Pilgrim, to be somewhat grotesque:

> His heed was balled, that shoon as any glas,
> And eek his face, as he hadde been enoint.
> He was a lord ful fat and in good point,
> His eyen stepe, and rollinge in his heed,
> That stemed as a forneys of a leed; (198-202)

The Pilgrim intends to give a description of a man in robust good health. At a time when the vast majority of the population had a subsistence diet, it was a mark of a man's social status to carry some excess weight. However, the PinkMonkey author succinctly summarizes the Poet's point: the Monk is a "fat hedonist." Physiognomy supports this conclusion, for glaring eyes were, according to Polemon of Laodicea's *de Physiognomonia* (2nd century AD) indicative of a "man given to folly, a glutton, a libertine, and a drunkard" (Bowden *Commentary* 275). The Monk's rich diet makes his skin shine, and looking for a superlative the Pilgrim comments that it looks as if it has been anointed with holy oil, reminding us (without meaning to) that this man has chosen the secular over the religious life (another parallel with the Prioress whose taking of wine has no "grece" in it). Those bulging, rolling eyes do not sound as attractive as the Pilgrim appears to find them, but it is the simile which describes them as glowing like a lead smelting furnace which is the Poet's master-stroke. Compare the description of the Miller, "His mouth as greet was as a greet forneys" (561). In each case, the Poet intends the reader to make the connection with the ever-burning furnace of Hell as described in Matthew 13:41-2:

> The Son of man shall send forth his angels, and they shall gather out of his kingdom all things that offend, and them which do iniquity; And shall cast them into a furnace of fire: there shall be wailing and gnashing of teeth. (King James Version)

The Monk's activities are dominated by his love of horses; ten lines are devoted to describing his horses and horse-related activities, as compared to four words in the portrait of the Knight. As an outrider, a horse would be essential to his work, but he should not actually own one. In fact, the Monk has a whole stable of the finest horses, and he rides a palfrey, a highly valued and expensive riding horse in the Middle Ages. We are told that the Monk "lovede venerie" (166) which is a deliberate parallel to the statement that the Knight "loved chivalrie" (46). Both statements come in the first three lines of the portraits, thus establishing a key-note for the understanding of each pilgrim, and the exploitation of rhyme makes it more likely that the reader will connect the two lines. The Poet's point is that the Knight is dedicated to something appropriate (and it still is appropriate even if the Knight is seen as a less than perfect embodiment of chivalry) whilst the Monk is dedicated to something inappropriate (and no argument he can offer will ever make it appropriate). He loves following the pricks (tracks) of hares and hunting them on horseback:

> … he was a prikasour aright:
> Grehoundes he hadde, as swift as fowel in flight;
> Of priking and of hunting for the hare
> Was al his lust, for no cost wolde he spare. (189-192)

Hunting and owning dogs were, of course, both forbidden by the Monk's order, but perhaps the most disturbing thing is his obsession with hunting: it consumes him (compare the Prioress, "In curteise was set ful muchel hir lest" [132]) and he spends lavishly on it.

The Poet has one more criticism to make. The Pilgrim tells us at the start of the portrait that the Monk "lovede venerie" (166) without seeming to be aware that the word involves a double entendre, for whilst the word does refer to hunting, 'venery' can also mean sexual pleasure. Similarly, in the above quotation, the words "prikasour" (189) and "priking" (191) repeat the same sexual double entendre we noticed in the first eighteen lines of The *Prologue*, and the word "lust" (192), given this context, speaks for itself. Perhaps the Poet means, by the Monk's single-minded pursuit of the hare (an animal noted for its fecundity), that we are to understand that he also hunts out sexually active women.

The reader now realizes the true implication of the detail that a "love-knotte in the gretter ende ther was" of the elaborately wrought pin which secures his hood (197). This little device is as ambiguous in meaning as the Prioress' broach and for the same reason: it can have both a sacred and a purely secular meaning. The love-knot could symbolize Christ or the foursome of the Trinity and Mary, or it could symbolize the purity of human love. In the Monk's case, however, the Poet wishes the reader to see it as emblematic of his inordinate sexual appetite – profane, not sacred, love.

That this is not reading too much into these lines is shown by the words which the Host speaks to the Monk immediately before the Monk tells his tale:

> God give that man confusion
> Who first brought you into the religious life!
> You would have been a great breeding cock.
> Had you as much freedom as you have strength
> To satisfy all your lust in procreation,
> You would have fathered many a creature.
> ("The Monk's Prologue" author's modernization)

The Host is frankly incredulous that the Monk should ever have become a cleric, adding that he is by nature such a lustful man that, if he were free to copulate as much as he wants to, then he would have fathered a great many children. Earlier, the Host decides to call the Monk (whose real name he says he does not know) "my lord Don John, / Or daun Thomas, or elles daun Albon." Now 'John Thomas' is English slang for the penis which makes the Host's intention clear.

It may be that the Host calls the Monk "Albon" after St Alban, the first British Christian martyr (3rd century). The Monk is a martyr precisely because he does have to restrain his sexual desires somewhat.

The final fifteen lines of the portrait are devoted to the Monk's physical appearance and his "array". The Monk's clothes are intended to convey his high social status. The wide sleeves of his cassock are trimmed with the finest grey fur, which almost certainly means that it is Russian gray squirrel, a luxury item at the time. It probably comes as no surprise that monks were not allowed to wear fur trimming on their garments, so by doing this the Monk is openly defying his order and associating with the secular world of the merchant class and the minor nobility.

The last few lines of the portrait are unusual because of their discontinuity: five main clauses, unconnected by conjunctions, and each end-stopped:

> His bootes souple, his hors in greet estaat.
> Now certeinly he was a fair prelaat;
> He was nat pale as a forpined goost.
> A fat swan loved he best of any roost.
> His palfrey was as broun as is a berie. (203-7)

There are thirteen unconnected main clauses in the preceding thirty-seven lines, giving an average main clause length of just under three lines, so these lines are stylistically different. Here the Pilgrim jumps from topic to unrelated topic (boots to horse to superlative to food to horse). There is no principle of organization, as though even the Pilgrim has lost interest in this man and just wants to get the portrait over with.

The Monk wears expensive boots which are another sign of his dressing in imitation of the rich and in direct contravention of the rules of his order. The leather is "souple" like the Monk who bends the rules to his own desires. The lines end with a reference to the Monk's appetite which makes him "a lord ful fat and in good point" (200). As a monk, he should be vegetarian, but we are told that this Monk enjoys swan best of all roast meats, implying that (again like the Prioress) he eats a wide range of roasted meats. Swan was a dish associated with (if not actually reserved for) royalty, and is a deliberate contrast with the Monk's earlier dismissive reference to common chicken ("a pulled hen" [177]). Since the twelfth century the king owned all unmarked swans on the River Thames. Even praise of his horse is achieved by a food simile, "as broun as is a berie." He rides a palfrey, a horse with a smooth ambling gait which was highly valued for riding. A good palfrey could cost as much as a knight's destrier, thus it functions as a status symbol and validates the comment that the Monk, "Ful many a deyntee hors hadde he in stable" (168).

Lines 208-272: The Friar

I found there friars from each of the four orders,
Preaching to the people for their personal profit,
Interpreting the Gospel just as they saw fit,
Desiring apparel for themselves, they twisted it as they liked.
Many of these master friars wear what they choose,
For to them money and preaching go together …
So long as Fortune is your friend, the friars will always love you.
(Langland. *The Vision of Piers Plowman* author's modernization)

[Friars] preach poverty to us, but they always have their hand stretched out to receive riches … Oh, how the friar conducts himself when he comes to a poor house! Oh, how he knows how to give a sermon! Even if the lady has little or nothing … [he] takes a halfpenny if she does not have a penny …
(John Gower *The Mirror of Mankind* Norton Anthology)

In Chaucer's England, there were four orders of Friars: Franciscans, Dominicans, Carmelites, and Augustinians. Monks and friars took similar vows of Poverty, Chastity and Obedience to the rules of their order, but, unlike monks, friars went out into the world to minister to the spiritual needs of the laity, particularly the poor and the sick. This meant that they duplicated the rôle of parsons in preaching, saying mass, taking confession, and accepting offerings, and this was the cause of some resentment and friction.

The Mendicant Friars (Franciscans and Dominicans) lived by begging, but this activity, which St. Francis had allowed only when actually necessary, had by Chaucer's time become very profitable, so much so that friars purchased the exclusive begging rights to an area from their order. The potential for corruption was enormous since there was no way to check on the amount which the friar actually raised by begging over and above what he paid for his license (Bowden *Guide* 57).

Probably the most famous friar in medieval literature is Friar Tuck who appears in the tales of Robin Hood and is noted for his humor and his love of good food and wine. However, as Pollard notes, "about the time Chaucer wrote, they [friars] must have been especially unpopular, as in 1385, in consequence of riots in which their houses were pulled down, a proclamation had to be issued for their protection" (52).

Pilgrim:
1. The Pilgrim finds the Friar a deeply impressive man. One indication of this is the company the man keeps. Explain.
2. Approval is also given of the Friar's theory and practice of confession. What arguments does the Friar use to support his approach to giving absolution and how does the Pilgrim indicate his approval?
3. The Friar is "the beste beggere in his hous" (252). What details are given to explain his success?
4. The appearance of the Friar also wins the Pilgrim's admiration. Give details.
Poet:
Everything that the Friar does is stunningly inappropriate to his vocation. The comic irony results from the Pilgrim presenting as eminently reasonable that which is totally indefensible. Amongst the many inappropriate interests and activities of the Monk, the following are the most important: a) sexual misconduct; b) gaining money by false pretenses; c) the cultivation of friendships with the wealthy; d) disregarding the needs of the poor and the sick.
5. Suggest a rather reprehensible explanation of why the Friar might have arranged many marriages of young women at his own cost.

6. What other indications are there in the portrait that the Friar is sexually promiscuous?

7. The Friar is said to be, "Curteis … and lowely of servise" (250) in what appears to be a virtual repetition of this line describing the Squire, "Curteis he was, lowely, and servisable" (99). What ulterior motive does the Poet include which exposes the hypocrisy of the Friar?

8. How does the Poet bring home the immoral reality of the Friar's skill at begging?

9. What elements of the Friar's appearance and social interaction with others are implicitly criticized at the end of the portrait?

> There was a Friar, easygoing and merry,
> Who was a limiter [i.e., licensed to beg within a particular, or limited, district], a very impressive man.
> 210 In all of the four orders of Friars there was none who knew
> So much about sweet conversation and fine language.
> He had arranged a number of marriages
> For young women and paid all the expenses out of his own pocket.
> He was the pillar of his Order.
> 215 He had a close friendship
> With the franklins in his district
> And also with the women of high social standing in the town;
> He had the power of taking Confession for serious sins
> As he said himself, with more authority than the parish priest,
> 220 Because he was licensed by his Order.
> He heard Confession in a very gentle way
> And getting absolution from him was a pleasure;
> He was an easy man when it came to giving out punishments
> Wherever he knew he would get plenty of money.
> 225 To give a donation to a poor Order
> Is a sure sign that a man is truly repentant
> For if a man offered a gift after confession
> The Friar was ready to vouch that he really was sorry for what he'd done;
> Because many men's hearts are so hard
> 230 That they cannot cry, although their sin hurts them deeply.
> Therefore instead of crying and praying
> Men must give silver to the poor Friars.
> His cape was stuffed full of knives
> And pins to give to young women.

235   Certainly he had a very pleasant voice;
     He sang and played well
     And at singing popular songs he was the best.
     His neck was as white as the lily;
     He was as strong as a professional fighter.
240   He knew well all of the taverns in every town
     And every innkeeper and barmaid
     Better than any lepers or beggar women;
     For such an important man as he
     It was not appropriate, he thought,
245   To be acquainted with sick lepers.
     It was not respectable or profitable
     To have dealings with such poor people,
     But only with rich people and food merchants.
     And wherever profit was likely
250   He was courteous and humble in his manners.
     Nowhere was there any man so effective.
     He was the best beggar in his friary;
     And paid a rent for begging rights;
     No other friars dared to come onto his patch;
255   Even if a widow was extremely poor
     So pleasant his reading of 'In principio' was
     That he would have a farthing before he left her.
     What he made from begging was much more than the sum he paid
     for his begging license.
     He knew how to play just like a puppy.
260   He was very useful at lovedays [days appointed for the settlement
     of disputes by arbitration]
     For he was not like a person locked away in a cloister
     With a threadbare old cloak like a poor scholar,
     But he dressed like a Master of Arts or a Pope.
     His cloak was made of fine heavy wool
265   It was rounded like a bell just out of the mould.
     He lisped a little, out of affectation,
     To make his English sound sweet on his tongue;
     And when playing the harp after he had sung
     His eyes twinkled in his head just
270   Like the stars in the frosty night.
     This worthy limiter was called Hubert.

Superlatives are rained down on the Friar: he is "a full solempne man" (209), "a noble post" to his order (214), and "Ther nas no man nowher so vertuous" (251). The adjective "worthy" is held back until the final line of the Friar's portrait, by which time it is clear that the word only applies in the sense that his corruption has given him wealth and high social status. The Friar is a limiter (i.e. he is licensed to solicit alms within certain assigned limits) which is a particularly ironic designation given because there is no rule of his order, nor any moral law, which he will not break in pursuit of his own pleasure. Arnold Williams writes that he is one of the small group of pilgrims who has "no mitigating virtues." Whilst the Prioress and the Monk simply ignore the obligations of their orders to live lifestyles which suit them, the Friar actively exploits his religious position and perverts the holy sacraments, endangering the souls of others in doing so, for his own financial and sexual gain. In this, he prefigures the Pardoner.

It is said that you can judge someone by the company he keeps, and it is on this principle that the Poet builds the irony of the Friar's portrait:

> Ful wel biloved and famulier was he
> With frankeleyns over al in his contree,
> And eek with worthy wommen of the toun; (215-7)

He consorts with country landowners, minor gentry and wealthy women (the word "worthy" carries no implication of moral virtue here). The description of his social circle continues:

> He knew the tavernes wel in every toun
> And everich hostiler and tappestere
> Bet than a lazar or a beggestere;
> For unto swich a worthy man as he
> Acorded nat, as by his facultee,
> To have with sike lazars aqueyntaunce.
> It is nat honest, it may nat avaunce,
> For to deelen with no swich poraille,
> But al with riche and selleres of vitaille.
> And over al, ther as profit sholde arise,
> Curteis he was and lowely of servise.
> Ther nas no man nowher so vertuous.
> He was the bests beggere in his house; (240-52)

Tavern keepers and barmaids he knows rather than poor people and sick lepers. Now the entire purpose of the friars (and what made them different from the monks) was to go out into the secular world and revive it with spiritual life. The Poet chooses the Pilgrim's words with great care. The Friar, who is supposed to live by begging, will have nothing to do with "beggestere"! The Friar regards himself as "worthy," but he is so only in the sense of being wealthy and associating with those of high social class. This section ends with two praise-lines, but once more it is the juxtaposition with details which entirely negate the praise which is ironic. The Friar is "Curteis" (courteous) and "lowely of seriyse" (humble), but these are ploys not virtues, means to the end of enriching himself. The Poet intends a parallel and a contrast with this line describing the Squire, "Curteis he was, lowely, and servisable" (99). For all his comic excesses, the Squire serves out of a sense of respect for his father and for the ideals of knighthood, whilst the Friar serves only his own self-interest. The final line is another superlative: the Friar is the most virtuous man anywhere, which is an improbable conclusion given what has just been said of him. However, the word "vertuous" is deliberately ambiguous. Whilst the Pilgrim is presumably using the word in its moral denotation, the Poet uses it to mean power, strength, and effectiveness - the same meaning which was referenced in the description of the "licour / Of which vertu engendred is the flour" (3-4). This statement of the Friar's power is appropriately followed by a detailed description of his devious, even ruthless, but highly effective begging techniques. (The word will be used of the Parson on line 517 where the context will make clear that it carries both denotations.)

Victims are not entirely absent from the *Prologue*:

> For thogh a widwe hadde noght a sho...
> Yet wolde he have a ferthing, er he wente. (255-7)

This is clearly a reference to Jesus' warning in Mark 12:38-40 against "scribes, which love to go in long clothing, and *love* salutations in the market places, and the chief seats in the synagogues, and the uppermost rooms at feasts: which devour widows' houses, and for a pretense make long prayers: these shall receive greater damnation" which comes just before the story of the widow who willingly donated "two mites, which make a farthing" (Mark 12:41-3 King James Version). The description of the abuse of clerical power fits the Friar exactly and he is shown to reverse the entire point of Jesus' parable by tricking the poor widow out of her two mites.

The Friar is licensed by his order to hear confessions for more serious sins than the local parish priests. The Pilgrim comments approvingly:

> Ful swetely herde he confessioun,
> And plesaunt was his absolucioun:
> He was an esy man to yeve penaunce,
> Ther as he wiste to have a good pitaunce. (221-4)

It is significant that the positive words used all refer to the effect upon the sinner of the Friar's way of taking confessions and not to the motivation of the Friar: the result is sweet, pleasant and easy. In contrast, when he describes the conscientious Parson dealing with his parishioners' sin of not paying tithes, the Pilgrim uses positive words which describe his moral principles:

> Benigne he was, and wonder diligent,
> And in adversitee ful pacient,
> And swich he was ypreved ofte sithes.
> Ful looth were him to cursen for his tithes, (485-8)

The Parson is forgiving because he is naturally kind, diligent and patient, and because he knows the terrible consequences of excommunication. The Friar's true motivation is hinted at in line 224: his hearing of confession is only sweet, pleasant and easy where he gains financially. (Compare Langland's Friar who tells Lady Lucre, "'Don't worry ... I will give you absolution – for a small offering, of course – shall we say a horse-load of wheat'" [*The Vision of Piers Plowman*, author's modernization].) This is hard for even the naïve Pilgrim to defend, so he does what he did in presenting the Monk's view that monks should not stay studying in their cloister: he closely paraphrases the Friar's own argument:

> For unto a povre ordre for to yive
> Is signe that a man is wel yshrive;
> For if he yaf, he dorste make avaunt,
> He wiste that a man was repentaunt;
> For many a man so hard is of his herte,
> He may nat wepe, althogh him soore smerte.
> Therfore in stede of wepinge and preyeres
> Men moote yeve silver to the povre freres. (225-32)

Once again, the reader appears to hear the Friar's own forceful defense of his practice, particularly in the emphatic use of alliteration, "For many a man so hard is of his herte, / He may nat wepe, althogh him soore smerte." The argument is, of course,

101

patently absurd since the entire point of confession is for the sinner to have a change of heart. Notice the repetition of the word "povre" to describe the Friars, making it sound as though giving money to them is a genuine act of charity. Again a contrast with the Parson puts the Friar's arguments in their correct moral context:

> But rather wolde he yeven, out of doute,
> Unto his povre parisshens aboute
> Of his offring and eek of his substaunce. (489-91)

The Parson is truly "povre," but rather than excommunicate sinners he himself pays their tithes. It is significant that the Pilgrim does not immediately follow this paraphrase of the Friar's argument with an exclamation of approval such as he did the Monk ("And I seyde his opinion was good" [183]). All that the Pilgrim can find to marvel at is the Friar's effectiveness, which is hardly in doubt:

> He was the beste beggere in his hous;
> And yaf a certeyne ferme for the graunt;
> Noon of his bretheren cam ther in his haunt;
> For thogh a widwe hadde noght a sho,
> So plesaunt was his '*In principio*',
> Yet wolde he have a ferthing, er he wente.
> His purchas was wel bettre than his rente. (252-8)

Here the Pilgrim gives us the cost-benefit analysis in business terms: the Friar pays a certain amount for his begging license in a particular area and by his efficiency he always makes a good profit. He does this partly by maintaining his monopoly in that area, but also by exploiting another advantage. St. John's Gospel ("In the beginning was the Word...") was long thought to be special, even magical, and there were restrictions on when it could be read and by whom. As with most things that are banned, this made people even more interested in hearing it read, and the friars happily filled this gap in the market. Pollard quotes the author of *Jack Upland* (1401) telling the friars, "Ye win more by yere with *In Principio* than with all the rules that ever your patrones made" (55). The Poet ensures that the reader gets a clear view of his victims: he will squeeze a farthing out of the very poorest woman.

The Squire's hypersexuality is treated by the Poet with indulgence and gentle comedy: it is much more likely that he stays up all night pining for his lady love than actually having sex with her. Either way, his strong libido is appropriate to his youth, which is clearly related to the outburst of life in spring described at the start of the poem, and to his status. This is clearly not the case for the three clerics, but in relation to sex they are presented very differently. The Prioress appears to have sublimated her desires entirely into the pursuit of the ideals of Courtly Love; the Monk's sexual activity is hinted at in his portrait through double entendre, but the Poet gives no actual details. In contrast, the Friar's sexuality is spelled out in the clearest terms. Firstly, he is shown to be expert at seducing women with his love-making and false promises:

> In alle the ordres foure is noon that kan
> So muchel of daliaunce and fair langage. (210-11)

It seems ironically superfluous to comment that he is the most skillful seducer in the four orders of friars, since (at least in theory) there should be relatively little competition. The Friar is shown to travel prepared with seduction gifts, kept ironically in the hood of his habit:

> His tipet was ay farsed ful of knives
> And pinnes, for to yeven faire wives. (233-4)

It is a subtle touch by the Poet to make the point that the Friar can afford to be choosy: he is interested only in attractive women. Nor does the Poet avoid the consequences of the Friar's sexual promiscuity, although he deals with it euphemistically: young girls get pregnant, and he buys them off by securing them a husband and paying the expenses of the marriage. The register of the bishop of Bath and Wells for 1321 records the case of a friar who had reneged on his promise to provide a dowry for a young woman by whom he had fathered two children (Bowden *Commentary* 124):

> He hadde maad ful many a mariage
> Of yonge wommen at his owene cost.
> Unto his ordre he was a noble post. (212-4)

The praise-line which follows the details of the Friar's sexual corruption gains obvious irony by the juxtaposition. The reader must decide whether the metaphor of the Friar as a pillar or column is a phallic joke – for myself, I have not the faintest doubt of it.

The Poet's final comment on the Friar's sexuality is the height of ironic understatement:

> In love-dayes ther koude he muchel help, (260)

Jane Austen, no less, defined love-days as "a day formerly appointed for an amicable adjustment of differences." Bowden points out that a love-day was a day appointed by the civil courts for the amicable reconciliation of specific court cases, and thus that the Friar meddles in civil affairs, "an act expressly forbidden in the Rules of the Mendicant Orders" (*Guide* 59). The practice of love-days had fallen into disrepute long before Chaucer's day having declined into bribery, coercion, and the victory of the more powerful party in the dispute. The Poet's irony rests on the fact that, while it would indeed be appropriate for a friar to use his position and his negotiating skills to bring together arguing factions, this Friar, who actually abuses his skills and position of trust to seduce young women, would certainly enter fully into the profitable corruption of love-days.

The description of the Friar's clothing is satirical:

> His tipet was ay farsed ful of knives
> And pinnes, for to yeven faire wives. (233-4)
> … he was nat lik a cloisterer
> With a thredbare cope, as is a povre scoler,
> But he was lyk a maister or a pope.
> Of double worstede was his semicope,
> That rounded as a belle out of the presse. (261-5)

The exact nature of a "tipet" is a little unclear, but the Ellesmere Manuscript shows the Friar wearing a very loose hood which drapes like a stole on his shoulders. At the rear, the hood falls half-way down the Friar's back forming a very deep 'pocket' in which he carries his seduction gifts forming a visual symbol of the way in which this man perverts the rule of his order for his own pleasure and self-interest. His habit appears in the illustration to have decorative trimming, like that of the Monk: it is said to be made of the finest quality woolen cloth and to be trimmed with fur.

Where the Monk strikes the Pilgrim as having the qualities to be an abbot, the Friar dresses up in a way that reminds the Pilgrim of a Master of Arts or a Pope! He certainly does not look like someone who spends his whole time in the cloister studying and wearing a threadbare habit. In this context, the closing comment about the Friar's clothes is particularly satirical: his habit resembles a newly cast bell. Obviously this reminds us of the Friar's gluttony (all three of the clerics in this group have 'fuller figures'), but the simile of the bell recalls a parallel simile used to describe the bells on the Monk's bridle (170-1), and with the same implication: the Friar may have the same shape as a bell, but that is his only association with bells because he never hears the bells of his cloister.

The portrait says little about the Friar's physical appearance

> And certeinly he hadde a murie note:
> Wel koude he singe and pleyen on a rote;
> Of yeddinges he baar outrely the prys.
> His nekke whit was as the flour-de-lys;
> Therto he strong was as a champioun. (235-9)

Like the obnoxious Pardoner, he sings inappropriate ballads rather than hymns. His throat is white which is surprising since friars were supposed to spend most of their time outside. Ironically, the white lily symbolizes the Virgin Mary and thus represents innocent beauty, chastity and purity, and it was also a symbol of Easter representing Resurrection and immortality. However, it is an ambiguous symbol for Jason Johnson states that, "According to medieval thinking, this outward characteristic [the white neck] reflects a lecherous heart" but he offers no evidence for this assertion. Like the Prioress who intones nasally when she sings, the Friar speaks in an affected way:

> Somwhat he lipsed, for his wantownesse,
> To make his Englissh sweete upon his tonge;
> And in his harping, whan that he hadde songe,
> His eyen twinkled in his heed aright,
> As doon the sterres in the frosty night.
> This worthy limitour was cleped Huberd. (266-71)

More emphasis is placed on his inappropriate singing and harping, and then the fourth image is used to describe the Friar. Perhaps strangely, the Pilgrim makes a rather beautiful, poetic comparison between the Friar's sparkling eyes and the stars in the night sky on a clear, cold evening. However, knowledge of contemporary physiognomy casts a more sinister light. The *Secreta Secretorum*, a mid-12th century Latin translation of a 10th century Arabic encyclopedic treatise, says that "ryght opyn eighyn and glysinynge" indicates a shameless man (Bowden *Commentary* 275). These lines leave us in no doubt about the personal magnetism of this man and his attractiveness, but the use of the word "worthy" after all that we have learned of his corrupt exploitation of his position (an exploitation which not only takes money from the guilty and the innocent alike, but also puts their mortal soles in jeopardy), is bitterly ironic.

Chapter Six: The Merchant, The Clerk, The Sergeant of the Law, The Franklin, The Five Guildsmen, and The Cook

From consideration of three representatives of traditional Church orders, Chaucer moves on to the rising middle class. Each of these pilgrims (though in different ways) is representative of the entrepreneurial middle class where a man could rise in status through his own efforts.

Lines 273-286: The Merchant

[Wool merchants] contrive all kinds of trickery and conspiracy in order to collect great quantities of you [i.e., wool]. And then they take you overseas as if you were the mistress of their ships. And in order to get you, the people come to bargain in covetousness and envy. Foreign exchange, usury, and bargaining... (John Gower *The Mirror of Mankind* Norton Anthology)

I have lent lords and ladies my merchandise,
And been their broker after, and bought it myself.
Currency dealing and usury ("Eschaunges and chevysaunces") - in such business I deal,
And lend to folk who will lose a part every florin they borrow.
(Langland. *The Vision of Piers Plowman* author's modernization)

The reference in the portrait to the towns of Middleburg and Orwell, two ports important to the wool and cloth trade from the 1380s, suggest that this pilgrim is a member of either the Merchants of the Staple, principally exporters of wool, or the Merchant Adventurers, principally importers of cloth from the Low Countries, or conceivably both since membership was not exclusive. From 1384 to 1388 the wool staple was at Middleburg, a port on the Dutch coast, the closest English port to which was Orwell.

Pilgrim:

1. The Merchant is an outwardly impressive man. What details does the Pilgrim give to illustrate this trait concerning: a) his clothes; b) the way he interacts with others (his manner of speaking particularly); c) his bearing (literally the way he holds himself)?

2. What evidence does the Pilgrim give to support the impression that the Merchant is a successful businessman?

Poet:

The Merchant is a fake: the impressive façade hides the fact that he is in debt, or at least is operating on credit, and therefore always close to going bankrupt.

3. In the light of this, comment on the Poet's intention in including the following details: a) his "forked beard" (272); b) his wearing "mottelee" (273); c) having the Pilgrim admit on the final line that, "I noot how men him calle" (286).

4. It is obviously vital for this man's business that the seas between England and Holland are kept free from pirates: no irony there. The irony is in the way in which the poet expresses the Merchant's desire, "He wolde the see were kept for any thing" (278). Explain what the Poet is implying here. (If you do not see it, ask yourself: Who does the Merchant want to keep the seas clear? Who is paying?)

5. It is even questionable whether this man is really a merchant at all. Explain how he makes his money. What word might we apply to the Merchant today?

	There was a merchant with forked beard,
	In a gown of multicolored cloth he sat high on his horse;
	Upon his head he wore a Flemish hat of beaver fur;
275	His boots were fastened attractively and elegantly.
	He spoke his opinions rather pompously,
	Always proclaiming the growth of his profits.
	He wanted the sea kept free of pirates at any cost
	Between Middleburgh and Orwell.
280	He was skilled at making money by dealing in French gold coins.
	This worthy man used all his wits;
	There was no one who knew he was in debt,
	So dignified was the management of all his business affairs
	With his buying and selling and his currency trading [usury].
285	Truly, he was a worthy man,
	But, truth to say, I do not know his name.

In both his clothes and his bearing, the Merchant is an impressive man, and the Pilgrim is duly impressed, "For sooth he was a worthy man with ale" (285). This portrait is one of the few which describes an entire outfit. He is dressed fashionably, though not extravagantly, giving an outward appearance of firmly based prosperity without appearing to flaunt his wealth. An expensive beaver fur hat of Flemish manufacture, of the kind favored by the nobility, indicates his involvement in trading with Flanders, and his boots have elegant fastenings. The Merchant rides a tall horse, or perhaps he sits upright in the saddle, or (more probably) both, and in his conversation he repeatedly stresses the profits he has made in business.

So far so good; the worst one might say is that the Merchant is a little self-centered and rather pompous. The Poet, however, has planted two clues in the physical description which the reader is supposed to notice. Firstly, the Merchant has "a forked berd" (272), which points to his having a dual nature, and secondly he is dressed in "mottelee" (273). Motley is variously explained as variegated cloth or more specifically as "cloth woven from threads of two colors" (Kirkham and Allen 36), and thus it implies that the Merchant is similarly composed of diverse, incongruous elements, implying that in this case appearance and reality do not match. These two details should alert the reader to the central contradiction in the character of the Merchant which David Williams describes thus, "While on the one hand he is described as solemn, worthy, and stately, on the other hand he is also a thoroughgoing materialist, deceitful, and totally dedicated to profit making" (39).

The Pilgrim reports faithfully the tenor and tone of the Merchant's conversation in lines which actually highlight the gap between appearance and reality:

>His resons he spak ful solempnely,
>Sowninge alwey th'encrees of his winning. (276-7)

The word "solempnely" links back to the Friar who was described as "a ful solempne man" (209). Any parallel with the despicable Friar must make the reader suspicious that this pilgrim is likewise not what he seems to be, or (as is clear from the quotation above) is not what he advertises himself to be. Once alerted, the reader has no difficulty in seeing the true significance of details which the Pilgrim notes with approval. The Merchant "wolde the see were kept [safe for trade] for any thyng" between Middleburg, at the mouth of the Scheldt, in

Holland, and Orwell, a seaport in Essex (278). He pays his taxes (in this case the subsidy of tonnage and poundage paid to the crown), and he expects the King to do whatever is necessary to keep the seas free of pirates. His profits depend on it: self-interest rules.

The Pilgrim next praises the Merchant's business acumen, "Wel koude he in eschaunge sheeldes selle. / ... With his bargaines and with his chevissaunce" (280-4). What is interesting in these lines is the Poet's emphasis on the possessive pronoun "his" which suggests, at the very least, the Merchant's full control of these business arrangements. However, it emerges that his 'trading' takes the form of currency speculation, an activity which Bowden identifies as "obviously illegal practice, for the English government held a monopoly on the right to buy and sell foreign currency" and seen by the Church as sinful since wealth was generated without actual labor (*Guide* 109). Bowden identifies "chevissaunce" as "a euphemistic word for what amounted to medieval 'usury' [i.e., the lending of money at interest]" which the Church condemned (*Guide* 107). The term "bargaines" also carries negative connotations "suggesting a transaction with unpleasant consequences or a struggle for mastery" (Reale in Lambdin and Lambdin 97). Pollard quotes the Ordinance Against Usurers of 1338 denouncing, "certain persons ... who maintain the false and abominable contract of usury, under cover and colour of lawful trading which ... they call 'exchange' or 'chevisance'" (58). The business skill which the Pilgrim so admires thus turns out to be the manipulation of deals using credit, money-lending, and the fooling of those with whom he trades so that they do not perceive that he is close to being bankrupt:

> This worthy man ful wel his wit bisette:
> Ther wiste no wight that he was in dette, (281-2)

These lines have balanced alliteration of the consonant 'w' which has the effect of slowing the rhythm and adding force to the second, the undercutting line. It thus emerges that the Merchant is neither "worthy" in the moral nor in the economic sense: he appears to be the Bernie Madoff of his day – a con man always on the point of going under.

The final four lines illustrate the Poet's use of juxtaposition:

> So estatly was he of his governaunce
> With his bargaines and with his chevissaunce.
> For sothe he was a worthy man with alle,

> But, sooth to seyn, I noot how men him calle. (283-6)

Firstly, the impressive terms "So estatly" and "governaunce" are undercut by the negative terms "bargaines" and "chevissaunce." Then the Poet repeats the word "soothe … sooth," as a way of drawing the reader's attention to the contradiction between the two 'truths' stated. The Pilgrim makes no causal connection between the Merchant's worthiness and his own inability to recall his name. Indeed, it seems counter-intuitive since the man is so impressive, but even this does not strike the Pilgrim. The Poet, however, knows that the reader will get the message: the Merchant is a fraud, all show, and certainly not worth remembering.

Lines 287-310: The Clerk

> [Scholars] have left off the virtue of study, and now they apply their studies vigilantly to vices. Scarcely one studies for the sake of the necessary subject matter … A cleric used to go to school with a patient spirit, but now worldly glory is his master. He rambles here and there, a lazy, wandering drunkard, wayward and given to lust. (John Gower *Vox clamantis* or *The Voice of One Crying Out* in Miller 218)

The Clerk's appearance is a total contrast to that of the previous four pilgrims: the Clerk is one of only four pilgrims (the Knight, Lawyer, and Reeve are the others) whose dress is actually below their social status. The description of the Clerk derives from contemporary stereotypes of the poor student rather than from the stereotype of the riotous student used by Gower above.

In Chaucer's day, students typically entered Oxford University at the age of fourteen. Their first course of study was the *trivium* (grammar, logic, and rhetoric). The Clerk's age is not given, but since he "unto logic hadde longe ygo" (288) he has evidently passed the *trivium* and is presumably either a Bachelor or Master of Arts at a university which "was noted throughout Europe for the study of logic and for the masters who did the teaching and the writing" (Dillon in

Lambdin and Lambdin 109). Since he is clearly a potential candidate for a benefice, he must be a cleric in minor orders.

Pilgrim:

The Clerk is an obsessive character - a dedicated student who prefers learning over worldly pleasures and pursuits. The Pilgrim does not express his approval as overtly as he does with other characters, but it is clear that he is impressed with the Clerk's knowledge and gravity.

1. How many books does the Clerk own in his personal library? Why would this be an impressive number in Chaucer's day?

2. The Clerk appears to have no income because he has not taken a paid position in the Church which was the normal career path of Oxford graduates. So how exactly does he get the money he needs to study?

3. On what does the Clerk spend the money that he gets, and on what things does he resist spending money?

4. The Clerk comes across as learned and wise. What about his social interaction with others helps to foster this impression?

Poet:

It is easy to dismiss the Clerk as a harmless eccentric, but a careful reading shows that the Poet finds much about the Clerk to criticize.

5. What are the consequences (for himself and for his horse) of the Clerk's obsession with books?

6. The Clerk is "holwe" in more than the literal sense (i.e., half-starved). What is really hollow about him becomes clear when the reader examines the uses to which the Clerk puts his massive learning. This is what the Poet will later say of the poor Parson of a town in an appreciative portrait which all commentators agree to be entirely without irony, "first he wroghte, and afterward he taught" [499] and "Christes lore... / He taughte, but first he folwed it himselve" [529-530]. What light does this description shed on the portrait of the Clerk?

7. There is something contrived about the way in which the Clerk interacts with others. Explain.

8. The second line of the portrait (288) appears simply to record the depth of the Clerk's learning, but there is a sting in the tail. Explain.

9. The Pilgrim's innocent joke that though he was a "philosophre / Yet hadde he but litel gold in cofre" (299-300) now appears to be

more cutting. Why does the Poet regard this pilgrim as worthy of scorn?

> A scholar from Oxford was with us also,
> Who had long ago begun the study of logic.
> His horse was as thin as a rake,
> 290 Nor was he himself too fat, I can tell you,
> But he looked hollow and of a serious disposition.
> His jacket was completely threadbare;
> Because he had not yet secured an ecclesiastical living,
> Nor was he interested in holding a secular office.
> 295 For he would rather have at his bed's head
> Twenty books, bound in black and red leather,
> Of Aristotle and his philosophy
> Than have rich robes, a fiddle, or fine harp.
> Yet for all that he was philosopher,
> 300 He had but little gold in his coffers;
> But all that he could borrow from his friends
> He would spend on books and learning,
> And then he'd pray earnestly for the souls
> Of those who gave him the wherewithal to stay in school.
> 305 He gave study his utmost care and attention.
> Not one word more than was necessary did he speak;
> And that was said with due formality and dignity
> And brief and pithy and full of meaning.
> His speech was suffused with moral virtue;
> 310 And willingly would he learn and happily teach.

Although the Pilgrim uses not one superlative in his description of him, at first reading the Clerk appears to be harmless enough. Bowden concludes that he is "a worthy individual" (*Commentary* 162), and some commentators have mistakenly found him admirable and even placed him amongst the idealized portraits. (Critics tend to make this mistake because they are teachers!) It is particularly tempting to do so because this portrait comes between that of the Merchant and the Lawyer who pursue their professions with the sole goal of enriching themselves. In contrast, the Clerk is the eternal student taking his obsession with buying books and studying a little too far to the detriment of his health and at the expense of his friends who nevertheless seem willing enough to subsidize his habit. Yet it all seems worth it, for when the Clerk speaks he does so with respect and dignity, and his subject is ever moral virtue. Surely the final complement, "And gladly wolde he lerne and gladly teche" is unambiguous enough (310)? Commentators have traditionally thought so.

Derek Brewer finds the line quoted to be a "quite explicit" complement to Oxford University and, commenting that the Clerk "demonstrates the analytical, and pedagogical, side of his [Chaucer's] mind," concludes that "the praise of the Clerk of Oxenford could well be taken for Chaucer himself" (206). Hirsh, writing in 2003, who firmly rejects the idea that the Knight is an idealized portrait concluding that "there is no more ambiguous noble representation in all of literature" (46) and that his portrait, "probably represents a serious and complex meditation on the problems of chivalry, and perhaps on those of warfare itself" (47), nevertheless believes that the Clerk's is an idealized portrait citing as his defining characteristics, "his dedication to study, his prayers for those who have assisted him financially, his modest and pithy style, and the 'high meaning' which he is said to reveal" (51-2).

Normally either praised as admirable or dismissed with a smile as a harmless obsessive, the Clerk is actually a more deeply flawed human being than most readers realize. Consider the following comment made by Wetherbee, and see if you can spot the self-contradiction in the critic's interpretation:

> Chaucer gives no clear sign of anything but admiration for this figure, but in a post-plague world where there was a desperate need for literate and conscientious parish clergy, the Clerk's remoteness is perhaps open to question … his activity is confined to an academic setting. In the absence of any sure indication of higher purpose, his sheer singlemindedness is potentially as self-interested as the materialism of his fellow-professionals. (27)

The contradiction is that the critic is convinced that there is no "clear sign" of the writer's intention, yet he understands precisely the grounds on which the Clerk is presented as morally flawed.

In reality, the Clerk has repeatedly slipped under the radar of readers who have missed the very real faults of this man, and the Poet's merciless exposure of them. The portrait begins with the statement that the Clerk is a serious student of "logik" which Dillon comments "quite illogically prompts him [the Pilgrim] to observe the physical poverty of the Clerk" (Dillon in Lambdin and Lambdin 111). What Dillon misses here is the Poet's use of ironic juxtaposition: the Clerk, who is so brilliant in logic, appears not to understand that his horse is emaciated because he needs feeding, "As leene was his hors as is a rake" (289). Only after this joke at the Clerk's expense does the Poet make the same observation about the man himself:

> And he nas nat right fat, I undertake,
> But looked holwe, and therto sobrely. (290-1)

The Ellesmere illustration shows the Clerk dressed far too well. In fact, his coat is threadbare, and he does not wear the short jacket favored by the more fashionable of the pilgrims. These details have been carefully given before the explanation: the man has not yet got himself a church benefice, "For he hadde geten him yet no benefice" (293), and is too unworldly to consider one of the secular positions for which his university training would have prepared him. Only when the reader has understood the Poet's criticism of Clerk is the irony of the word "yet" clear: it is not that he has not yet got a benefice, but that he will never get a benefice.

The Clerk is poor through choice: he would rather spend his money on books than on "robes riche, or fithele, or gay sautrie" (298). The Pilgrim's defense is impressive, since the three items named are synonymous with extravagance and frivolity. The Poet, however, counts on the reader not to have forget what the Pilgrim has forgotten which is that the whole point is that he buys books with the money he should be using to buy basics like food, and that as well as starving himself (which, though stupid, is the man's right) he is also starving his horse (which is simply cruel).

The Pilgrim now makes an indulgent joke: amazingly although he is a philosopher (as were those who searched for the Philosopher's Stone which would turn base metal into gold), he is poor:

> But al be that he was a philosophre,
> Yet hadde he but litel gold in cofre; (299-300)

All commentators have to acknowledge the irony here, but (they assure us) it is just a little joke. The BestNotes author comments, "There are no ironic overtones in the Clerk's portrait apart from the pun on his being a philosopher and yet being poor." In fact, these two lines are not a minor and unimportant aberration; they fit into the irony of the entire portrait: the Pilgrim intends us to understand that the Clerk pursues study for its own sake and not for monetary reward, but then the Poet shows us that the Clerk has indeed found the Philosopher's Stone for he maintains a steady income through the simple expedient of sponging off his friends:

> But al that he mighte of his freendes hente,
> On bookes and on lerninge he it spente,
> And bisily gan for the soules preye
> Of hem that yaf him wherwith to scoleye. (301-4)

The key word here is the verb "hente" which is normally rendered by the morally neutral word 'borrowed'; however, the word also had the denotation 'caught' which changes the implication of the line significantly. The Poet shows us a man who tricks his friends into giving him money, presumably by playing on their sympathy, and in return prays for their souls, which is a pretty sweet deal. The picture so far is not attractive: the work-shy Clerk, by living off of his friends' generosity, has sufficient money to feed himself and his horse adequately, but he chooses to do neither.

The Clerk has chosen to specialize in logic rather than theology, a choice which is reflected in his wish to have:

> Twenty bookes, clad in blak or reed
> Of Aristotle and his philosophie, (296-7)

As so often, what is not included in the portrait is as important as what is included. Indeed, we may say of the Clerk exactly what we are told of the Doctor, "His studie was but litel on the Bible" (440). The reader will perhaps object that the important thing is what the Clerk does with the learning which is the product of his single-minded endeavor. The Pilgrim is, of course, fulsome in his praise of the man's economy with words: he speaks seldom, but what he says is always to the point, always powerful and authoritative:

> Of studie took he moost cure and moost heede,
> Noght o word spak he moore than was neede,
> And that was seyd in forme and reverence,
> And short and quik and ful of hy sentence;
> Sowninge in moral vertu was his speche, (305-9)

The Pilgrim entirely misses what the Poet unerringly sees: the Clerk is a poseur who carefully waits for just the right moment to impress his listeners with his erudition. That his speech is "ful of hy sentence" appears to mean only that he makes good sense, but the word "sentence" also carries the denotation 'sententious' which implies pompous moralizing and self-righteousness. The Poet's most barbed comment, however, is given in pointing out that the Clerk's morality is limited to his speech: his words are, "Sowninge in moral vertu," just as the Merchant's words are "Sowninge always th'encrees of his winning" (277). The repetition of the same word and the same grammatical structure is surely no accident, for in each case the appearance is deceptive. The Clerk does not do anything with his learning, "And gladly wolde he lerne and gladly teche" (310). Contrast this with what we are later told of the conscientious Parson:

> But Cristes loore, and his apostles twelve
> He taughte, but first he folwed it himselve. (529-30)

As the portrait of the Parson will emphasize, actions are more morally significant than theories. The problem with the Clerk is that his learning has no product; it does not affect how he acts, "Of studie took he moost cure and moost heede" (305). The word "cure" (care) is carefully chosen by the Poet for it calls to mind the Latin phrase 'cura animarum' (cure of souls), that is the obligation on a priest to care for the souls of his parishioners. This is the end to which study should be put.

Now the reader thinks back to a word used earlier which seemed innocent enough, a mere objective observation by the sympathetic Pilgrim that the man "looked holwe" and understands that the Poet intends the word to be a damning condemnation of the Clerk's character (291). The Clerk is indeed a hollow man since the appearance of virtue which he cultivates so assiduously hides a moral vacuum. His friends' money has not been well spent: his studies appear to be without purpose. The apparent contrast between this portrait and that of the Merchant and the Lawyer was noted earlier, but now the reader sees a fundamental similarity: each of the three presents a false face to society, hiding the reality of the moral vacuum within.

Lines 311-332: The Sergeant of the Law

> There stood scores of men wearing silk scarves [a lawyer's
> badge of office]
> Important lawyers they seemed to be who served at the bar
> And pleaded cases for money and controlled the law,
> But for the love of God they would not once open their lips,
> You might as easily catch mist on the Malvern Hills

116

As get a syllable out of their mouths until money is produced...
The men of Law who argue their cases in court
Were to receive the least pardon of all,
Because the Psalm denies salvation to those who take bribes
Especially from innocent, unsuspecting folk.
(Langland. *The Vision of Piers Plowman* author's modernization)

Throughout the country everyone is complaining about ... men of law, but the name they bear is an empty one, for law includes justice but none of them pay any attention to that; they have, rather, the pretense without any good faith. I bear witness to these people that right gets but little if wrong pays generously.
(Gower *The Mirror of Mankind* Norton Anthology)

The Sergeant of the Law, who has a social status similar to the Knight, is one of England's elite members of the legal profession ranking "immediately after the judges of the king's bench and common pleas" (Manly *New Light* 133). (He has been compared to a member of the U.S. Supreme Court.) "Not only was it required by law that the judges of both the king's courts, the court of common pleas and the court of the king's bench, should be chosen from the number of the sergeants at law, but sergeants were often appointed by patent and commission to serve in the itinerant courts for specified terms [see lines 316-7]" (Manly *New Light* 145-6). He has spent many years studying at university to reach his current rank, but unlike the Clerk he has certainly put his learning to practical use in the real world. As a king's sergeant-at-law, he has every opportunity to build his personal fortune.

Pilgrim:
1. Even the Pilgrim finds nothing impressive about the lawyer's appearance. What aspects of the lawyer's conduct on the pilgrimage and his conduct of legal affairs do impress the Pilgrim?

Poet:

2. Comment on the contribution made to this portrait by lines 315 and 324.

3. Since the Lawyer is skilled at what he does, and since there is no indication that he is actually corrupt or that he does anything illegal, what does the Poet find to be the man's moral shortcoming and how do we know?

> A high-ranking barrister, prudent and wise,
> Who had frequently met his clients in the porch of St. Paul's Cathedral,
> Was also there, an outstanding talented man.
> He was discreet and exceptionally dignified –
> 315 He seemed that way because his words were so wise.
> He had very often been a judge in the Court of Assizes,
> Authorized by royal letters of appointment and with the King's full commission to hear all cases.
> Because of his expert knowledge and for his high reputation,
> He had many retainers of clothing and grants of yearly income from great men to secure his services.
> 320 There was nowhere a greater purchaser of land:
> All his contracts gave him absolute possession;
> The land deals he made could not be contested.
> There was nowhere so busy a man as he,
> And yet he appeared to be busier than he actually was.
> 325 He had a record of all the cases and legal decisions
> Made since the time of King William I.
> Furthermore, he knew how to compose and draw up a legal document,
> So that no one could find a flaw on which to base a challenge;
> And he could recite accurately every statute word for word.
> 330 He rode only in a homely coat of mixed colors,
> Girded with a band of silk, with narrow stripes;
> About his clothing, I have nothing more to say.

The Lawyer is one of the few pilgrims who dresses modestly. However, he wears a "medlee cote" (331) which alerts us to look for a disparity between appearance and reality as did the "mottelee" coat of the Merchant (273). The silk trimming likewise suggests the man's wealth. Apart from this, the portrait is almost the reverse of that of the Yeoman: where that portrait concentrates exclusively on observable details of the man's physical appearance, clothing and equipment, this portrait concentrates almost exclusively on the man's professional skills and achievements which are formidable. The result is that the Lawyer emerges as a type rather than an individual.

He has an encyclopedic knowledge of the law and can quote precedent verbatim; he writes contracts which leave no opportunity for legal appeal; when he makes land purchases, either for himself or for a client, his title is always absolute and uncontestable. As a result, he has risen high in his calling and has a great reputation: he has been a judge at the Assize Courts; he has served on the King's authority; he collects lucrative retainers from many rich clients; and he has become a great landowner by investing his wealth in land purchases. The evidence in this case appears to justify superlatives with which the Pilgrim typically begins the portrait:

> A Sergeant of the Lawe, war and wys,
> That often hadde been at the Parvis,
> Ther was also, ful riche of excellence. (311-3)

The final phrase of the first line brings the rhythm to a halt. The parenthetical use of commas isolates the alliterated monosyllables "war and wys" thus giving them emphasis. This is important because they are the keynote to this man's character: he is deliberate, cautious and brilliant in everything that he does.

The Poet, however, has another story to tell. Every detail which the Pilgrim relates he owes to the word of the lawyer, and when the Pilgrim comments:

> Discreet he was and of greet reverence –
> He semed swich, his wordes weren so wise. (314-5)

The Poet here repeats a word which he has just used to describe the Clerk's way of speaking "in forme and reverence" (307). There the word means 'with appropriate respect,' but here it describes the man himself and means 'worthy of respect.' I would argue that in both cases the respect is pure affectation. Here the Poet uses the forceful dash to interrupt the praise-line with an ironic comment. The word "semed" carries the implication that all is not what it might seem to be to a naïve observer like the Pilgrim. To ensure that the reader gets the point, the Poet repeats the word 'seemed':

> Nowher so bisy a man as he ther nas,
> And yet he semed bisier than he was. (323-4)

This has to be the ultimate put-down! It is the first instance of the Pilgrim making a consciously negative comment about one of his companions. The man is a fake, not because, like the Merchant, he is in debt, but because his entire professional persona is an act. He is an obsessive, like the Clerk, but he does not love the law for its own sake as the Clerk loves study. Bowden believes that "he has more 'fees and robes' than can honestly be explained" (*Commentary* 171), but there is no actual evidence of corruption. The truth is that, rather like the Doctor, this man uses his undoubted skills for the sole purpose of enriching himself. There really is nothing else to him: no personality, no humanity. This is hinted at in the Poet's use of ambiguity in the line:

> Al was fee simple to him in effect; (320)

The Pilgrim's praise of the Lawyer's ability to ensure that he has clear title to the land that he buys may also be read as an assertion that to him it is all about the money, and that he finds making money out of the law very 'simple.' Now the reader may reconsider the early description of the Lawyer as "ful riche of excellence" (313) and see that the word "riche" is a pun: the Lawyer is not only rich in legal ability, he is also wealthy because of his legal ability. The Poet describes the unchallengeable legality of his documentation thus:

> Therto he koude endite, and make a thing,
> Ther koude no wight pinche at his writing; (327-8)

Manly draws attention to the particular wording suggesting that "pinche" is a pun on the name Pynchbeck, the historical lawyer who Manly identifies as the model for the portrait (*New Light* 157). Another possible pun is on the word 'pinch' meaning frugality and meanness (as in 'penny-pinching') which certainly seems appropriate to the lawyer being described.

It is only at the end of the portrait that the Man of Law's appearance is described, and, as with the Knight, there is an ironic contrast between the scale of this apparent achievements and the relative poverty of his dress:

> He rood but hoomly in a medlee cote,
> Girt with a ceint of silk, with barres smale; (330-1)

Like many of the more avaricious pilgrims (the Doctor again comes to mind), the Lawyer spends very little of his money, except on the acquisition of land: he is a miser as is shown by the fact that he is poorly dressed. Even the Pilgrim appears to be embarrassed about the contrast between the Sergeant's own account of himself and what he can see with his own eyes, "Of his array telle I no lenger tale" (332).

Lines 333-362: The Franklin

Either: As a representative of the minor landed gentry, the Franklin is socially superior to most of the other pilgrims. His status is at least equal to that of the Knight and the Man of Law, and he is certainly richer than the former and possibly the latter. This Franklin accepts the social obligations which go with his position having served in parliament, and as sheriff, auditor, and justice of the peace. The portrait contains no overt criticism about the way in which he has fulfilled these rôles.

Or: As a freeholder, the Franklin ranks below the landed gentry. His status is below that of the Knight and the Man of Law, though he may be richer than the former and possibly the latter. The Franklin (rather like the Prioress) aspires to 'gentillesse,' and makes a great show of fulfilling the social obligations which go with gentility. Despite having served in parliament, and as sheriff, auditor, and justice of the peace, this Franklin is insecure about his status, and the portrait satirizes his social climbing.

These are roughly the two opposing positions taken by critics in their interpretation of the Franklin. As Sembler points out in his review of the critical debate, the problem is not in Chaucer's text but in the lack of historical evidence relating to "the rôle and place of franklins in late medieval English society" (Lambdin and Lambdin 135-44). Thus, Cooper states:

> One matter can be resolved: the Franklin is not inherently a social climber or a nouveau riche. The evidence is strongly that franklins were landed members of the minor gentry, with a long-standing stake in land ownership (45),

while David Williams says the opposite:

In the social aspect of his portrait, we see the Franklin as a nouveau riche, a person recently risen from a lower class due solely to financial success, who attempts to deny and camouflage his roots and convince himself and others of his inherent nobility by acquiring and displaying what he perceives are the accoutrements and accomplishments of his new class. (Williams 43)

In my view, the evidence appears to point to Williams being the more nearly correct. For example, Brown and Butcher point out that the unusual term "vavasour" (362) "in all probability derives from a French literary tradition in which the vavasour has an ambiguous position on the fringes of aristocratic life" (60). They go on to conclude that:

Absent from traditional estates satire ... [the Franklin] represents a social stratum in the upper reaches of the peasantry which, in the peculiar conditions of the fourteenth century, and especially those after the Black Death, began to take on some of the political and administrative functions of a declining chivalric group, the knights, while never acquiring a heritable nobility or gentility" (61).

Certainly, Chaucer's intentions in the text appear to make more sense if the reader understands the status of the Franklin to be ambiguous and insecure. This is not to claim that there is anything but gentle irony in this portrait. Indeed, the Franklin comes closest of all of the Pilgrims to the status of the historical Geoffrey Chaucer, himself the son of a wealthy London wine merchant who rose through government service in a number of prestigious posts including, in 1386, being appointed Knight of the Shire for the country of Kent.

Pilgrim:
1. What important official positions in the government and administration of the country has the Franklin held (presumably with some ability)?
2. In what other ways does the Franklin appear to carry out the obligations of a country gentleman? (Note the comparison to "Seint Julian" [342].)
Poet:
3. How do the simile on line 334 and the metaphor on line 347 influence our view of the Franklin?

4. Do you feel that this is the portrait of a man who is the backbone of the social fabric or a man in the grip of deadly sin, a glutton, proud and uncharitable? How would the Poet's statement "he was Epicurus owene sone" have influenced the medieval reader in answering that question (338)?

A Franklin there was in his company;
White was his beard as is the daisy;
335 Of sanguine temperament he was.
First thing in the morning, he loved bread dipped in spiced wine sauce;
To live in pleasure was his constant aim,
For he was a true son of Epicurus,
Who held the opinion that sensual gratification
340 Was the truest form of happiness.
A great householder was he;
Saint Julian he was in his own district.
His bread, his ale were always the same high quality;
A man with a better stocked wine cellar was nowhere to be found.
345 His house was never without baked pies
Both fish and meat, and that so plenteous
It seemed to snow food and drink in his house,
Of every dainty that a man could imagine.
According to the season of the year
350 He changed his midday meal and his supper.
Full many a fattened partridge he had in pens,
And many a bream and many a pike in his fish-pond.
Woe to his cook, unless his sauces were
Spicy and sharp, and all his kitchen implements were ready.
355 His dining table always standing in his hall
Was ready covered through the whole day.
At sessions of the magistrate's court, he was lord and president,
Often he was appointed Member of Parliament for the shire.
A dagger and a silk purse
360 Hung from his girdle, white as morning milk.
He had been sheriff and an auditor of taxes;
And nowhere was a more respectable landowner.

This is one of the more individualized portraits in terms both of the man's household and of the four offices he has held. Bowden concludes that he is "someone who is likely to have been immediately identified by his contemporaries" (*Commentary*, 174), and tentatively supports Manly's identification of the Franklin with Sir John Bussy of Lincolnshire, a man often associated with the Sergeant of Law Pynchbeck, who had a reputation amongst his enemies as an upstart (*Commentary*, 177). The Franklin gives every indication that he represents 'old' (i.e. inherited) wealth and title, in contrast to the Man of Law who seems to be largely a self-made man (i.e., a buyer of land rather than an inheritor of land). This, however, is the key to one of the central ironies of the portrait: although the line, "An housholdere, and that a greet, was he" (341) establishes that the Franklin has the wealth to support his gentry status, the portrait gives the impression that he tries somewhat too hard to exemplify the manners appropriate to the status which he has actually attained. Significantly, he wears, "An anlaas and a gipser al of silk" (359). Wearing a large hunting dagger and a purse of silk establishes his view of himself as amongst the wealthy gentry class. It would help to know definitively whether the Poet uses the word "vavasor" to mean simply "a feudal tenant ranking directly below a baron" (Mirriam-Webster) or whether the word still retained the negative connotation of its possible Latin origin from *vases vassōrum* meaning "vassal of vassals" (The Free Dictionary).

Of the man's appearance, we learn only that:

> Whit was his berd as is the dayesie;
> Of his complexioun he was sangwin. (334-5)

Interestingly, his face combines the same two colors "white and reede" (90) as the embroidered jacket of the vivacious Squire, and the Franklin is similarly compared to a flower. In a group where personal attractiveness is at a premium, this is an opening which disposes the reader positively to regard the Franklin, a man of the sanguine complexion: healthy, vigorous and confident, with "a large desire and capacity for all kind of self-indulgence" (Pollard 63). Unfortunately, this tendency is exclusively expressed in his love of good food; ten different items of food and drink are mentioned in the portrait:

> To liven in delit was evere his wone,
> For he was Epicurus owene sone,
> That heeld opinioun that pleyn delit
> Was verray felicitee parfit. (337-40)

Epicurus (341–270 BC) held that pleasure and pain are the measures of what is good and evil. His philosophy has been completely

124

misunderstood as being hedonistic, that is, as reducing life to the pursuit of physical pleasure. In reality, he was an anti-hedonist who lived a life of "the greatest temperance and simplicity ... content ... with a small cup of wine ... [and] no better fare than barley cakes and water" (Pollard 64). Pollard comments that the misunderstanding of Epicurus' philosophy did not become general until the sixteenth century (64) which means that Chaucer's original readers would have been more alive to the Franklin's misunderstanding than is the modern reader.

Hallissy concludes that, "In every way, the Franklin's description contrasts with the religious tradition of asceticism that was so much a part of medieval Christianity" (37). This may be true, but the Franklin's gourmandizing really is presented as a victimless self-indulgence to be gently mocked but not denounced. The ironic tone of the Poet's description is set by the use of comic superlatives:

> His breed, his ale, was alweys after oon;
> A bettre envined man was nowher noon. (343-4)

For the only time in the *Prologue*, superlatives (whether intended seriously or ironically) do not refer to the person: his bread and ale are always of the very best quality, and no man has a better stocked wine cellar. Contrast the similarly worded, but entirely serious superlative used to describe the Parson, "A better preest I trowe that nowher noon is" (526). This gentle irony is continued in the metaphor, "It snewed in his hous of mete and drinke" (347), a comic hyperbole which presents an amusing visual image of excess. The picture is completed by the unusual detail of the hall table:

> His table dormant in his halle alway
> Stood redy covered al the longe day. (335-6)

It was the custom at the time to set up a table on trestles only for mealtimes. The fact that the Franklin orders the table to remain standing and ready for dining all day is a novel way of suggesting both his devotion to food and the high importance which he places on his duty as host.

The Franklin begins his day with a gourmet, luxury item. Bowden explains that, "A 'sop in wyn' was made with a sauce of wine, saffron, almonds, ginger, sugar, cloves and mace which was poured over bread" (*Guide* 118). The comment that:

> After the sondry seasons of the yeer,
> So chaunged he his mete and his soper (349-50)

reflects the best contemporary medical advice that a healthy diet should change with the months of the year, a recommendation based on astrology and aimed at maintaining the body's humoral balance. Further evidence that the Franklin takes his food seriously is presented in the account of his relationship with his cook:

> Wo was his cook but if his sauce were
> Poynaunt and sharp, and redy al his geere. (353-4)

The exaggerated reaction suggested by the word "Wo" is intended to be comic as, I believe, is the statement that the Franklin aims to be "Seint Julian … in his contree" (342). Saint Julian, patron saint of hospitality, was very popular in the period, so except for the arrogance implicit in comparing oneself to a saint, there is nothing suspect in this. Critics have, however, tended to overlook the rest of the line. That the Poet refers to the area in which he lives, using the possessive pronoun, as "his contree" shows the man's proprietorial self-importance, a point which is emphasized when the line is immediately followed by the repetition of the same possessive pronoun, "His breed, his ale" (343).

If the Poet makes gentle fun of the Franklin's misunderstanding of Epicurus, of his obsession with good food, and of his exaggerated sense of his own social position, there is no overt irony in the description of his administrative service:

> At sessiouns ther was he lord and sire;
> Ful ofte time he was knight of the shire…
> A shirreve hadde he been, and a contour.
> Was nowher swich a worthy vavasour. (357-62)

As previously stated, these are offices similar to those held by Chaucer himself, and government administration is, perhaps, no laughing matter. Higgs, however, suggests that, "Although he presides at local court sessions and serves as sheriff and Member of Parliament from time to time, his preoccupation with the surface of life cannot impart an ethical sense to his service…" (in George 108). This harsh judgment rests on the reasonable assumption that the reader is supposed to apply the irony of the first part of the portrait to its last six lines. The same may be said of my own suggestion that the Franklin appears to be accumulating offices with the same enthusiasm with which he accumulates food.

Lines 363- 380: The Five Guildsmen

> Everyone nowadays talks a great deal about one merchant,
> called Fraud, full of guile. From the Orient to the end of the
> Occident there is no city or town where Fraud does not
> amass his wealth. (John Gower *The Mirror of Mankind*
> Norton Anthology)

In large manufacturing towns, craft guilds were organized by
profession:

> Guilds have the dual function of restricting competition
> (only guild members may practice their profession in a
> town) and ensuring quality. Guilds issue strict rules on
> quality standards which are enforced by unannounced
> inspections resulting in confiscations and fines for offences.
> Membership of most guilds is divided into masters and
> apprentices, each master normally being allowed only one
> apprentice at any time. (Gies and Gies 273-4)

The Haberdasher (a seller of men's clothes, particularly headwear,
and accessories), Carpenter, Weaver, Dyer, and Tapestry-maker,
however, are not members of the trades which formed the great
guilds; they are members of a parish guild, that is, a religious guild
for all manufacturers in a small community such as a London
borough. Smith and Smith comment that such guilds "were founded
upon the wide basis of brotherly aid and moral comeliness, without
distinction (unless expressly specified) of calling or class" (quoted in
Gastle).

Their trades are not the ones from which aldermen were selected
at this time, and so their professions have brought them wealth, but
not the status to which they (and their wives) aspire.

Pilgrim:
1. What is it about the appearance of the five which impresses the
Pilgrim?
2. How does the Pilgrim assess the abilities of the five?
Poet:
3. How does Chaucer mock the pride of the Guildsmen and of their
wives?

A Haberdasher and a Carpenter,
A Weaver, a Dyer, and a Tapestry-maker
365 Were with us, clothed in the same livery
Of a dignified and a great parish guild.
Their outfits were new and heavily ornamented
Their daggers were not cheaply trimmed with brass
But all with silver; skillfully and neatly made
370 Were their girdles and their purses in every way.
Each man of them appeared fit to be a leading citizen
And to sit in a guildhall on a high dais running the affairs of their guild.
Each one of them, had the wisdom
To make him fitted to have been an alderman;
375 For they had enough property and money to qualify as one;
Their goodwives would certainly agree,
And their wives would certainly blame them if they did not actually became aldermen.
It is very pleasant to be called 'Madam' before one's name,
And to have a place at the head of the procession to mass on saints' days,
380 And to have one's train carried as if one were royalty.

The Five Guildsmen are not differentiated: they dress alike, and they share the same ambitions and high sense of their own worth. They are wearing their finest, and the Pilgrim is duly impressed: their garments appear to be new and of the finest cut, and their daggers are ornamented with silver. The Pilgrim accepts their own estimation of themselves as rising men destined to be aldermen in their community but as Lambdin and Lambdin comment, the Poet aims to satirize "the rising middle class [who] sometimes overstepped the bounds of propriety in an ostentatious attempt to outshine the gentry" (149).

Not surprisingly, the Poet draws the reader's attention to the inflated self-importance of these men and to the pushy ambition of their wives. These are manufacturers, and in comparison with the great trades guilds of London or York, their guild is insignificance, making the statement that they belong to "a solempne and a greet fraternitee" clearly ironic (366). Every item of their dress is chosen to assert their social status – or rather, the social status to which they aspire. The ostentation of the group is epitomized by their daggers decorated with inlaid silver. Technically they are breaking the sumptuary law which restricted such ornamentation to the gentry class (the very class to which they aspire) and above. The reader recalls that the Franklin is described as wearing "An anlaas and a gipser al of silk" (359), that is, a dagger and a silk puse, both appropriate to his gentry status.

The irony of their ambition to become aldermen lies in the Poet's careful selection of their professions. Gastle comments:

> Even though they represent several different professions, Chaucer's guildsmen ... derive from the lesser professions from which city aldermen were rarely elected ... their clothing alludes to a position far above their alloted station in London mercantile life and politics, and Chaucer's aristocratic audience most probably found such sumptuous dress subject for derision. They were dressed like aldermen, but could never be aldermen. The passage praises their wisdom, from which their ability to hold public office derives; but the "wisdom that he kan" seems to say more about their ability to dress smartly than act so, a characteristic they seem to have in common with their wives. (emphasis in original).

Wasserman and Guidry point out that "no carpenter ever served as a London alderman in the fourteenth century," and add that "of 260 aldermen elected in the fourteenth century only nine came from the lesser craft companies" (Lambdin and Lambdin 155). Even without the support of such historical research (unnecessary, of course, to Chaucer's intended audience), the Poet's irony is evident:

> Wel semed ech of hem a fair burgeys
> To sitten in a yeldehalle on a deis.
> Everich, for the wisdom that he kan,
> Was shaply for to been an alderman.
> For catel hadde they ynogh and rente, (371-5)

These men seem, in their own eyes, fit to stand on a dais running the affairs of their guild or to be elected to the post of alderman in the city government because they have wealth to equal those who are appointed to those positions. They do not, however, have the traditional status, and they never will have.

The Poet reserves his sharpest satire for the wives of the five, for it is actually their ambition which is driving their husbands on:

> And eek hir wives wolde it wel assente;
> And elles certeyn were they to blame. (376-377)

The last line makes it clear that the wives expect their husbands to enable them to rise to the status of ladies, and that the men will clearly be held responsible for any failure to do so. The implication is that these fine men are in reality hen-picked. In a description which foreshadows the Wife of Bath, these women look forward to being placed at the front of religious processions to the mass and to having someone carry the train of their cloak:

> It is ful fair to been ycleped 'madame,'
> And goon to vigilies al bifore,
> And have a mantel roialliche ybore. (378-80)

Religious services have been reduced to opportunities for social one-upmanship. Since in this the five wives share a failing with the Wife of Bath, it is appropriate to quote the words of the Parson concerning the sin of Pride which makes men always wish:

> to go in front of his neighbor to the offering, and such similar things, contrary to his duty, perhaps, but because he has his heart and his ambition set on a proud desire to be exulted and honored in public. ("The Parson's Tale" author's modernization)

Here the Parson specifically denounces those whose pride leads them to seek honor by receiving the offering before all other people. The Poet's really barbed satire, however, is reserved for the final line. The wives will take their husband's ambitious dressing-up to the level of vainglory: they will wear a long mantle which requires a servant to carry the train because they aspire (ridiculously) to the status of royalty.

Lines 381-389: The Cook

Derek Brewer remarks that with the portrait of the Cook, who he identifies with the historical figure Hodge (or Roger) of Ware, Chaucer shows us the pilgrim who is lowest on the social scale and adds that although he was "well aware of the low-life of London … [here] we have truly come to the margins of Chaucer's social life and knowledge" (144). Hieatt notes that Hodge of Ware "was found guilty of being a 'common nightwalker,' which means someone who is habitually in the streets after curfew and was suspected of keeping company with thieves and prostitutes" (Hieatt in Lambdin and Lambdin 203).

Pilgrim:
1. Unsurprisingly, the Pilgrim regards the Cook as a man at the very top of his profession. He is in awe of the range of the man's cooking skills and the variety of dishes which he is able to prepare superlatively. Make a list.
Poet:
2. One of the Cook's supposed skills is his ability to judge the quality of London ale. (Remember that at this time each tavern [and indeed most households] would brew their own beer so it tended to vary a lot in taste and strength.) Ask yourself: How does a man become an expert beer taster?
3. The genius of this portrait lies in the way Chaucer places the "mormal". Comment on the juxtaposition in the last two lines of the portrait of the detail of the "mormal" and the praise of the Cook's "blankmanger". What effects does Chaucer achieve?

> A Cook they had with them for the journey
> To boil the chickens with the marrow bones.
> Sharp tasting powder and spice.
> He was an expert judge of London ale.
> 385 He could roast, boil, grill and fry,
> Make stews and bake a lovely pie.
> But it seemed to me a great pity
> That on his shin he had an open sore.
> When it came to blankmanger [fish and chicken mould], he made the best!

The five Guildsmen, unwilling to take a chance with the food provided by the inns along the way, have hired their own cook to accompany them on pilgrimage; it is another ostentatious display of their wealth, an exercise in one-upmanship. However, it is the Poet's final joke at the guildsmen's expense that they have engaged such an inappropriate cook.

The range of the Cook's skills is, indeed, impressive, "He koude rooste, and sethe, and broille, and frie" (385), and he knows how to use spices such as "poudre-marchant tart and galingale" (383) to give his food flavor. The range of his dishes is equally impressive: spiced chicken boiled with the marrow bones, "mortreux" (a rich stew made with chicken and pork), pies of all kinds, and, of course, his specialty "blankmanger" or 'white dish' (a savory mold whose "basic ingredients were milk or almond milk, sugar and shredded chicken [usually capon] or fish and often combined with rosewater, rice flour, and mixed into a bland stew. Almond milk and fish were used as substitutes for the other animal products on fast days and Lent. It was also often flavored with spices like saffron or cinnamon and the chicken could be exchanged for various types of fowl, like quail or partridge. Spices were often used in recipes of the later Middle Ages since they were considered highly prestigious" [Webster's Online Dictionary]). Clearly these are sophisticated dishes designed to appeal to people of high status, and both "mortreux" and "blankmanger" are "found on aristocratic menus and in the cookery books that claim to come from the highest social circles" (Hieatt in Lambdin and Lambdin 205).

The first hint by the Poet that all is not entirely as it seems to the Pilgrim is the latter's praise of the Cook's skill in judging good ale, "Wel koude he knowe a draughte of Londoun ale" (384). The reader is not to think here of a connoisseur or even of a chef who can recommend exactly the right wine to accompany a meal. The Cook is an expert in ale, the drink of the common people, not in wine, and he has become an expert in judging good ale by drinking a lot of it! In fact, the man is a drunkard who later in the pilgrimage falls off of his horse because he is too inebriated to stay on it. Would that this were the worst, but it is not:

> But greet harm was it, as it thoughte me,
> That on his shine a mormal hadde he. (387-8)

Even the Pilgrim cannot help but notice, and express regret, that the man has an ulcer, a suppurating pustule on his shin; however, the joke is that the Pilgrim in no way links the "harm" of the ulcer to the man's cooking. In fact, in the very next line, he has entirely forgotten the "harm" and is driven to superlatives to describe the excellence of the Cook's specialty, "For blankmanger, that made he with the beste" (388). The naïve Pilgrim just does not join the dots. For one thing, the ulcer actually resembles the 'white dish' which suddenly makes it seem less appetizing, and for another, as. Thomas Carney Forkin explains, the significance of the mormal goes much deeper than mere hygiene in the kitchen:

> The modern reader who understands a mormal as simply a dry-scabbed ulcer; sore; an abscess, neglects the innuendo Chaucer has ascribed to Roger by inflicting him with this particular unsightly excrescence. It is Lydgate's [John Lydgate (c.1370–c.1451) monk and poet.] use of the mormal that offers the best source of comparison to Chaucer's. In the Falle of Princes Lydgate writes:
>
> > Of glotonie & riotous excesse...Kometh uncouth
> > feveres...Goutes, mormalles, horrible to the siht.
>
> Lydgate explicitly states that one will become afflicted with feveres, goutes, and mormalles, by living a life of glotonie & riotous excesse. Chaucer expects his audience to keep these imbalances of the humours in mind while reading the Cook's Prologue where a further perspective into the character of Roger is afforded the reader ... Knowing that one becomes afflicted with a mormal through glotonie & riotous excesse, Chaucer assumed that his audience would take these sins as being implicit characteristics of the Cook. (31-2)

It has even been suggested that the suppurating sore might be a symptom of the plague or of venereal disease. It is enough to put the reader off his food, or at least off this Cook's food!

Later in the *Prologue* before the Cook's own tale, the Host (himself an inn keeper and thereby qualified to judge) tells him:

> From many a pie have you drained the blood,
> And many a Jack of Dovere have you sold
> That has been twice hot and twice cold.
> Many a pilgrim has uttered Christ's curse on you,
> Because your parsley has made them feel ill,
> Which they ate with your stubble-fed goose,
> For in your shop there are many flies.
> ("Prologue to the Cook's Tale" author's modernization)

He accuses the Cook of adulterating his pie-fillings, selling twice-reheated dishes, giving his customers food poisoning, and having an unclean kitchen infested with flies. Of course, the Host insists that he is only joking, but then goes on to say, in effect, that many a true word is spoken in jest.

Chapter Seven: The Shipman, The Doctor, and The Wife of Bath

Lines 390-412: The Shipman

 Chaucer was familiar with Dartmouth having been sent there on government business in 1374. Various historical figures have been suggested as his models including: John Hawley, who in 1378 owned a ship called the Magdaleyne and had a reputation as a privateer; Piers (or Peter) Risshenden, who was one recorded master of the Magdaleyne; and John Piers, "who lived in the west of England from 1385 to 1388, captured a ship named the *Magdaleyne* in 1383, killed its crew, and threw them overboard" (King in Lambdin and Lambdin 215). If inconclusive, the mere proliferation of these examples shows that the actions of the Shipman are quite typical. He is clearly a man of vast experience and expertise at sea. An expert in navigation, he knows how to keep his ship safe, and has survived every storm he has been caught in. Morally, however, there is much for the Poet to criticize.

Pilgrim:
1. What details of the Shipman's knowledge and skills does the Pilgrim give to illustrate that this man is an exceptional sea captain?
2. What evidence is given of the Shipman's bravery?

Poet:
3. The Poet immediately follows the Pilgrim's assertion that "certeinly he was a good felawe" (397) with two details which entirely undercut the assertion. Explain in detail. (Be sure to comment on the tone of the line, "By water sente hem hoom to every lond" [405].)
4. In the light of your last answer, what is the real significance of the fact that the Shipman wears a "daggere hanginge ... / ... under his arm adoun" (394-5)?
5. How does line 392 mock the Shipman?

6. The Shipman's vessel "ycleped was the Maudelaine" (412). Research the connotations of St. Mary Magdeline in Chaucer's time. Do you think that the Poet has any ironic intention in selecting this particular name?

390   A ship's master was there who lived in the far West of England;
        For all I know, he might have come from Dartmouth.
        He rode upon a cart horse as well as he could
        In a gown of coarse woolen cloth which came down to his knees.
        A dagger he had, hanging on a cord
395   Around his neck down under his arm.
        The hot summer sun had given him a dark tan;
        And certainly he was a good fellow.
        Many a drink of wine had he taken from the barrel
        On the voyage home from Bordeaux, while the merchant was sleeping.
400   He had no time for tender feelings.
        If he was involved in a sea battle and he got the upper hand
        He sent his prisoners home by water [i.e. threw them overboard!].
        But of his craft, to work out accurately the tides,
        The currents, and the dangers round about him,
405   The harbors, the influence of the moon, and navigation,
        There was not a sailor better than him from Hull to Cartagena.
        He was bold and yet clever in deciding what to do;
        His beard had been shaken by many storms.
        He knew all of the safe places to put into harbor
410   From Gotland to Cape Finisterre,
        And every creek in Brittany and in Spain.
        His ship was called the Magdalene.

The Shipman is appropriately dressed both for his calling and his social status in a mantle, or cloak, made of coarse woolen cloth possibly of Irish manufacture. He combines vast experience of the seas and the coastlines from Gotland (a Swedish island in the Baltic Sea) to Cape Finisterre (in North West Spain) with outstanding skills in seamanship and navigation – at least, this is the picture relayed by the Pilgrim who cannot be working from first-hand knowledge. The man hails from the West of England (perhaps even Dartmouth) long known for producing gallant seamen, and his face is bronzed by exposure to the "hoote somer" (396). More importantly, he is the master of his craft, knowing how to calculate the tides and currents and how to estimate dangers, which explains how he has survived despite the fact that with "many a tempest hadde his berd been shake" (408). He knows every harbor, haven and creek where he can find protection from a storm, and he is a master of navigation using both his knowledge of the moon and reading his compass. The Pilgrim slips into superlatives, "Ther nas noon swich from Hulle to Cartage" – a comparison which subtly (and improbably) extends the area of the Shipman's expertise to the western Mediterranean Sea (406). The Pilgrim seems unaware that he is describing a violent man, a callous murdering thief; indeed, far from moral outrage, the Pilgrim seems lost in admiration for this "good felawe … Hardy … [and] wys" (397-407). The Poet also uses the term "felawe" to describe the Summoner ("A bettre felawe sholde men noght finde" [650]) and the adulterers whom he lets off ("He wolde suffre … / A good felawe to have his concubyn" [652]). The use of the word indicates both that the Poet is referring to men well down the social ladder and also men of low moral standing, what he will later term "churls".

The Poet begins the unmasking with mockery: the Shipman is (almost literally) a fish out of water. He may be at home with his feet on a heaving deck, but the sight of him on a horse is comic, "He rood upon a rouncy, as he kouthe" (392). A "rouncy" is a carthorse:

> The rouncy horse was used to carry heavy objects and farm the land. They were usually heavier than the destrier, palfrey, and the courser. These horses were the farmer's horse and were usually poorly trained. Rouncy horses had good endurance because they had to work in the fields or travel all day long. There was no special breeding that was associated with the rouncy. It was a horse for the lower class. (Del Dotto, and Prescott 13)

Whoever rented this horse to the Shipman quickly estimated his inexperience and took advantage of it. For another thing, he rides as well as ever he is able, which is to say very badly. Nor is the man dressed in a manner which seems appropriate to his apparent success in his vocation for he wears a gown of coarsely woven woolen cloth, hardwearing, no doubt, but hardly a conspicuous sign of financial success. Under his arm (where it is ready for instant use), he wears a dagger on a lanyard which is symbolic of the man's violent nature, and is certainly incompatible with the judgment that the man is a "good felawe," although it has been noted above that, as Kirkham and Allen point out, this word "has overtones of low class or disreputable" (46).

The Pilgrim now has a problem, for he is about to describe how the Shipman routinely steals wine which he is transporting to England from Bordeaux, while the merchant who has employed him is asleep, using the simple expedient of taking a tankard and drawing himself a draft, and how he throws captured pirates overboard to drown. How is it that even the gullible Pilgrim cannot see that these are actions calling for moral censure? The theft of wine is obscured by euphemism: the Shipman is said to "ydrawe" wine while the merchant sleeps (398), an action which is justified by the comment that, "Of nice conscience took he no keep" (400). The Pilgrim implies that only the overly-scrupulous would find fault with such action which is undoubtedly the Shipman's view of the matter as well. No doubt the barrel would be topped up with water in London, and no one any the wiser.

The ruthless action he takes to dispose of his enemies is dismissed firstly by presenting it as simply the fortunes of war (the victims are pirates after all) and secondly by hiding the reality of murder in euphemism:

> If that he faught, and hadde the hyer hond,
> By water he sente hem hoom to every lond. (401-2)

The Shipman sends his enemies home by water to every country from which they originate – the joke is surely the Shipman's own, repeated verbatim by the Pilgrim.

The Poet takes a very different view of the Shipman's immorality. Firstly, he prefaces the description of his crimes with the Pilgrim's judgment, "And certeinly he was a good felawe" (397). As so often, the praise-line is followed by details which entirely undercut it. Immediately after these details the portrait goes on to extol the Shipman's navigational skills:

> But of his craft to rekene wel his tides,
> His stremes, and his daungers him bisides,
> His herberwe, and his moone, his lodemenage,
> Ther nas noon swich from Hulle to Cartage. (403-6)

The word "But" functions to alert the reader that what is about to be said marks a radical departure from what has just been said. In this case, the Poet expects the reader to see the ironic contrast that his man, so skillful in setting the right course by sea, lacks a moral compass.

The Poet's final thrust at the Shipman comes when the Pilgrim mentions, as always without making any connection to what he has just told us, the name of the man's vessel, "His barge ycleped was the Maudelayne" (412). At first, it merely seems ironically inappropriate that so sinful a man should name his own ship after a saint, but the fact that he chooses Saint Mary Magdalene adds layers of irony, for, in 591, Pope Gregory the Great declared that Mary Magdalene was a prostitute, a judgment which was not reversed by the Roman Catholic Church until 1969 during the papacy of Pope Paul VI. The Poet expects us to see a clear parallel: the Shipman sells the use of his vessel as a prostitute sells the use of her body, and in the process each steals from their 'employer' while he sleeps.

Lines 413-446: The Doctor of Physic

Fraud the apothecary deceives people in his shop more than I can explain; but when he conspires with the physician as his companion, he deceives people a hundred times more. The physician writes out the prescription, and the apothecary compounds it. But he sells for a florin that which is not worth a button. Thus the apothecary whispers his guile into our physician's hood. (John Gower *The Mirror of Mankind* Norton Anthology)

To understand this portrait, the reader has to enter the medieval mindset. To the modern reader, this doctor is a medical disaster, and no one would want to be treated by him; to the medieval reader, however, this doctor offers state of the art medical treatment. Many of the things he does (like consulting the patient's horoscope) we find laughable, but the people in the Middle Ages would have taken these as signs of the man's skill. As Gies and Gies write, "The real shortcoming in medical education is its subservience … to astrology and numerology" (286). Medieval medical theory offered a complete explanation of the cause of illness and the interventions necessary to restore the patient to health. So impressive was the theory that people hardly noticed that the patients kept dying!

It is not entirely clear if the Doctor is both a physician and a surgeon which in Chaucer's day was an unusual, but not unheard of, combination:

> With us ther was a Doctour of Phisik;
> In al this world ne was the noon him lik,
> To speke of phisik and of surgerye, (413-5)

The phrase "To speke of" could mean 'in the fields of' implying that he is the greatest healer in either discipline, or it could literally mean 'in speaking about' implying that he boasts of his knowledge in both disciplines. Neither reading definitively identifies him as a surgeon, nor do the details in the portrait relating to his medical practice include surgery. Surgery was the inferior branch of medicine being regarded as a craft which an apprentice learned over a period of seven years from a master surgeon who had been licensed by the London authorities, just as one might learn any other craft. In contrast, a physician (assuming that he studied in England and not at one of the continental universities such as Salero, Montpellier, or Paris) was a graduate of Oxford or Cambridge University where the entire faculty of medicine was composed of clerics. To become a Master of Medicine at Oxford such as our Doctor, a "student was required to spend at least seventeen years attached to the university before he could even think about setting himself up in private practice" (Eleazar in Lambdin and Lambdin 229).

Rather than follow the usual medieval approach of satirizing doctors' incompetence and lack of care of their patients, Chaucer goes out of his way to stress that this Doctor really does know his stuff. Nevertheless, exactly like the Shipman, the man is not without his moral failings – to say the least.

Pilgrim:
1. When the Pilgrim says of the Doctor, "He was a verray, parfit praktisour" (424), he is telling us the truth, at least about the Doctor's medical practice. Give details of the Doctor's skills in diagnosis (416-426), his grounding in medical knowledge (431-436), his own healthy diet (437-439).
2. How is the Doctor's success reflected in his appearance?

Poet:

3. The Doctor is actually running a scam in collaboration with his pharmacist. How does the scam work to the mutual profit of each?

4. What is implied by the detail in line 440?

5. In one way, the Doctor's conduct during times of "pestilence" (444) is admirable compared to that of many doctors of the time. However, there is another aspect of his conduct which is less admirable. Explain.

6. In the last two lines of the portrait, the Poet comes close to making an outright joke at the Doctor's expense. Explain.

>   With us there was a Doctor of medicine;
>   In the whole world there was not another who was his equal,
> 415 In knowledge of medicine and surgery,
>   Because he was so well informed about astrology.
>   He kept a close watch on his patients
>   And used his knowledge of astrology to choose the best hours to
>   give his treatments.
>   He knew exactly what star signs to engrave on
> 420 A medicinal charm to help his patient to recover.
>   He knew the origin of every illness,
>   (Whether caused by too much hot, or cold, or wet, or dry humor)
>   And how they had started and what part of the system was to
>   blame.
>   He was a true, perfect practitioner.
> 425 As soon as he knew the cause, and the root of the problem,
>   At once he prescribed the sick man his remedy.
>   His pharmacists were always ready
>   To send him drugs and medicines,
>   For each of them ensured that they made a profit from this
>   relationship -
> 430 Their friendship had been going on for years.
>   He had a deep knowledge of Esculapius,
>   And Deyscorides and also Rufus,
>   Old Ypocras, Haly and Galen,
>   Serapion, Razis and Avycen,
> 435 Averrois, Damascien and Constantyn,
>   Bernard, and Gatesden, and Gilbertyn.
>   He was very moderate in his diet,
>   For he didn't eat to excess
>   Choosing what was nutritious and easily digested.

440   He didn't spend much time studying the Bible.
        He was dressed in blood-red cloth and blue-grey cloth
        Lined with two kinds of silk;
        And yet he was careful with his money;
        He kept what he had earned in Plague time.
445   For gold in medicine is a great cure,
        Therefore he had a special love for gold.

This portrait, which contains no physical description, is largely of a type: the moral shortcomings highlighted (lack of religious devotion and price-fixing) are criticisms found in many other estates satires. Only the man's miserliness adds a hint of individuality. The Pilgrim begins with a familiar superlative, "In al this world ne was the noon him lik" (414), and the portrait justifies this assertion by providing abundant evidence that, "there is no branch of his profession in which he is not an expert" (Kirkham and Allen 48). The first major discord is sounded by the description of the Doctor's clothes:

        In sangwin and in pers he clad was al,
        Lined with taffata and with sendal;
        And yet he was but esy of dispence; (441-43)

Taavitsainen quotes the injunction in *Treatises of Fistula in Ano* by the English surgeon John Arderne (1307–1392) that in dress doctors should "shew the manner of clerkes" (Brown 389), and Bowden quotes Arderne's injunction that the doctor "should be clean and soberly dressed, 'nought likkenyng himself in apparalyng ... to mynistralles'" (*Commentary* 209). Thus, not only does his wearing of expensive cloth and very vibrant silk set him apart from other doctors who, belonging to the middle class, did not dress in lavish style, but his extravagance in his dress is at odds with his general parsimony. Thus, even a superficial reading of the portrait indicates that the central contradiction in the Doctor's character relates to money.

The theory and the practice of medieval medicine, in which astrology and medical diagnoses go hand-in-hand, strike the modern reader as absurd; however, by the standards of the period the Doctor offers exemplorary treatment. The prominent Islamic physician Rhazes (865-925) wrote, "Wise physicians are agreed that all things here below, air, water, the complexions, sickness, and so on, suffer change in accordance with the motions of the planets" (quoted in Vigneswaran 1). The Doctor casts the patient's horoscope charting the position of the stars at the moment of birth, at the onset of the disease and at the time of the physician's consultation. Combining these three configurations, the Doctor "could discover what planets were favorable to the cure of the illness and what malefic or 'antagonistic' planets were present, in order that he could 'fortunen the ascendent' – that is, make discs of metal, bearing representations of a particular planet together with magic formulae which could be applied to the patient" (Bowden *Guide* 92-3). An additional form of diagnosis which we would actually recognize today is urinoscopy. The Ellesmere illustration shows the Doctor examining what may well be a flask containing a urine sample.

The basis of the Doctor's practice relies on the four humors: blood, yellow bile, black bile, and phlegm each of which is related to a specific season, element, and organ. Yellow bile, for example, represents the summer, and when it gets hot and dry a person becomes choleric. Successful treatment rests on balancing the humors within the patient:

> He knew the cause of everich maladie,
> Were it of hoot, or coold, or moiste, or drie, (421-2)

In order to restore humoral balance, the Doctor would bleed his patient and prescribe medicines, "For example, an excess of phlegm (the cold and moist humor) might be counterbalanced by a hot and dry medicine like a mixture of sugar and/or cardamom dissolved in wine or oil" (Eleazar in Lambdin and Lambdin 236).

The Doctor uses his knowledge of the position of the planets, the relevant signs of the zodiac, the season and the time of day to treat his patients, since each of these impacts the patient's humors:

> ... he was grounded in astronomye
> He kepte his pacient a ful greet deel
> In houres by his magik natureel. (416-418)

Pollard's explanation is still the clearest:

> [E]very part of the human body was supposed to be under the domination of one of the twelve Signs or Constellations ... Aries governing the head, Taurus the neck, etc. Knowledge of these relations was thought [to be] essential ... a physician was supposed to choose the part of the body at which to bleed a patient according to the sign then in the ascendant. Complications were introduced by the sign under which the patient was born, which was thought to rule his destiny through life; by the sign in the ascendant when his

> illness began, etc., etc. The skill of the astrologer-physician would be exercised in calculating the hours when the balance of contending influences would be most favourable to his patient, and choosing these for the application of his remedies. (71)

The day was divided into four segments of six hours during each of which one humor would be dominant: noon until six was dominated by melancholy, six until midnight by phlegm, midnight until six by blood, and six until noon by choler. Once the doctor diagnosed a patient's illness as resulting from an excess of a particular humor, he would know which hours would tend to accentuate the imbalance and which would be favorable in his attempts to restore the humoral balance of the patient (Hussey et al. 175).

To ensure the efficacy of the remedies he prepares and the charms he makes, the Doctor also monitors the phases of the moon which are grouped in four separate quarters. When in the first and second quarters the size of the moon increases, or waxes, the Doctor will perform any procedures that require growth because it was believed that as the moon increases in size, so does the part being treated. In the third and the fourth quarters, when the moon begins to shrink, or wane, the Doctor uses his natural magic to minimize something such as phlegm or an abscess.

Another astrological method the Doctor uses on his patients is determining their ascendant (the rising star at the exact moment a person is born) and how it affects their health. A person's rising sign, also known as their zodiac sign, was thought to predict his or her strength, immunity, and what illnesses and diseases they are vulnerable to:

> Wel koude he fortunen the ascendent
> Of his images for his pacient.
> He knew the cause of everich maladie, (419-421)

The Pilgrim praises the Doctor's use of complex charts and tables such as those of the ascendants to determine the cause of an illness. This description of his skill in diagnosis and treatment leads to a second superlative, "He was a verray parfit praktisour" (424), although the Poet intends the word "praktisour" to be a pun on the word 'practicer,' that is, one who plays upon and exploits the vulnerability and gullibility of his dupes (Halverson 18).

The Doctor is knowledgeable on the works of medical authorities:

> Wel knew he the olde Esculapius,
> And Deiscorides, and eek Rufus,
> Olde Ypocras, Hali, and Galien,
> Serapion, Razis, and Avicen,
> Averrois, Damascien, and Constantin,
> Bernard, and Gatesden, and Gilbertin. (431-436)

What is particularly impressive about this list is that, although it begins with those classical authorities whom one would expect, it also contains the names of Moslem writers from the Middle East and of near-contemporary doctors from Britain. This man certainly keeps up with the medical literature of his day! The result is that this Doctor gets to the root cause of every illness and successful diagnosis leads to the prescription of the most efficacious remedy. The Doctor applies his knowledge to managing his own healthy diet:

> Of his diete mesurable was he,
> For it was of no superfluitee,
> But of greet norissing and digestible. (437-439)

Perhaps he believes that by others seeing his success with his health, they will want to become his patients.

Although the Doctor is praised for the theoretical basis of his treatments and for the promptness of providing medication, not a word is said about his patients getting better. Moreover, the Poet knows that his motives are not unselfish. After using his mystical methods to diagnose his patients' sickness, the Doctor is ready to prescribe medicine:

> The cause yknowe, and of his harm the roote,
> Anon he yaf the sike man his boote. (425-426)

He refers them immediately to the pharmacists with whom he has an arrangement:

> Ful redy hadde he his apothecaries
> To sende him drogges and his letuaries, (427-428)

The Pilgrim approvingly records the Doctor's close relationship with his pharmacists since it means that the patient gets the drugs he needs immediately, but what the Pilgrim does not recognize is the ulterior motive: together they have a highly profitable scam. The Poet's implication is that the Doctor over-prescribes: he prescribes drugs that his patient does not actually need, and he prescribes expensive drugs when cheaper alternatives exist. The patient is then told that he can only get these drugs from particular apothecaries who abuse the artificial monopoly to inflate prices. Not only does the Doctor receive payment from his patients, but he also gets a percentage from the pharmacists, thus exemplifying the medieval proverb that doctors, "Take while the patient is in pain" (quoted in Gies and Gies 286). The Poet ironically describes this arrangement as a mutually beneficial friendship whilst making it clear that this drugs scam has been going on for years:

> For ech of hem made oother for to winne –
> Hir frendshipe nas nat newe to biginne. (429-430)

Notice the Poet's coy use of the euphemism "frendshipe" to describe a criminal conspiracy.

The reader can now see the full significance of the throw-away comment that, though he is deeply read in medical theory, "His studie was but litel on the Bible" (440). Bowden quotes the medieval proverb "where there are three physicians, there are two atheists" (*Guide* 46) and reminds us that it was the extensive study of medical texts written by Moslem authors (such as those mentioned in the portrait) which caused doctors to have a general reputation for agnosticism (*Commentary* 207). This line is particularly shocking since the Doctor is a clerk by dint of his university education with a place in the hierarchy of the church; Laura Hodges points out that it is quite possible that he was also technically a priest (199). Despite this, his actions indicate a lack of moral focus: his motive for practicing medicine is to acquire wealth, in which he parallels the Man of Law:

> For gold in phisik is a cordial,
> Therefore he lovede gold in special. (445-446)

This is the Poet's joke. The naïve Pilgrim says that because potable gold is health-giving, the Doctor has a high regard for it (gold was considered to be the purest of metals and therefore a kind of cure-all but particularly good for the heart); the perceptive Poet implies that the Doctor loves medicine only because of the gold he makes out of it.

The Doctor of Phisik is not fond of spending his money, "he was esy of dispence" (443) though even the obtuse Pilgrim notices that he does make an exception for the lavish clothing that helps him maintain an image of prosperity. The Doctor's parsimony has, however, a moral dimension, "He kepte that he wan in pestilence"

(444). The Black Death, or Bubonic Plague, spread to England in 1348 killing between a third a half of the population and recurring at other times, so it would be a horror within the experience of Chaucer's audience. On the positive side, the Doctor appears to be one of those few doctors who actually stayed to treat the sick, but his motive is to make money, and his avarice leads him to hold on to his earnings during the time of the Black Death rather than make any contributions to relieve the sufferings of the sick. The full significance of this detail becomes clear when we consider that:

> medieval medicine was much more than the survival and modification of classical learning ... Judaism, Christianity, and Islam all demanded of their followers the practice of charity ... the relationship between clerical duty and medical care was a strong one throughout the medieval period, and charity was thought to be the best motive for medical practice. (Getz quoted in Vigneswaran 2)

The Doctor has the expertise of an experienced medieval physician, but his actions prove that his main motive for practicing medicine is to become wealthy. The lines:

> For gold in phisik is a cordial,
> Therefore he lovede gold in special. (445-446)

are often contrasted with similar lines describing the Clerk:

> But al be that he was a philosophre,
> Yet hadde he but litel gold in cofre; (299-300)

The conclusion which critics draw is that whilst the Clerk pursues his calling for its own sake, the Doctor pursues wealth. In fact, both men are shown by the Poet to be obsessively self-centered: the Doctor puts his financial gain before the needs of others by cheating his patients, and the Clerk puts his thirst for learning above the social obligation to actually use that learning in the service of his fellow man.

Lines 447-478: The Wife of Bath

In 1347, England exported 30,000 sacks of wool and 4,422 cloths, but the average for the years 1392-5 was

19,000 sacks and 43,000 cloths. The reason for the change was that in 1375 the Crown levied a tax of 33% on exports of raw wool and only 2% on finished cloth. The tax was designed to increase the quality and the amount of domestic cloth production. To further this end, Hussey reports that, "Flemish workers were encouraged to immigrate, and English workers to improve their skill" (Hussey et al. 39).

Howard places the portrait of the Wife of Bath (later identified as Dame Alisoun) in its socio-historical context:

> Of all the 'middle-class' members, the Wife, a cloth-maker, ranks lowest; where the wives of the Guildsmen aspire to walk at the head of a procession in a 'mantel royalliche ybore,' she is content with (but insisted on) going up first to the offering in her parish church. (96)

Women were, of course, born into one of the Three Estates, but women also had a separate and more significant classification, based entirely on their relationship with men, into virgin, wife, or widow. Alisoun is a widow who has buried five husbands, in the process raising her status considerably, and as a widow she is in the strongest position a medieval woman could be in: she legally owns property in her own right.

Pilgrim:
1. This larger-than-life character really impresses the Pilgrim. What details does he give in praise of: a) her skills as a weaver; b) her clothing; c) the way she interacts socially with the other pilgrims?
2. One outstanding feature of this character is the number and variety of pilgrimages she has been on. List the places she has visited and give brief details of their religious significance.

Poet:
Once again, it is the moral failings of the character which the Poet attacks.
3. The adjectives "good" (447) and "worthy" (461) sound like moral approval, but what did these words actually mean in Chaucer's time?
4. The Wife's religious devotion (implied by her enthusiasm for pilgrimages) is seriously undercut by her unchristian behavior when making the offering at Mass. Explain.
5. By now the reader can see that the Wife is competitive in everything she does – perhaps even aggressive. What details of her

clothes and her accessories are inserted by the Poet to reinforce this point?

6. Although now middle-aged, the Wife has obviously been sexually active (perhaps even hyperactive) for most of her adult life.

a) What physical features indicate her passionate nature?

b) What exactly is implied by the statement that, as well as five husbands, she had "oother compaignye in youthe" (463)?

c) At first reading, the line "she koude muchel of wandringe by the weye" (469) appears to refer to the Wife being much-travelled. Explain the deeper meaning intended by the Poet.

> A wealthy widow there was from near Bath,
> But she was a little deaf and that was a pity.
> At weaving she had such skill,
> 450   That she was better than the cloth-makers of Ypres and Gaunt.
> In the whole parish there was no woman
> Who she allowed to go to the alms-offering in front of her;
> And if any of them did do so then she was so angry
> That she was out of all charity for them.
> 455   Her head-cloths were of very fine material;
> I dare swear that they weighed ten pounds,
> That is the ones she wore on her head on Sundays.
> Her stockings were of a fine scarlet red
> Tightly fastened, and her shoes made of supple new leather.
> 460   Bold was her face and attractive and of a ruddy complexion.
> She was an admirable woman all of her life:
> She had married five husbands at the church door
> Without mentioning other boyfriends she had had when she was young –
> But we do not need to speak about that at present.
> 465   She had been to Jerusalem three times,
> She had crossed many a foreign river;
> She had been to Rome, and Boulogne,
> At the shrine of St. James in Galicia (northwest Spain), and at Cologne.
> She knew a lot about wandering by the wayside.
> 470   Gap-toothed she was, to tell you the truth.
> Upon a walking horse she sat,
> Her forehead covered by a wimple and a hat on her head
> Which was as big as a buckler or a shield;
> She wore an overskirt around her large hips,

475   And on her feet a pair of sharp spurs.
           In company she laughed and chatted a lot,
           She knew the cures for lovesickness without a doubt,
           About love she knew all the tricks of the trade.

The Wife of Bath herself recognizes the influence of two planets at her birth in forming her temperament:

      For certainly, I am all Venusian
      In feeling, and my heart is Martian.
      Venus gave me my lust, my sexual appetite,
      And Mars gave me my sturdy hardiness.
      ("The Wife of Bath's Prologue" author's modernization)

Venus makes her sanguine, a "lover of company, fine clothes, gossip and merriment" (Hussey et al. 168), while Mars makes her choleric, "intemperate, brazen, and bent on conquest, a feminine counterpart of the thick-set Miller" (Hussey et al. 161). The influence upon the Wife of the planet Mars is best seen in contrasting her character with that of the Prioress who is entirely of a sanguine temperament: where the Prioress is delicate and refined in all that she does, the Wife is immodest and self-assertive.

The Pilgrim leaps straight into superlatives to describe the Wife's skill in weaving:

      Of clooth-making she hadde swich an haunt,
      She passed hem of Ypres and of Gaunt. (449-50)

Bath was indeed an important commercial centre of the wool trade, and the local cloth, called Bath Beaver, was known throughout England. As so often, the Pilgrim seems in this portrait to be giving the Wife's version of herself, probably using her own words, rather than judging for himself. It is by no means clear from the portrait whether weaving is the Wife's profession (at that time it was still a cottage industry there being no factories) or a part-time occupation. As Brown and Butcher point out, the status which is claimed for the Wife in the above lines makes her "and unusual if not unique figure" for:

      Unmarried women and widows, among the less prosperous,
      might scrape a living performing low-paid labour in trade or
      craft, engaging in by-employments, serving as domestic
      labour in more prosperous households, or by prostitution.
      Exceptionally, it was possible for single women to trade, by

special licence, as a *femme sole* or *sola mercatrix*. (Brown and Butcher 27)

No one but the Wife herself would compare Bath Beaver with the fine woolen cloth produced at Ypres and Gent which had a Europe-wide reputation for high quality. Hussey offers what is almost certainly the correct interpretation of these lines, "When Chaucer notes that she surpassed 'hem of Ypres and of Gaunt' it is possible that he means alien residents in England at the time, rather than the workers at home in Flanders (Hussey et al. 39). This certainly sounds more likely, but either way, it is an arrogant and unrealistic boast.

The portrait of the Wife of Bath is the only one which offers two detailed descriptions of the character's clothing: her Sunday attire, and what she is wearing on the pilgrimage. More than any other character, her garments illuminate her character. The portrait begins with the Wife's Sunday church clothes:

> Hir coverchiefs ful fine weren of ground;
> I dorste swere they weyeden ten pound
> That on a Sonday weren upon hir heed.
> Hir hosen weren of fyn scarlet reed,
> Ful streite yteyd, and shoes ful moiste and newe. (455-9)

Everything about this description implies the ostentatious display of wealth and excess. Even if we assume that the coverchiefs are themselves elaborately ornamented, and that they are arranged on and supported by wire frames, the idea that they might weigh ten pounds is comic hyperbole. Note also the repetition of the superlatives "full" and "fine," the bright red of her stockings, and the combined detail that her shoes are of the finest leather and that they are new. The red of the hose which she wears immediately suggests her passionate nature; the wearing of red hose was associated with the nobility, so it is also a sign of the Wife dressing above her station. The phrase "scarlet reed" is not redundant repetition (458): it tells us both that her hose is dyed red and that the hose is 'escarlate,' a particularly fine and expensive woolen cloth (Shuster). Every item of the Wife's clothing is aimed to impress upon others her social status – she is even meticulous in ensuring that the back seams of her hose are straight. There is an unlikely parallel between the Prioress and Alison in that each appears to "countrefete" (139) the behavior of the social class to which they aspire, but to which they were not born, the Wife having gained status and wealth by each successive marriage which perhaps accounts for Alison's aggressive self-assertion in being the first to the offering.

The contrast between the Wife's Sunday best and her pilgrimage clothes could hardly be greater:

> Ywimpled wel, and on hir heed an hat …
> A foot-mantel aboute hir hipes large, (472-4)

The keynote here is practicality, reminding us that the Wife is a seasoned traveler. She wears a wide-brimmed hat to protect her face from the elements. A wimple serves the same purpose, even at the expense of hiding her forehead, and she wears an overskirt to protect her gown (Shuster). These clothes much more realistically reflect the Wife's true position in society.

The Wife is conventionally religious and makes regular offerings to the Church on Sundays. She has been on pilgrimages to holy places throughout Europe:

> And thries hadde she been at Jerusalem;
> She hadde passed many a straunge strem;
> At Rome she hadde been, and at Boloigne,
> In Galice at Seint-Jame, and at Coloigne. (465-8)

The Pilgrim uses this impressive list to suggest a high level of devotion, but the Poet would have the reader see the Wife as a serial palmer, one whose motives for undertaking a pilgrimage are recreational rather than religious, for he describes her as sociable and good company, "In felaweshipe wel koude she laughe and carpe" (476). Her extensive travels also indicate the Wife's financial independence and her self-assurance, for such travel was very expensive and involved some degree of personal risk.

The first adjective used in this portrait is "good" (447) which coincidentally is the first adjective used to describe the very next pilgrim, the Parson. The difference in meaning is dictated by the context in which the words are used: whilst the Parson is "good" in the moral sense, the same word here simply indicates that the Wife is the mistress of her own house and therefore has a high standing in the town. This same point is re-enforced later in the portrait when we are told:

> She was a worthy womman al hir live:
> Housbondes at chirche dore she hadde five, (461-2)

The Poet's irony here works by juxtaposing what appears to be an approving moral judgment with a detail which undercuts it. As the

Wife will explain in her "Prologue" there were those in the Church who found the notion of a widow remarrying to be a sin. The word "worthy" carries no hint of moral approval; this woman's relatively high social status (literally her worth in monetary terms); her financial independence is seen to rest on having buried husbands and inherited their estates and not on her conduct.

The Pilgrim's sharp eye for detail allows the Poet to make it clear that the Wife's sexual morality is extremely suspect. She has married five husbands and been widowed five times. (We learn later in the *Tales* that she married the first four men because they were rich and old and only the last for love.) These marriages have been conducted, as was the custom for a woman of her class, "at chirche dore" (462):

> couples usually spoke their vows at the church door, the most public place in the village. Here the priest inquired if there was any impediment, meaning kinship in the degree forbidden by the Church. The bridegroom named the dower which he would provide for his wife, giving her as a token a ring … Vows were then exchanged, and the bridal party might proceed into the church where a nuptial Mass was celebrated. (Gies and Gies 177)

There are clear hints, however, of extra-marital affairs before her first marriage and of subsequent infidelity. The Pilgrim speaks euphemistically of "oother compaignye in youthe" (463), a detail which he simply attempts to skate past, "therof [I] nedeth nat to speke as nowthe" (464). Ironically, the very lengths to which the Pilgrim is forced to go in his effort to minimize the implications of what he says has the effect of drawing it to the reader's attention. Promiscuity is also suggested by such details as:

> She hadde passed many a straunge strem …
> She koude muchel of wandringe by the weye.
> Gat-tothed was she, soothly for to seye. (466-70)

The first two lines are intended by the Pilgrim to relate to the Wife's extensive experience of religious travels throughout Europe, but the Poet intends a metaphorical interpretation: the Wife finds it hard to stick to the straight and narrow path of salvation. The Medieval reader would immediately think of Mathew 7:13-4, "Enter ye in at the strait gate: for wide is the gate, and broad is the way, that leadeth to destruction, and many there be which go in thereat: Because strait is the gate, and narrow is the way, which leadeth unto life, and few there be that find it" (King James Version).

The detail of the gap between her front teeth, which the Pilgrim records as adding to her attraction, complements the previous line, for physiognomy saw being gap-toothed as a sign of a bold nature given to aggressive, wanton and immoral behavior, uncontrolled appetites, lust, and hypersexuality. It has been suggested that the very first hint of this aspect of the Wife's character is given in the innocuous-sounding line, "Of clooth-making she hadde swich an haunt," (449). The word "haunt" means 'skill,' but it also means a 'much frequented place' which, in terms of her sexual history, is a pretty good description of the Wife (crossref-it.info).

The Wife's dominant characteristic is her assertiveness. She rides upon an "amblere' (471), that is a palfrey, the most expensive and highly-bred type of riding horse of the Middle Ages, proving once again her affluence. The palfrey was the preferred choice of nobles, knights and ladies for long journeys because its gait provided a smooth and comfortable ride which accounts for the detail that the Wife sat her mount "esily" (471). This being so, it is entirely superfluous that the she wears "on hir feet a paire of spores sharpe" (475). The Poet is highlighting that the Wife must be in control in all situations. The Ellesmere illustration shows her with an equally superfluous whip in her hand, which is not described in the portrait. However, later she will tell the company:

> … when I shall have told you all my tale
> Of the tribulation that is in marriage,
> Of which I have been an expert all my adult life,
> That is to say, myself have been the whip,
> ("The Wife of Bath's Prologue" author's modernization)

She claims to have literally had the whip hand in her marriages.

The Wife wears a wimple, as befits her status as a widow, but one suspects that the adverb "wel" implies that her wimple is as ornate and flattering as is that of the Prioress. She is:

> Ywimpled wel, and on hir heed an hat
> As brood as is a bokeler or a targe; (472-3)

Impressed by the size of the Wife's hat, a simile springs innocently to the pen of the Pilgrim emphasizes only the immense size of the Wife's hat, but to the Poet it is another indication of her assertive, combative character. John Clements explains the place of the "bokeler" in medieval combat:

A buckler differs from a shield in that the latter is carried by straps and worn on the arm whereas the former is held in single-hand in a "fist" grip. It is difficult to trace the history of the weapon as many times any type of round shield or small targe would be called buckler, regardless of whether it was held in the fist or worn on the arm. The buckler was a small, maneuverable, hand-held shield for deflecting and punching blows ... Bucklers were typically round and frequently between 8 to 16 inches in diameter.

The second comparison is even more significant since a "targe" was a larger round shield, generally between 18 and 21 inches, usually attached to the forearm.

The Wife's martial spirit is initially shown, most inappropriately, in her determination to be the first to reach the altar with her offering at Mass:

In al the parisshe wif ne was ther noon
That to the offringe bifore hire sholde goon;
And if ther dide, certeyn so wrooth was she,
That she was out of alle charitee. (451-4)

The Pilgrim presents this detailed description without comment, the unspoken implication being that, like her many pilgrimages, it is another indication of her devotion. The Poet, however, relies upon the reader to understand that being first to the altar was reserved for the person with the highest social position, and that the Wife is merely asserting her worthiness in its purely social sense. This point is hammered home by the comment that if she is beaten by another lady she is furious ("wroth") and full of hard thoughts against her rival ("out of alle charitee"). Wrath is, of course, one of the Seven Deadly Sins and charity one of the Seven Heavenly Virtues. The final detail which fits into the pattern of the Wife's assertiveness is the Pilgrim's sympathetic remark that "she was somdel deef, and that was scathe" (448). It is later revealed in "The Wife of Bath's Prologue" that she is deaf in one ear because, during an argument over the relative position of men and women in marriage, her last husband threw a heavy book at her and hit her on the side of her head knocking her to the floor. However, at this point in the *Prologue*, the reader may speculate that her deafness is more psychological than it is physical: the Wife of Bath only hears what she wishes to hear.

In contrast to the detail given in describing the Wife's clothes and her conduct, surprisingly little physical description is given and the details are spread throughout the portrait:

> Boold was hir face, and fair, and reed of hewe. (460)
> Gat-tothed was she, soothly for to seye. (470)
> A foot-mantel aboute hir hipes large, (474)

The Pilgrim finds the Wife physically attractive commenting on her ruddy complexion, the gap between her front teeth and her large hips. Everything points to someone who has been sexually active, and who puts her experience to good use:

> Of remedies of love she knew per chaunce,
> For she koude of that art the olde daunce. (477-8)

Kirkham and Allen gloss her knowledge of remedies as "aphrodisiacs and seduction techniques" (52). This makes even clearer the irony of the fact that she remains childless.

Chapter Eight: The Parson and The Plowman

Lines 479-530: The Parson

Parsons and parish priests complained to their bishop
That since the plague-time their parishes were impoverished,
And asked permission and license to live in London
And sing requiems for money since silver is sweet.
(Langland. *The Vision of Piers Plowman* author's modernization)

The Black Death, which hit England particularly hard between 1348 and 1349, between 1361 and 1362, in 1369, and in 1375, had a significant impact on parish priests. The population of England declined drastically (estimates range between 20% and 63%). Entire villages were abandoned and many others were impoverished so that income from tithes plummeted at a time when the stipends paid to priests were also low. Pollard quotes Simon Sudbury (Archbishop of Canterbury from 1375 until he was killed in the Peasants' Revolt of 1381), "It has come to our ears that rectors of our diocese scorn to keep due residence in their churches, and go to dwell in distant and perhaps unhonest places, without our license, and let their churches out to farm to persons less fitted. Lay persons with their wives and children sometimes dwell in their rectories, frequently keeping taverns and other foul and unhonest things in them." As Pollard notes, the real irony here is that licenses to farm out a rectory were quite easy to obtain (80-1).

There is good reason to conclude that parish priests were particularly at risk of catching the plague because of their obligation to care for the sick. The result was that in Chaucer's day the number of qualified parish priests was relatively small and, just as the peasants did, priests used this to their advantage. Many simply abandoned their villages and found lucrative positions in the larger cities or with noble patrons. Pollard writes, "According to Dugdale there were thirty-five chantries at St. Paul's served by fifty-four priests" (83). As a result of this lucrative competition, many of the priests who remained at their posts were poorly educated.

The Parson is the only devout and conscientious cleric described in the *Prologue*. Later in the *Tales*, the Host will claim to "smelle a Lollere in the wynd," yet his very presence on the pilgrimage guarantees that he is not a follower of John Wycliffe (i.e., a Lollard). Nevertheless, many of the qualities attributed to the Parson spring directly from criticisms by Lollards and others of the abuses of parish priests, leading Bowden to comment that Chaucer invests the Parson "with many of the characteristics of the Wyclifites" (*Commentary* 10). His portrait (and that of his brother the Plowman) involves no irony for the simple reason that there is no difference between appearance and moral reality: for the first time in the portraits what you see really is what you get.

This study argues that the only morally idealized portraits in the *Prologue* are the Parson and his Plowman brother. As Hussey writes:

> They have both resisted the call to the towns where the one might have made more money in a trade and the other in a fashionable chantry. The parish priest is a symbol of the ideal place of the church in village life, the centre of stability in it, and the spiritual home of a man who exercises the pastoral task to which he has been called. These brothers, Parson and Plowman, are twin pillars of the village at its best. (Hussey et al. 34)

Even those who argue for more idealized figures (by co-opting characters such as the Knight, the Squire, the Yeoman, and the Clerk) still come up with a tiny minority. The reason is expressed effectively by Leo Tolstoy in the opening sentence of *Anna Karenina*, "Happy families are all alike; every unhappy family is unhappy in its own way." The *Prologue* is quintessentially a comedy of manners which explores the infinite variety of ways in which, and the various degrees to which, people can be corrupt; as Swanson puts it, "roguery, not saintliness, makes good poetry" (Brown 407). In contrast, as refreshing as the two idealized portraits are, as important as they are in restoring our faith in human nature, and as essential as they are in functioning as the 'gold standard' against which all of the other pilgrims are to be judged, two is enough.

All truly good people are good in the same way which perhaps explains why neither portrait is brought to life with the kinds of individualizing details which animate the other pilgrims: they are concepts rather than people. Swanson is the only critic I am aware of who has argued that neither the Parson nor the Ploughman is quite as ideal as they appear to be (see Brown 408-9). If his argument is ultimately unconvincing, he is, nevertheless, quite right to point out that Chaucer is here drawing an abnormal situation: the Parson is "an exemplary priest because he can afford to be one: he has the security of tenure which allows him to live up to the ideal," and he has a prosperous benefice which allows him to pardon the occasional defaulting on tithes. Similarly, the Ploughman is wealthy enough to be able to work for his poorer neighbors without wages. There can have been relatively few real-life models.

Pilgrim/Poet:
1. Why is irony neither appropriate, nor indeed possible, in the case of the Parson? Essentially what is it about him that makes him immune from criticism?
2. The Parson's virtues highlight the moral failings of many of his fellow pilgrims. Select about five details of this portrait and for each show how they highlight a moral failing in one of the other pilgrims.

	There was a good, religious man
480	Who was a poor village Priest,
	Although he was rich in holy thought and works.
	He was also a learned man, a scholar,
	Who accurately preached Christ's gospel;
	His parishioners he taught devoutly.
485	Kind he was and wonderfully hard-working,
	And very patient when things got difficult,
	Which he had proved many times.
	He was unwilling to have anyone excommunicated for not paying tithes,
	On the contrary, he would rather give,
490	To his poor parishioners
	Out of his own income from offerings and also from his possessions.
	He could make do with very little.
	His parish was large, and the houses far apart,
	But he never neglected, in rain or thunder,
495	In sickness or difficulty, to visit
	The farthest house in his parish, be it great or small,

On foot, and a staff in his hand.

This noble example to his sheep he gave

That first he did good and then taught others to do the same.

500 He took those words out of the Gospel

And he also added this figure of speech:

If gold rusts, what will iron do?

Meaning that if a priest, in whom we trust, is evil

Then no wonder that a simple man rusts [i.e., goes bad];

505 And it is a shame, if priests will only realize it,

For the shepherd to be covered in shit and the sheep to be clean.

A priest really ought to set an example

By his purity, about how his sheep should live.

This parson didn't hire out his benefice [i.e., the living of his parish]

510 And leave his sheep stuck in the mud

And run up to London to St. Paul's

To try to get a paid position in a chantry praying for the souls of the dead,

Or to be paid to be chaplain to a guild [trades union];

Instead he stayed at home and took care of his flock

515 So that the wolf didn't get hold of them;

He was a shepherd not a mercenary.

And although he was holy and virtuous

He was not scornful of sinful men,

Nor was he proud and superior in the way he spoke,

520 But in his teaching he was thoughtful and kind.

To draw people towards heaven by the goodness of his life,

By setting a good example, that was the way he sought to influence people.

But if there was any evil person who was unwilling to change

Whether he was of high or low class,

525 Immediately, he would sharply reprimand him.

There was not a better priest anywhere.

He didn't want any ceremony or reverence,

Nor did he find fault with little things his parishioners did wrong,

The rules of Christ and his twelve Apostles

530 He taught, but first he followed them himself.

The portrait of the Parson is not individualized in any way: he has no name; neither he himself not his dress is described; he is associated with no religious or academic institution; there is not even a hint of where in England his parish is located. Swanson memorably

159

calls him "one of the most striking [of] nonentities" (Brown 407). This, then, is a description of a character type – a type moreover which the Poet knows to represent an ideal seldom found in the real world of his day:

> [The] Parson ... is the epitome of simple virtue, a credit to his profession and a witness to man's moral perfectibility. The Narrator lists his virtues with an unusual reverence, and the complete absence of irony suggests that for once, at least, Pilgrim Chaucer and Chaucer the Author see things in exactly the same way. (Williams 36)

Although there is no irony directed at the Parson, in another way his portrait is heavily ironic, for he is partly defined by the things he does not do, like having multiple livings and getting substitutes to perform his duties. The Poet's clear implication is that, in the world beyond, these kinds of abuses are common, and it is against this corruption that the entire portrait is an ironic attack.

The position of parson, or rector, in a village was in the gift of the lord of the manor. It was termed a living because the appointee received the revenues attaching to the post in return for carrying out (either personally or by substitute) the duties of parish priest. Rectors were generally either the younger sons of noble families or local freemen who had been ordained into the clergy; the former were more likely to hold a number of livings concurrently, whilst the latter were more likely to hold just one. The practice of taking the revenues of several parishes and appointing substitutes to perform parish duties was called 'pluralism' and was open to abuse. It is reported that Bogo de Clare, younger son of an earl, had an income of £2,200 in 1291 from twenty-four parishes and other religious posts (Gies & Gies 198).

Chaucer's Parson appears to be a local man since his brother farms land in the parish, yet it is made clear that he has had a university education which makes him the intellectual equal of any parson of noble birth. This is also unusual, for most local freemen got their training from other parish priests or, if they were lucky, by attending monastic or cathedral schools. The few who were able to attend university normally found more lucrative positions within the Church than that of parish priest with the result that most parsons were poorly educated. Indeed, John Peckham, Archbishop of Canterbury (1279–1292), recorded that priests in general showed an "ignorance which casts the people into a ditch of error" (quoted in Gies & Gies 199). Many priests of the time also married or lived openly with a concubine simply ignoring their vow of celibacy.

The Parson is one of the few pilgrims whose physical appearance and costume are not described at all. Laura Hodges points out what the Poet is implying, "The omission of costume is a literary signal that the character is metaphorically clothed in his/her actions or virtues and may be judged accordingly" (Hodges 7). The portrait begins with antithesis:

> And was a povre Persoun of a toun,
> But riche he was of hooly thoghte and werk, (480-1)

This is the very opposite of almost every portrait so far: the pilgrims are almost all materially wealthy but spiritually poor; they have money but lack morality. The description of the Parson, which deals exclusively with the man's "condicioun" (38), is composed of a number of abstract qualities which the Parson exemplifies: he is devoutly orthodox, kindly, diligent, patient in adversity, virtuous and fair. However, he exemplifies these qualities by his actions:

> And in adversitee ful pacient,
> And swich he was ypreved ofte sithes (486-7)
> That first he wroghte, and afterward he taught (499)

Amongst the actions which prove the Parson's faith are: paying the tithes of poor parishioners, visiting every house in his parish no matter how far away or what the status of the parishioners and rebuking in no uncertain terms those sinners who show no repentance. These actions illustrate that, "Cristes loore and his apostles twelve / He taughte, but first he folwed it hymselve" (529-30).

Despite the size of his rural parish, and the fact that he keeps no horse, the Parson travels regularly to every part undeterred by storms:

> Wyd was his parisshe, and houses fer asonder,
> But he ne lefte nat, for reyn ne thonder,
> In siknesse nor in meschief to visite
> The ferreste in his parisshe, muche and lite, (493-6)

Notice that each line is composed on a pair. In the first three lines, the pairs are complementary ("Wyd... fer," "reyn... thonder," "siknesse... meschief"), but in the fourth line they are opposites ("muche... lite"). Four pilgrims are explicitly associated with travel:

the Knight and the Wife of Bath who have each traveled throughout Europe and the Middle East; the Pardoner who (if we believe him) has traveled to Rome and who has certainly traveled the length of England; and the Parson, who, by way of contrast, has served God by staying in his own parish.

The Parson is also defined by the things he does not do. Chaucer here makes use of the common complaints against priests found in other estates satires. Unlike many priests in his situation, he does not pay a substitute to do his duties and seek in London a remunerative position in a chantry (where priests are paid to sing hymns for the souls of the dead) or as priest to a guild or brotherhood. He is described as a true shepherd to his flock, a metaphor which is appropriate to his rural roots and which also serves to present the Parson as a Christ-figure:

> He sette nat his benefice to hire
> And leet his sheep encombred in the mire...
> But dwelte at hoom, and kepte wel his folde,
> So that the wolf ne made it nat miscarie; (509-15)

This is a clear echo of Christ's parable of the shepherd who goes to find one stray sheep. Although the Parson is a learned man that "Cristes gospel trewely wolde preche" (483), it is stressed that he teaches mostly by setting a good example (which makes him actually unique amongst the pilgrims who are members of the clergy):

> This noble ensample to his sheep he yaf,
> That first he wroghte, and afterward he taughte.
> Out of the gospel he tho wordes caughte,
> And this figure he added eek therto,
> That if gold ruste, what shal iren do?
> For if a preest be foul, on whom we truste,
> No wonder is a lewed man to ruste; (498-504)

The Parson uses gold as a symbol of spiritual purity, unlike pilgrims such as the Doctor who seek it for its monetary value. This poetic metaphor is followed by the more down-to-earth assertion that a "shiten shepherde" cannot expect to keep "clene sheep" (505), and here we can see the Parson's skill at presenting the truths of the Gospel in language that uneducated country people can understand. He applies common sense to enforcing the Gospel and is said not to have "a spiced conscience" (528), but when he encounters an unrepentant sinner, "What so he were, of heigh or lough estat" (524) he rebukes him soundly. This man is no soft touch! He represents

162

robust Christianity at it best. For once, the Poet joins the Pilgrim in his use of superlatives, "A bettre preest I trowe that nowher noon is" (526).

The significance of the portrait of the Parson does not lie solely in its depiction of a good man. The Poet's description is carefully constructed to resonate with other portraits so that the implied contrasts cannot be missed by the reader. The Parson is described as "a povre Persoun of a toun" (480), a phrase identical to that used to describe the sort of humble priest on whom the Pardoner preys:

> But with this relikes, whan that he fond
> A povre person dwellinge upon lond,
> Upon a day he gat him moore moneye
> Than that the person gat in monthes tweye; (703-6)

Perhaps this particular parson is too robust a Christian to be exploited by the Pardoner, but he clearly exemplifies the kind of honest country priest he normally exploits. The Parson is also described as "a lerned man, a clerk" (482), identifying him as the intellectual equal of the Clerk of Oxenford. The essential contrast, however, is that the Parson gives primacy to practice over theory. Whilst it is the financial poverty of the Clerk which is stressed, it is the Parson's spiritual wealth (which results from his putting morality into practice) which is emphasized, "But riche he was of hooly thoght and werk /… first he wroghte, and afterward he taughte" (481-99). Recall that the Clerk's fault was precisely that he does nothing with his learning.

The Parson is not the first character to be described as lenient in taking confession and imposing punishment. It is said of the Friar:

> Ful swetely herde he confessioun,
> And plesaunt was his absolucioun:
> He was an esy man to yeve penaunce,
> Ther as he wiste to have a good pitaunce.
> For unto a povre ordre for to yive
> Is signe that a man is wel yshryve; (221-6)

The difference between the Friar and the Parson is, of course, in the direction in which the money flows! Whilst the Friar essentially accepts bribes to secure a mild punishment, the Parson will sooner pay out of his own pocket than have one of his parishioners default on their tithes and so be excommunicated:

> Ful looth were him to cursen for his tithes,
> But rather wolde he yeven, out of doute,

Unto his povre parisshens aboute
Of his offring and eek of his substaunce. (488-92)

The Parson knows that his parishioners would pay if they had the money, and that they will pay when they are able, and he treats them accordingly. Unlike the Friar who dresses and bears himself "lyk a maister or a pope" (263) and the Prioress whose whole life is lived "to ben holden digne of reverence" (141), the Parson has no time for "pompe and reverence" (527), and while the Friar is careful to associate with "everich hostiler and tappestere / Bet than a lazar or a beggestere" (241-2), the Parson serves all of the people in his parish "muche and lite" (496) and applies the same standards to each sinner, "What so he were, of heigh or lough estat" (524). The detail that the Parson "koude in litel thing have suffisaunce" (492) is a jibe at those pilgrims who indulge excessively such as the Franklin of whom it is said, "It snewed in his hous of mete and drinke" (347) or the Friar who is so fat that his "semicope, / ... rounded [is] as a belle out of presse" (264-5). An even more pointed contrast, however, is with those pilgrims who similarly make do with little but for very different reasons such as the Clerk who starves both himself and his horse to feed his book-buying habit or the Doctor who maintains a diet which is "of no superfluitee" (378) as part of his general reluctance to spend money for "he was but esy of dispence" (443).

Although the Parson rides a (presumably) hired horse on the pilgrimage to Canterbury, the portrait makes it clear that he travels his wide parish, "Upon his feet, and in his hand a staf" (497). This description brings to mind Christ and contrasts with that of the Monk who has, "Ful many a deyntee hors ... in stable" (168). The parallel with Christ is extended in the line which concludes, "He was a shepherde and noght a mercenarie" (516). It is tempting to see the use of the word "mercenarie" as a direct reference to the Knight, and if Terry Jones is correct in saying that Chaucer's readers would have immediately identified the Knight as a mercenary then it is not impossible, for Merriam-Webster gives the word's derivation thus, "Middle English, from Latin *mercenarius,* irregular from *merced-,* *merces* wages... First Known Use: 14th century." The word was certainly used to describe priests who farmed out their benefices, but even if we concede that a deliberate military reference here is unproven, the contrast between the wondering Knight who seeks glory, booty, and prestige throughout Europe but is never at home to fight for his king and the Parson who refuses to hire out his living and go to London to make money, "But dwelte at hoom, and kepte wel his folde" (514) could not be clearer. What is indisputable is that the word "mercenarie" is intended as a reference to John 10:12:

> But he that is an hireling, and not the shepherd, whose own the sheep are not, seeth the wolf coming, and leaveth the sheep, and fleeth: and the wolf catcheth them, and scattereth the sheep. (King James Version)

A final, and perhaps surprising, contrast which is made between the Parson and many of the other pilgrims is his plain speaking. Whilst the Prioress takes great pains to make her voice pleasing and to avoid swearing, "Hire gretteste ooth was but by Seinte Loy" (120), and the Knight "never yet no vileynie ne saide / In al his lif unto no maner of wight" (70-1), the Parson appears to have a robust, agricultural vocabulary which calls a spade a spade. He supports his dedication to his flock with the sort of metaphor which his parishioners would understand, "shame it is, if a prest take keep, / A shiten shepherde and a clene sheep" (505-6), and it is clear that when confronted by an unrepentant sinner this man does not mince his words, "Hym wolde he snybben sharply for the nonis" (525). As so often we hear in this line the very tone of the pilgrim and in this case the sharp, hard alliteration convinces the reader that here is a man who is not to be trifled with.

As usual, what is not in the portrait is as important as what is in it. The most common adjective in The *Prologue* is "worthy": it is used of the Knight (43, 47, 68), the Friar (243), the Merchant (285) and the Wife of Bath (461), but it is not used in the portrait of either the Parson or the Plowman because, in socio-economic terms, they have neither worth nor value, while their moral worth is self-evident.

Lines 531-543: The Ploughman

> ... the poor lesser folk (who should stick to their work) demand to be better fed than the one who has hired them. Moreover, they clothe themselves in fine colors and handsome attire, whereas they were formerly clothed (without pride and without conspiracy) in sackcloth. (Gower *The Mirror of Mankind* Norton Anthology)

> ... the servants of the plough ... are sluggish, they are scarce, and they are grasping. For the very little that they do they demand the highest pay ... They desire the leisure of great men... (John Gower *Vox clamantis* or *The Voice of One Crying Out* Miller 233)

> A man who lives by his own honest labor is blessed in body and soul. (Langland. *The Vision of Piers Plowman* author's modernization)

The Plowman is not a landless peasant, much less a serf, for if he were he would not be required to pay tithes; he is a landowner or, at the very least, a free tenant. Donald Howard sets this portrait in its historical context:

> [A]gricultural laborers were at a premium in the late fourteenth century because the Black Death and subsequent plagues had wiped out over a third of the work force. Serfs demanded freedom and agricultural smallholders chafed against the old manorial impositions. Their discontent was constant, the Peasant's Revolt of 1381 being the most violent expression of it ... so it is the more surprising to find a small tenant farmer like the Plowman living in peace and perfect charity without a trace of discontent. To the extent that he can be thought a reality rather than an ideal, he would indeed have seemed an anachronism. (94)

At a time when real agricultural laborers were taking advantage of their new economic power to demand greater freedom and higher wages, Chaucer's Plowman appears to be entirely content with his lot in life. Partly this is Chaucer's nostalgic wishful thinking: he portrays things as he feels that they ought to be (and as he nostalgically believes they were in the past) not as he knows them to be. However, Blamires points to the portrait as evidence of Chaucer's social and political conservatism:

> *implicitly* Chaucer reacts to the spectacle of a clamorous peasantry. His version of a Ploughman is an epitome of peasant docility and altruism, who lives in peace and will work for free ... In the prevailing labour context, this representation constitutes an aggressive act of establishment propaganda. (Emphasis in original Brown ed. 135)

There is no Ellesmere illustration, and the Ploughman tells no tale.

Pilgrim/Poet:

1. In what sense(s) does Chaucer intend us to understand the Ploughman to be the "brother" of the Parson?

2. How is the Ploughman's moral virtue illustrated in actions?

> With him there was his brother, a Plowman,
> Who had hauled many a cartload of dung,
> He was an honest and true laborer,
> Living in peace and perfect charity.
> 535 He loved God most with his whole heart.
> At all times, whether he prospered or suffered,
> And next, he loved his neighbor just as much as he loved himself.
> He'd thresh the grain, construct ditches and dig,
> For every poor person for Christ's own sake,
> 340 All without pay, if it lay in his power.
> He paid his taxes to the Church, regularly and in full
> Both for what he earned by his own toil and from selling his farm produce.
> In a humble smock, he rode upon a mare.

A similarity between the portraits of the Yeoman and the Plowman, each of whom occupies a position at the bottom of the social range presented in the *Prologue*, is that they both lack individuality. The essential difference is that only the portrait of the Plowman contains material related to his spiritual and moral condition. The Yeoman is an expert woodsman, but, aside from some vanity expressed in his dress, he may or may not be a good man: there is simply no evidence one way or the other. In contrast, the Plowman is the only member of the laity who is idealized; he lives a life which exemplifies his faith in and his duty to God. The lines:

> God loved he best with al his hoole herte
> At alle times, thogh him gamed or smerte,
> And thanne his neighebor right as himselve. (535-7)

are a paraphrase of Luke 10:25-8:

> And, behold, a certain lawyer stood up, and tempted him, saying, Master, what shall I do to inherit eternal life?
> He said unto him, What is written in the law? How readest thou?
> And he answering said, Thou shalt love the Lord thy God with all thy heart, and with all thy soul, and with all thy

strength, and with all thy mind; and thy neighbour as thyself.

And he said unto him, Thou hast answered right: this do, and thou shalt live. (King James Version)

Jesus goes on to tell the parable of the Good Samaritan leading to the conclusion that one's neighbor is anyone in need, or "every povre wight" (539) as it is expressed in the portrait. Thus, the Plowman lives by what theologians call the Golden Rule.

As with the Parson, the Poet gives no physical details of the Plowman who is presented as a character type - a type which, like his brother, represents an ideal seldom found in the real world. The only physical details are of his "array": he wears a smock and rides upon a mare (the only pilgrim who is said to do so), both of which are appropriate to his status and therefore suggest his humility. No one with any pretentions to gentility would ride a mare.

The remainder of the portrait is concerned with his actions: he is a hard worker, lives in his community "in pees and parfit charitee" (534), loves God in good times and bad, loves his neighbor as himself, helps out poor men in need without seeking reward, and pays his tithes promptly and in full both for his labor and for the money he has made selling his produce. What is stressed is how completely he is integrated into his community, just like his brother. Appropriately, the Pilgrim/Poet illustrates the man's hard work by describing the least pleasant of agricultural chores, "[He] hadde ylad of dong ful many a fother" (532) and tasks which are physically demanding, "He wolde thresshe, and therto dike and delve" (538). The last line stands in contrast to the critical comment on laborers, "Ditchers and diggers that do their work ill" in Langland's *Piers Plowman*.

The portrait is literally a list of superlatives, but the use of the adjective "ful" seems particularly well chosen recalling as it does the repeated use of the same word in the portrait of the Prioress. When we read that the Plowman, "His tithes paide he ful faire and well" (541), it is hard not to believe that the Poet intends us to recall the sentence "Frenssh she spak ful faire and fetisly" (124). The almost identical grammatical structure serves to highlight the difference between the two statements, for the Prioress takes pride in a dilettante skill whilst the Plowman humbly, and without question, pays his obligation to the Church.

The Plowman is frequently regarded as "the lowest ranking pilgrim" (Kirkham and Allen 59), but is presented as both literally and spiritually the Parson's brother. This is made clear by the repetition of the word "hire": the Parson will not "sette his benefice to hire" (509), and the Plowman:

> ... wolde thresshe, and therto dike and delve
> For Christes sake, for every povre wight,
> Withouten hire, if it lay in his might. (538-40)

They are equally motivated to work for the glory of God and not for pecuniary benefit, which in itself sets them apart from most of their fellow pilgrims. Together they represent the fourteenth century ideal (already an anachronism) of clergy and laity devoutly serving God. He is called a plowman, rather than a farmer, because of the Biblical associations of the term, for example in Galatians 6:7, "Be not deceived; God is not mocked: for whatsoever a man soweth, that shall he also reap" (King James Version). This principle is exemplified by each of the brothers. The portrait of the Ploughman is immediately followed by extreme contrast, for the remaining five pilgrims prove to be the least attractive of the whole party.

Chapter Nine: The Miller, The Manciple and The Reeve

These three pilgrims have something fundamental in common: they are each in positions of trust because people place their property in their hands. Each in some way manages that property in return for an agreed fee and (at least in theory) returns the profits to the owner. The potential for corruption is clear, and each of these three pilgrims is manipulative, self-serving, and dishonest. The status of all three men has risen as a result of the criminal application of their skills; what differs is their social functions and the social status and wealth of those from whom they steal which determines the scale of their ill-gotten gains. Together they represent what Wetherbee terms "a grotesque, predatory hierarchy" (31).

This section begins with a fine example of Chaucerian comedy:

> Ther was also a Reve, and a Millere,
> A Somnour, and a Pardoner also,
> A Maunciple, and myself - ther were namo. (544-6)

Here the Pilgrim includes himself not only with five of the lowest status pilgrims, but, more importantly, with the five worst predatory rogues in his entire gallery.

Lines 547-568: The Miller

In most villages, the gristmill (water-powered in hilly regions and wind-powered in flat) was owned by the lord of the manor to whom the miller, a free tenant, paid a fixed annual fee. Local farmers brought their grain and received back ground meal, or flour, minus an agreed percentage called the miller's toll, or multure, which ranged from a sixteenth to a twenty-fourth of the original weight of grain (Gies and Gies 81). Since most millers were in a monopoly position, and since their

profit depended on the size of the toll they took, millers had a reputation for taking more than they should and for substituting flour from poor quality grain for good. The dishonesty of this Miller is almost certainly the origin, otherwise unexplained, of the animosity between the Reeve, the lord of the manor's agent, and the Miller. Gies and Gies record this medieval riddle. Question: What is the boldest thing in the world? Answer: A miller's shirt, for it clasps a thief by the throat daily (81).

Pilgrim:
1. The Miller's most obvious quality is his skill as a wrestler and his enormous strength. What details does the Pilgrim give to illustrate these qualities?
2. The Miller is also an expert at his trade. This is the surface meaning of the detail "he hadde a thombe of gold" (Chaucer 565). Explain.
Poet:
3. This portrait is notable for its vivid imagery. Find each of the similes and metaphors used to describe the Miller and explain the significance of the comparisons made.
4. What is the significance of the fact that "a swerd and bokeler bar he by his side" (560)?
5. Explain exactly how the Miller cheats his customers (i.e. steals from them).
6. What significant detail is given of the Miller's social interaction?
7. Why do you think that the Poet chooses to make the Miller a player of bagpipes?

> There was also a Reeve and Miller,
> A Summoner, and a Pardoner also,
> A Manciple, and me – there were no others.
> The Miller was a very strong fellow;
> Big of muscle and big of bone.
> That was proved by the fact that wherever he went
> 550 At wrestling he would always win the prize of a ram.
> He was a thickset, strong-looking chap;
> There was not a door anywhere that he couldn't wrench off its hinges
> Or break it down by running at it with his head.
> His beard was as red as any pig or any fox,
> 555 And it was as broad as a spade.

Right on the tip of his nose he had
A wart and on it stood a tuft of hairs,
Red as the bristles on any pig's ear;
His nostrils were black and wide.
560   A sword and small round shield he carried by his side.
His mouth was as big as a great furnace.
His loud talk was all ribald stories and course jokes
Mainly about sex and lewdness.
He was skillful at stealing corn and at taking three times the legal
toll on corn that he ground;
Yet he had a golden thumb, I can tell you.
565   A white coat and a blue hood he wore.
He played the bagpipes well
And with them he played up out of London.

The portrait of the Ploughman is appropriately followed by that of another rural character, the Miller, but the contrast could not be more extreme. The Miller (later called "Robyn" by the Host) is so ugly both physically and morally that even the naïve Pilgrim finds little to admire, though he remains true to form in that he finds nothing to condemn either, yet there is plenty.

Bowden quotes the opinion of the *Secreta Secretorum* that a man of the Miller's strong, squat build will be, "'Shameless, immodest and loquacious' as well as 'bold and easily angered'" (*Commentary* 247). His "course appetite, quarrelsome temper and brutishness prove him choleric; excessive heat having twisted his nature out of shape" (Hussey et al. 161). Winny identifies his controlling planet as Mars and quotes Bartholomaeus Anglicus (c.1203–1272), the Franciscan encyclopaedist as stating that Mars is "red and untrue and guileful" and John Maplet (*The Dial of Destiny* 1581) as concluding that the predominance of Mars makes men "wild and savage rather than properly puissant; and more venturous - rash and bold than considerate and politic" (Hussey et al. 166).

The portrait begins by emphasizing the Miller's most outstanding quality, his brute strength:

The Millere was a stout carl for the nones;
Ful big he was of brawn, and eek of bones.
That proved wel, for over al ther he cam,
At wrastlinge he wolde have alwey the ram. (547-50)

The word "carl" (roughly 'churl') establishes the Miller as an ill-bred fellow, but there is no denying the sheer strength and will to win which make him a wrestling champion. His association with the ram reminds us that the ram is traditionally associated with strength, aggression, force, energy, virility, and fearlessness, associations which are supported by the detail that he carries, "A swerd and bokeler... by his side" (560) - as ready for instant use as is the Shipman's dagger and pointing to the same short temper in their owners.

There is no getting around the physical ugliness of the Miller, so the Pilgrim uses the simple expedient of presenting details without comment. The portrait ends, however, on two notes of apparent approval, even praise, which are each prefaced by the phrase 'well could'. The Pilgrim is impressed by the Miller's cunning in stealing grain and in taking three times his agreed fee:

> Wel koude he stelen corn and tollen thries;
> And yet he hadde a thombe of gold, pardee.
> A whit cote and a blew hood wered he. (564-6)

The scams that the Miller works here must have been very common: the farmer brings in grain to be turned into flour, but has no way of telling exactly how much flour his grain will make, leaving him totally at the mercy of the miller. A miller can quite easily steal grain before he grinds it, and/or he can take his agreed percentage of the flour and then double- or in this case triple-dip. The next line has caused some confusion. It clearly opens as though it is meant as a counterbalance to the admission that the Miller is a thief (albeit a skilled one). The simplest explanation is that a miller would test whether grain was ready for grinding by putting some of the grain in the palm of his hand and rolling it around with his thumb. Experience would teach a miller to know by the feel of the grain if it was still too damp for grinding or just right. Thus, implies the Pilgrim, he may be a thief, but he is a very expert miller!

It is significant that the only reference to the Miller's dress in the portrait comes immediately after the details of his stealing. Had the Miller dressed appropriately to his status, he would have worn a white coat and matching hood, but he wears blue as a sign that "Robyn believes that he is of an upper class, and he is arrogant enough to wear the hood" (Lambdin and Lambdin 275). A final note of approval is struck by the Pilgrim's commendation of the Miller's skill of the bagpipes:

> A baggepipe wel koude he blowe and sowne,
> And therwithal he broghte us out of towne. (567-8)

Not only does he appear to play the pipes well, but characteristically he takes the lead as the pilgrims leave London.

The Poet has placed into the mouth of the Pilgrim all of the details which will expose the Miller's corruption; typically, the Pilgrim sees everything and understands nothing. This is the first portrait to give a really detailed physical description of the pilgrim's body and particularly his face: ten lines out of twenty-five describe his physical appearance, and only three lines his clothing and accessories. To illustrate the man's extraordinary strength, the Pilgrim notes without comment:

> He was short-sholdred, brood, a thikke knarre;
> Ther was no dore that he nolde heve of harre,
> Or breke it at a renning with his heed. (551-3)

Running at doors head-first would explain the Miller's short neck and high shoulders. However, the reader is left to wonder just how much call there was for pulling doors off their hinges or breaking them down even in the Middle Ages, and the answer is probably no more than there is today. Gies and Gies make the point that the medieval house, made of wattle-and-daub, was "insubstantial [and that] 'House breaking' by burglars was literal" (137). The Poet's implication is clear: the Miller breaks into houses. He is a burglar of a particularly violent and brazen type.

The Miller's red beard suggests comparisons with a fox and a pig:

> His berd as any sowe or fox was reed,
> And therto brood, as though it were a spade.
> Upon the cop right of his nose he hade
> A werte, and theron stood a toft of heris,
> Reed as the brustles of a sowes eris; (554-8)

Foxes are traditionally associated with cunning, theft and trickery, and pigs with sloth, greed and filth. The portrait concludes by describing the Miller's nose and mouth:

> His nosethirles blake were and wide...
> His mouth as greet was as a greet forneys.
> He was a janglere and a goliardeys,
> And that was moost of sinne and harlotries. (559-63)

174

What comes out of his mouth is humor of the crudest and most vulgar kind being all about sex: the Miller has a potty-mouth. However, looking into these orifices is even more revealing of the man's character. His nostrils are black, suggesting evil, and his mouth is like a great furnace. The Poet intends the reader to identify the "greet forneys" with the mouth of Hell itself since the representation of Hell as a furnace is traditional, for example in Matthew 13:42, "And shall cast them into a furnace of fire: there shall be wailing and gnashing of teeth" (King James Version).

The Poet intends more than does the Pilgrim by the statement, "he hadde a thombe of gold, pardee" (565). It is a reference to the traditional saying that an honest miller has a thumb of gold which has two possible negative connotations. It could mean that since every honest miller has a gold thumb, and since a gold thumb is not possible, therefore there are no honest millers. Alternatively, it could mean that, since every miller covertly uses his thumb to tip the weighing scales in his favor (and so make more gold by cheating), it follows that there are no honest millers. A golden thumb indeed! In fact, the very force of this line lies in its ambiguity: like so many of the corrupt pilgrims, the Miller is actually very good at his job, as is the Doctor, the Lawyer, and so many others – even the despicable Pardoner when he gets up into the pulpit. That is an essential element of the Poet's irony because it makes their corruption all the more lamentable.

As a final comment on this man, the Poet makes him an expert on the bagpipes - imagine the different connotations had he been an expert on the lute or the flute. The bagpipes are a folk instrument traditionally associated with the common people, and contemporary accounts mention them being played on pilgrimages. Thus, the Lollard William Thorpe complains of pilgrims that "have with them both men and women that can well sing wanton songs; and some pother pilgrims will have with them bagpipes" (quoted in Bowden *Commentary* 29). However, even more significantly bagpipes are associated with the devil (see *Luther as the Devil's Bagpipes*, 1535). Some commentators in addition suggest a sexual double entendre here, though they are too coy to explain it. Whilst that assertion is unproven, it is undeniable that the general connotation of bagpipes is negative; they are (shall we say) an acquired taste. Shakespeare's Shylock makes the obvious point:

Some men there are love not a gaping pig,
Some that are mad if they behold a cat,
And others, when the bagpipe sings I' th' nose,
Cannot contain their urine. (*The Merchant of Venice* 4.1)

The Poet leaves us to wonder just how happy the pilgrims were with the Miller's insistence on playing them out of London town.

Lines 569-588: The Manciple

There were only two Inns of Court in London, the Middle and the Inner Temple. Each was a residential college for lawyers, and the manciple was in charge of purchasing supplies. Fisher points out that the inclusion of a manciple (not a type represented in estates satire) is an unusual choice for Chaucer to make simply because there were so few in England at that time (Fisher in Lambdin and Lambdin 281). Manly adds to this the observation that the portrait itself is "thinly drawn" and concludes, "He is not an individual; he is not even a well-drawn, rounded type: he is merely a stalking horse from behind which Chaucer shoots a playful arrow at his learned masters of the Temple – capable of managing great estates but not wise enough to defeat the low cunning of their servant" (*New Light* 257). Certainly the idea that the target of the Poet's satire is not the Manciple but his masters, makes a great deal of sense. Nevertheless, the portrait seems somewhat out of place bracketed as it is by country people, although his professional function has many similarities with that of the Reeve which follows: he has more opportunities for fraud than the Miller but fewer than the Reeve. That seems to be the reason for including the Manciple at this point.

Pilgrim:
1. What skill does this man have of which the Pilgrim stands in awe? How does the portrait support the view that this man is very good at what he does?

Poet:
2. What is your answer to the question posed on lines 575-7?

3. What exactly is implied by line 588?

There was a fine Manciple of one of the Inns of Court,
570 From whom all stewards might take example
Of how to be wise in the purchasing of provisions;
For whether he paid cash or bought on credit,
He always watched the markets for the best time to buy
So that he always came out ahead and always made money.
575 Now is it not a sign of God's fair grace
That such an uneducated man's intelligence should surpass
The wisdom of a host of learned men?
He served more than thirty lawyers,
Who were expert and skillful in the law,
580 Of whom there were a dozen in that institution
Worthy to be a steward administering the lands
Of any lord in England,
Making him live within his means
Honorable and debtless (unless he was crazy),
585 Or enabling him to live as economically as he desired;
And also able to come to the help of anyone in the shire
In any legal case that might befall or happen.
And yet this Manciple hoodwinked them all.

The portrait gives no indication of what the Manciple looks like or what he wears; he is described entirely in terms of how he performs his duties as steward of one of the Inns of Court. The Pilgrim praises his outstanding abilities: he uses his knowledge of the market to make purchases at the moment when the price is lowest; he knows when it is to his advantage to pay cash and when to buy on credit; he has built up a substantial net worth; he serves educated men who have the potential themselves to become the stewards of noblemen and to run their households effectively, and yet he outshines even these men. The Pilgrim's enthusiastic approval takes the form of a rhetorical question:

Now is nat that of God a ful fair grace
That swich a lewed mannes wit shal pace
The wisdom of an heep of lerned men? (575-7)

It must be a sign of God's grace that a man like the Manciple, who has had little formal education, can outshine some of the brightest minds in the land. As so often, the reader hears in these lines the voice of the person being described, and in this case can actually hear the contempt which the Manciple has for his so-called betters. The adjective "lewed" obviously reflects the Manciple's perception of how the trainee lawyers look down on him, whilst the word "pace" suggests how easy he finds it to outwit them – he does it at a walk, without breaking sweat. Dismissively, the Manciple refers to the lawyers as "an heap of lerned men" suggesting that he regards them as one would a pile of dirty rags thrown onto the floor. It is as though these learned men consider themselves above such mundane tasks as marketing and balancing accounts. They seem to live in some elevated, rarified ivory tower, and this is probably the reason why the Manciple takes such evident self-satisfaction in demonstrating daily his superiority to them.

The bulk of the portrait does not describe the Manciple at all; it describes the capacities and potential of the lawyers and lawyers-in-training. It is here that the Pilgrim uses superlatives: thirty of them are "expert and curious" in the law (579); a dozen are able enough to run the household "Of any lord that is in Engelond" (582); these same men are "able for to helpen al a shire" with any legal case that might present itself (586). Indeed, there is little in the portrait to raise the reader's suspicions, until the Poet hits us with the last line:

And yet this Manciple sette hir aller cappe. (588)

There is no further explanation; the reader has to work it out for himself.

Looking back we note the Manciple's skillful business dealings, the fact that he is a relatively poor man who has worked his way up from the bottom, and the fact that the portrait seems to imply the delight he takes in being more skillful that his supposed superiors. The Poet is implying that the Manciple uses his position of trust to enrich himself; he is fiddling the books! In this context, the Pilgrim's naïve belief that the Manciple's success is indeed a sign of God's grace is deeply ironic: it is rather a sign of the man's deception and criminality.

The fact that the Manciple is dishonest is not lost on the Host who later in the pilgrimage warns him that it might not be such a good idea to be so insulting to the Cook because he might get his revenge by finding evidence of embezzlement by examining the Manciple's recordkeeping ("rekenynges, / That were nat honeste"):

"But yet, Manciple, in faith you are too particular,
Thus openly to criticize him for his vice.

Another day he will perhaps
Get revenge on you and trap you.
I mean that he will speak of seemingly trivial things,
Like finding errors in your accounts,
That would not appear to be honest, if they ever came to be examined."
"No," replied the Manciple, "that would cause a great deal of trouble,
In that way, he could easily catch me in his trap;"
("The Manciple's Prologue" author's modernization)

Notice in the last two lines of the quotation how quickly the Manciple agrees with the Host that having someone examine his books might be a big problem because he could find himself caught in a trap.

Lines 589-624: The Reeve

A reeve was the chief assistant of the lord of the manor's bailiff. His chief duties were: ensuring that villagers fulfilled their labor service, ensuring that villeins did not absent themselves from the manor without permission, supervising the composition of plow teams and the grazing of livestock in the village, collecting rents, selling surplus produce from the lord's land, and keeping the demesne accounts which were  audited annually (Gies and Gies 145). The reeve was thus "the most important of the village officers," but his duties placed him in a difficult position since he was always a villein himself. He was elected by the tenants of the lord of the manor to oversee the running of the manor in the interest of the lord, a conflict which led many to "avoid the office if possible, and even pay fines to be released from having to serve in it" (Gies and Gies 84). Nowhere was the conflict more evident that when the Reeve was carrying out his duty of "hailing them [his fellow villagers] before the manorial court when they failed in their service" (Gies and Gies 84).

This Reeve has clearly turned elective office into a lifetime appointment mainly by becoming indispensible to his lord. His injustice towards and exploitation of the poor (and that of those in similar positions) has recently been linked very clearly to the oppressions which led to the Peasants' Revolt of 1381 (see Blamires "Chaucer the Reactionary"). Accepting this linkage, Hirsh comments:

> Chaucer's trenchant description shows nothing more clearly than a sympathy for those whom the Reeve exploits. He does not present such persons simply as victims, however, but, in the person of the Ploughman, represents them as empowered by a moral integrity and a social power quite unknown to the Reeve. (53)

If nothing else, such perspectives qualify the received wisdom that Chaucer's poetry does not deal with the social and political crises of his day, and that the *Prologue* carefully excludes the victims of those pilgrims who abuse their positions.

Pilgrim:
1. Physically unattractive, the Pilgrim nevertheless finds plenty to admire in this man. How does the Pilgrim establish the Reeve's management skills?

Poet:
2. There is an insinuation of corruption about this man who seems to have made himself very rich in the service of his lord. Identify the Poet's hints.
3. What does the physical description of the Reeve suggest about his character? (Which pilgrim does he seem to resemble physically?)
4. With what detail of the portrait of the Manciple would you compare lines 608-612?

      The Reeve was a thin, choleric man.
590   His beard was shaved as close as ever he could;
      His hair was close cropped up to his ears;
      The hair on the top of his head was cut short like a priest's.
      His legs were extremely long and lean,
      Like a stick; there was no calf to be seen.
595   He well knew how to manage a granary and a grain storage bin;
      There was no auditor who could make money by finding errors in his accounts.

He could accurately predict according to the amount of drought and of rain
What would be the yield of his lord's seed and of his grain.
His lord's sheep, his cattle, his dairy cows
600   His swine, his horses, his livestock, and his poultry
Were wholly in this Reeve's control,
And in accord with his contract he had managed the accounts,
Ever since his lord was only twenty years of age.
No man could accuse him of being in arrears in paying his bills.
605   There was neither farm manager, nor herdsman, nor other laborer,
Whose trickery and deceit he did not know about;
They were as afraid of him as they were of the plague.
His house was beautifully situated upon an open heath;
His place was shaded by green trees.
610   He could buy property more skillfully than could his lord.
He was very rich, but hid his wealth away.
He knew just how to subtly ingratiate himself with his lord,
By giving and lending him some of his [the lord's] own money,
For which he would receive thanks, and also a gift of a coat and hood.
615   In youth he had learned a good trade:
He was an excellent craftsman, a carpenter.
This Reeve sat upon a broken-down old horse
That was all dappled gray and was called Scot.
He had on a long outer coat of blue-grey,
620   And by his side he wore a rusty sword.
Of Norfolk was this Reeve of whom I tell,
Near to a town called Bawdeswell.
He had his coat hitched up under his belt, like a friar,
And always he rode as the last of our company.

Bawdeswell was (and is) a rural village almost in the centre of Norfolk on the northeastern boundary of Breckland District. There is no evidence that Chaucer was personally connected with the village though he may have passed through it on his travels in eastern England. However, McDonald states that "there was a societal stereotype that associated the people of Norfolk with fraudulence and deceitfulness," and quotes medieval documents as calling Norfolk men "crafty and treacherous" (McDonald in Lambdin and Lambdin 297). Except the Wife of Bath, no other pilgrim is assigned so precise a place of origin, and in other ways this portrait is uniquely detailed:

there is a description of his house, and even his horse is given a name.

The Pilgrim's usual enthusiasm is becoming progressively muted as the portraits continue – gone are the superlatives and the hyperbole. Perhaps this is because having described the truly good and virtuous Parson and Ploughman, even the Pilgrim is beginning to see through the facades presented by the churls who make up the remaining portraits: the Miller, the Manciple and the Reeve dishonestly exploit their positions for personal gain whilst the Summoner and the Pardoner will prove to be the most despicable of the pilgrims.

The portrait of the Reeve (later called "Osewold" by the Host) begins with a physical description:

> The reve was a sclendre colerik man.
> His berd was shave as ny as ever he kan;
> His heer was by his eris ful round yshorn;
> His top was dokked lyk a preest biforn
> Ful longe were his legges and ful lene,
> Ylik a staf, ther was no calf ysene. (589-94)

The Reeve's lean form is derived from his choleric humor, but this is a more significant indicator of his character. A person of the choleric temperament is energetic, intelligent, ambitious, aggressive, and wants to be in charge of everything and to dominate others. In this case, the Reeve clearly inherits the choleric tendency to be highly organized, all of which explains his success in manipulating his lord and totally controlling those below him by fear. Winny, however, points out the importance of the fact that the Reeve is an old man. With ageing, when "the blood flowed sluggishly through the veins, the moisture of the organs and tissues dried up, and the vital heat of the body abated," the influence of Saturn, a cold dry planet, becomes greater (Hussey et al. 167). This, Winny argues, accounts for the Reeve's malice to others and his solitary nature.

Curry points to a second aspect of the Reeve's character in quoting from the Middle English *Secrata Secretorum* to the effect that those of choleric temperament are, "Desyrous of the company of women moore than hym nedyth" ("Reeve and Miller" 190). This tendency towards lust and lechery (which only becomes evident in later parts of *The Canterbury Tales*) is also indicated by the Reeve's thin legs. Should the reader wish to go further and see the sword as a phallic symbol (a sword is, after all, longer than it is wide) then the rusty sword would imply that this mean, dried up old man has long ago lost the ability, though perhaps not the desire, to procreate and is reduced to reminiscing over past exploits and empty boasting that he still has a colt's tooth – in fact, exactly what he does in "The Reeve's Prologue."

In so far that the quality about the Reeve which the Pilgrim most admires is the skillful way he conducts business and defrauds his employer, this portrait is something of a re-run of the Manciple:

> Wel koude he kepe a gerner and a binne;
> Ther was noon auditour koude on him winne.
> Wel wiste he by the droghte and by the reyn
> The yeldinge of his seed and of his greyn. (595-8)

The only difference is that he has a wider range of opportunities to defraud his master; for a laborer he is doing very well for himself financially. Not only is the Reeve a knowledgeable farm supervisor, but he also keeps his accounts immaculately. As a result, his lord places full trust in him to manage his entire estate. As Bowden comments, "The activities of Chaucer's Reeve seem to indicate that he serves as both bailiff and provost, and even as seneschal [chief manager]," so that he answers to no one but has complete control of the administration of his lord's estates (*Commentary* 250). Always prompt in the payment of his own bills, the Reeve is aware of the tricks and deceits of others and never gets taken in by them. (The saying, 'Set a thief to catch a thief' comes to mind!) This almost certainly explains the Reeve's antipathy to the Miller. In "The Miller's Prologue," the drunken Miller calls the Reeve, "Leve brother Osewold" and refers to his being married, which suggests that, in his professional capacities, the Reeve may have had to deal with this dishonest Miller.

Just as the Pilgrim praises the Manciple as being more skilled at purchasing and managing provisions than his so-called betters, so of the Reeve he says:

> He koude bettre than his lord purchace. (610)

He can buy property more skillfully, which means more cheaply, than his lord ever could. The Pilgrim makes it clear that the Reeve has reaped the just rewards of his hard and skillful work when he describes the beautiful location of his house:

> His woning was ful faire upon an heeth;

With grene trees yshadwed was his place. (608-9)

The picture is idyllic and indicates just how much the Reeve had raised his status by his own efforts. Hirsh sees this description of the Reeve's dwelling as evidence of his "aristocratic aspirations" (54) which is a serious over-statement; let us rather say of his aspirations to join the country gentry. The Reeve is wealthy, and he learned in his youth to be an excellent carpenter. If there is nothing for the Pilgrim to get too excited about here, there is certainly much to admire, not least the fact that the Reeve seems to have turned an unpopular, elected office into a permanent appointment.

As the praise for this pilgrim is muted, so is the criticism. Like many of the rich pilgrims, the Reeve is something of a miser:

Ful riche he was astored prively: (611)

He has literally hidden his wealth. Like the Manciple, the clear implication of the Poet is that the man becomes rich by cheating his employer:

His lord wel koude he plesen subtilly,
To yeve and lene him of his owene good,
And have a thank, and yet a cote and hood. (612-4)

The irony here is that by giving or lending his lord things that his lord already actually owns, the Reeve wins his lord's thanks and presents of clothes, a gift traditionally given for loyal service. The man's corruption is suggested by his emaciated figure:

Ful longe were his legges and ful lene,
Ylik a staf, ther was no calf ysene. (593-4)

These lines deliberately echo the description of the Clerk:

As leene was his hors as is a rake,
And he nas nat right fat, I undertake,
But looked holwe, and therto sobrely. (289-91)

another character who lives off what he takes from others.

Two details which combine to suggest the corruption into which the Reeve has fallen are his youthful induction into the trade of carpenter (significantly the trade of Christ's father) and the rusty sword which he carries:

He was a wel good wrighte, a carpenter…
And by his side he baar a rusty blade. (616-20)

By juxtaposing these details, the Poet implies that the Reeve's youthful purity and potential had been corrupted: the sharp blade which he used as a carpenter has become rusted and dull through disuse, symbolizing the man's corruption. The sword fairly obviously hints at the Reeve's temper and propensity for violence (compare the Shipman), though the rust on the sword also implies that he is past his fighting days or perhaps more damagingly that his anger is all bluster and that when it comes to action he is a coward.

Significantly the Reeve is twice compared to a cleric. Firstly, his haircut is priest-like:

> His heer was by his eris ful round yshorn;
> His top was dokked lyk a preest biforn (591-2)

and secondly, he wears a long surcoat:

> Tukked he was as is a frere aboute, (623)

The point of these comparisons to the Poet is how inappropriate they are. There was once something pure and shining about this man, but now he is tarnished, an anti-social miser. Walter detects an "ostentatious display of humility" in the Reeve's closely shaven cheeks and short hair both of which are associated with low status, particularly "an obedient and humble servant" ("Reeve and Miller" 190).

His character is, reflected, as so often in the *Prologue*, by the horse he rides:

> This Reve sat upon a ful good stot,
> That was al pomely grey and highte Scot. (617-8)

These lines are frequently misunderstood as describing a fine stallion (e.g., Kirkham & Allen 66). Such a horse would certainly be incongruous for this miserly, dried up, bitter old man. However, the word "stot" comes from the Old English meaning a hack, jade, or worthless horse - what Pollard calls a "low-bred undersized horse" (91). Thus, a "ful good stot" is an oxymoron. A stot was a draught horse used for farm work such as ploughing and harrowing because it was generally cheaper than a cart horse (Wikipedia article "Horses in the Middle Ages" which references Clark, John (Ed), 2004, *The Medieval Horse and its Equipment: c.1150-c.1450.*). This certainly fits with the Reeve's agricultural background and his reluctance to spend money. As a verb "stot" means to bound with a stiff-legged gait, to move unsteadily or to lurch, and in Northern English dialect it means to bounce or rebound. Putting these meanings together suggests that the Reeve pays for his miserliness with an uncomfortable ride. Although the description of the horse as a dappled grey sounds very attractive, the implication may be that the horse is, like the Reeve, graying with age. Just as the name of the

Shipman's vessel implies a comment on his nature, so too does the name of the Reeve's horse. 'Scot' was (and still is) a very common Norfolk name for a horse (Bowden *Commentary* 253), but the medieval reader would have two negative associations with the word 'Scot': firstly, the Scots have a national reputation for being frugal and mean, and secondly they were feared border raiders (or reivers) sweeping down from the north to carry off cattle, possessions and hostages. Both negative connotations are an exact fit for the Reeve.

Chapter Ten: The Summoner and The Pardoner

It is significant that four of the last five portraits (the Manciple is the exception) are of exceptionally ugly men of relatively low social status. More important is the trend by which each one of the five marks a progressive descent on the moral scale.

The Summoner and the Pardoner are friends (perhaps even lovers), but they are united by much more than social ties. Along with the Friar, they represent the most vicious of the many hypocrites, crooks, criminals and con-artists who the Poet has described because each one knowingly misuses the power entrusted to him by the Church in ways which place the eternal souls of their victims in jeopardy. Bowden characterizes Chaucer's attitude to these two characters as "extreme disgust … bitter detestation" (*Commentary* 262).

Lines 625-670: The Summoner

…the said Summoners make their summons to diverse people for malice … and these extortioners impute crimes to the poor, contriving that the poor shall pay a fine … Summoners demand that people appear for trial twenty or more leagues from their homes, sometimes to two places on one day, to the great oppression … of the said poor… (Parliamentary plea of 1378 quoted in Bowden *Commentary* 266)

In Medieval England there existed, in addition to the secular courts whose authority derived ultimately from the king, a system of church courts deriving their authority ultimately from the pope. These courts dealt with offenders who claimed benefit of clergy and with lay people who committed crimes such as usury, witchcraft, simony, slander, libel, sexual misconduct, and failing to pay tithes which had no redress in secular courts. The function of a summoner, or apparitor, was both to deliver the court order to the accused and to ensure that he/she appeared to answer the charges against them. Summoners were as close as the Middle Ages got to policemen.

The Ellesmere portrait shows the Summoner holding such a court order in his right hand in the act of delivering it; however, as Keller points out, as summoner to the archdeacon's court, he was compelled by law to walk when performing his duties - only summoners to the bishop's court were allowed to ride (Lambdin and Lambdin 302). Summoners also collected fines imposed by the courts for immoral behavior, and were paid a percentage of the fines levied on those who they brought to court. Together, these duties provided easy opportunities for corruption, for example by searching out 'crimes' to increase the number of summons issued, by writing a false summons and then taking a bribe to 'make it go away,' and by taking bribes from the guilty to ensure that they were never brought before the court. As a result, Summoners were much hated, especially by the poor who were the usual victims of their extortion.

Although it does not become evident in the *Prologue*, there is an enmity between the Summoner and the Friar which, like that between the Miller and the Reeve, appears to pre-date the pilgrimage. The source is almost certainly professional since each is seeking to make money from the same set of poor people. The Summoner gets his authority from the archdeacon and so it is limited to a particular diocese, whereas the Friar, who gets his authority from his order, is not so limited; the Summoner clearly resents this (Manly *New Light* 102-3).

Pilgrim:
1. Which words and phrases suggest naïve approval by the Pilgrim?
Poet:
2. The Summoner's face is so disfigured that it frightens the children. What are the exact details of the disfigurement? What aspects of the Summoner's life-style make his condition worse?
3. When he has had a few drinks, the Summoner likes to show off his learning by speaking Latin. How does Chaucer the Poet ridicule this affectation?
4. How does Chaucer justify his ironic statement that, "He was a gentil harlot and a kinde; / A bettre felawe sholde men nought finde"? Comment on the importance of lines 661-664.

5. Once again, the Poet implies that this pilgrim is not only promiscuous, but also that he uses his power and authority to seduce young women. Give details from the portrait of the man's sexual immorality.

6. As in some other portraits, the final line is the clincher. Explain.

625   A Summoner there was with us in that place,
        Who had a fiery-red, cherub's face,
        Which was pimply, with swollen lids and narrow eyes.
        As hot he was, and lecherous, as a sparrow;
        With black, scabby eyebrows and a thinning, ragged beard;
630   He had a face which scared little children.
        There was no mercury, peroxide of lead, or sulphur,
        No borax, white lead, nor oil of tartar, nothing would help,
        Nor any ointment that could cleanse or burn enough,
        To heal his white pustules,
635   Nor the carbuncles on his cheeks.
        He really loved garlic, onions, and also leeks,
        And drinking strong wine as red as blood.
        Then would he talk and shout as if he were mad.
        And when he had drunken his fill of wine,
640   Then would he utter no words except in Latin.
        Just two or three memorized phrases,
        Which he had learned out of some ecclesiastical law book;
        It is no wonder, for he had heard them all day long in court;
        And you know just as well as I do that a mocking jay
645   Can call out 'Walter' as well as can the Pope.
        But when someone examined him about other things,
        Then it became clear that he had used up his whole learning;
        Only 'Questio quid juris' ['The question is, which part of the law applies'] would he cry.
        He was a gentlemanly rascal, and a kind one;
650   A better fellow men could not find anywhere.
        For a quart of wine, he would let
        Some good fellow keep a mistress
        For a whole year, and enable him get away with it;
        Secretly, he too could pluck a finch.
655   And if he met another good fellow,
        He would tell him never to be afraid,
        In a case of sexual misconduct, of the archdeacon's excommunication,
        Unless a man's soul lies in his purse;

For the man should punished be with a fine.
660   'The purse is the archdeacon's concept of Hell,' said he.
But well I know he was certainly lying;
Every guilty man should dread excommunication,
For excommunication damns, just as absolution saves,
And every guilty man should also be careful to avoid a *Significavit*
[The first word of an order of imprisonment for a person found
guilty in a church court].
665   He had complete jurisdiction over
The young people of the diocese,
And knew their secrets, and gave them advice.
A garland had he set upon his head,
Large as a wreath of vine-leaves hung on a tavern's signpost;
670   He had a buckler made out of a loaf of bread.

There is very little for the Pilgrim to admire about the Summoner.
In most of the other pilgrims, the impressive external appearance
hides a morally corrupt nature, but in this case the Summoner is as
repulsive physically as he is morally (compare the Miller and the
Reeve). Neither is there much about this man's corruption which the
Poet finds particularly clever or funny; indeed, the voices of Pilgrim
and Poet are scarcely distinguishable any more.

The gradual transformation of the naïve Pilgrim is virtually
completed in this portrait: the Summoner (who embodies the sins of
avarice, gluttony, and lust) has not a single redeeming feature. There
is not even one word of praise for the efficient way in which the
Summoner hauls accused people to court. His drunkenness and his
pathetic attempts to sound learned, make him a rather pathetic figure.
In fact, there are only two positive lines in the entire portrait, a
superlative which recalls the earlier enthusiasm of the Pilgrim who
was so easily impressed by his new acquaintances:

He was a gentil harlot and a kinde
A bettre felawe sholde men noght finde. (649-50)

Even this is hardly unqualified praise since the word "harlot" means
rascal, rogue, villain, buffoon, jester, and once again the praise-line is
juxtaposed with details that entirely undermine it:

He wolde suffre for a quart of wyn
A good felawe to have his concubyn
A twelf month, and excuse hym atte fulle; (651-3)

His good fellowship is expressed in taking the smallest of bribes (a quart of wine) to let people get away with the very sins that he is supposed to bring them to court for – sins which, as we shall see, he is very ready himself to commit. These two praise-lines come half-way through a portrait in which there is absolutely nothing else to support them: they stand out like a sore thumb, bracketed before by a physical description which makes the Summoner appear truly repulsive and an account of his drunken ignorance, and after by a description of his systematic undermining of the values of the very court system which he is supposed to serve.

Six of the first eleven lines of the portrait describe the physical appearance of the Summoner's face. He is of the choleric temperament, the hot dry heat of Mars being reflected in his red complexion. The physical corruption visible on the Summoner's skin (we might diagnose infected acne and/or eczema) both results from his life-style and symbolizes the moral corruption which his life-style epitomizes. His favorite foods are strong, hot and spicy:

> Wel loved he garleek, oynons, and eek lekes,
> And for to drinken strong wyn, reed as blood; (636-7)

These foods would have further heated the Summoner's blood leading to the outbreaks on his skin. A medieval doctor might have diagnosed his skin disease as alopecia "a disease of the flesh growing out of an infection of the blood" (Curry "Summoner" 400) which marked the on-set of leprosy and would certainly have advised the patient to abstain from sexual activity which likewise heats the blood - something which the Summoner quite clearly does not do.

The Summoner's skin condition is the despair of medical science (the portrait gives an impressive list of the strongest medicines which appear to have no effect) because their origin is in the man's moral corruption. Curry explains the Poet's use of physiognomy in the description of the Summoner's face:

> Chaucer the scientist has first created, according to the best medical authority of his time, a perfect figure representing that type of leprosy called alopecia … The rascal is either criminally indifferent or foolishly ignorant; he might have learned from any physician of his time, or before, that lepra may be contracted by illicit association with women affected by it, that garlic, onions, and leeks produce evil humors in the blood, and that red wine, of all others, is the most powerful and heating of drinks … [H]aving once contracted

the disease by riotous and lascivious living and by the immoderate use of unwholesome meats and wines, he further aggravates it by the same foolhardy practices. (Curry "Summoner" 401-2)

The Summoner's sexual immorality is presented in a way that makes it appear tawdry, as can be seen by comparing him with the Squire. Of the Summoner, it is said, "As hoot he was and lecherous as a sparwe" (628), and of the Squire that, "So hoote he lovede that by nightertale. / He sleep namoore than dooth a nightingale" (97-8). The difference is in the contrast between the word "loved," which suggests emotion, and "lecherous" which suggests only unrestrained lust. Each man's passions are compared to birds, but the connotations are very different: nightingales are associated with poetry because of their beautiful, melancholy song (a point which reminds us that the Squire spends his nights writing love poetry rather than bedding his lady) whilst sparrows, not noted for their song, are "long associated with lechery" (Kirkham & Allen 68).

There is another rather crude reference to the Summoner's sexual voraciousness after the Pilgrim has recounted his willingness to overlook (for a price) a man's keeping a mistress, "Ful prively a finch eek koude he pulle" (654). Literally this modernizes as, 'In secret, he could pluck the feathers (or perhaps the guts) out of a finch,' which does not make the meaning clear. The surface meaning of the line seems to be that the Summoner exploits his victims as easily as plucking a finch – the finch being a very small bird. However, most critics are convinced that the line euphemistically implies that the Summoner not only allows other men to keep their mistresses, but that he secretly does the same. Bowden, citing the authority of Kittredge, says that this phrase was "a medieval impolite expression meaning 'he kept a concubine'" (*Commentary* 264). The phrase 'to pull a bird,' meaning to attract a woman, is still in use in England.

The man's moral corruption is, however, nowhere better seen than in the account of the way in which he discharges his duties. Not only does he turn a blind eye to adultery, but he reassures the offender that if he is caught he has nothing more to fear than a fine since being excommunicated by the archdeacon is not going to happen:

He wolde techen him to have noon awe
In swich caas of the ercedekenes curs,
But if a mannes soule were in his purs;
For in his purs he sholde ypunisshed be.
'Purs is the ercedekenes helle,' seyde he. (656-9)

Here the Summoner encourages men to ignore the ultimate sanction of the church: the threat of the loss of their eternal souls. He justifies this advice by accusing the system of being corrupt: the archdeacon will rather find offenders than excommunicate them because there is no money to be made by excommunication. And now something quite remarkable happens: for the first time, the voice of the Pilgrim is heard openly criticizing:

But wel I woot he lied right in dede;
Of cursing oghte ech gilty man him drede,
For curs wol slee right as assoilling savith,
And also war him of a *Significavit*. (661-4)

This is outright condemnation: the Summoner is a liar because guilty men should dread excommunication as they should revere and seek absolution, and because guilty men should also fear the writ of imprisonment that will follow conviction and excommunication. Contrast this outburst by the Pilgrim with his earlier enthusiastic defense of the Monk:

And I seyde his opinion was good.
What sholde he studie and make himselven wood,
Upon a book in cloistre alwey to poure,
Or swinken with his handes, and laboure,
As Austyn bit? ... (183-7)

The Pilgrim appears to have had enough! Yet Nevo perceptively makes a distinction between the Pilgrim's concern "with the purity of doctrine in respect of archidiaconal powers," and his apparent failure to see the Summoner's lies as part of his strategy for making money out of offenders, what she calls "the Summoner's pocket-lining motive in this transaction" (in Bloom ed. *Critical Interpretations The Prologue* 15). It appears that, despite the Pilgrim's growing confidence to speak up for moral and religious truths, he still remains naïve about the motivation and methods of the con-men he describes.

Given that the distinction between Pilgrim and Poet has narrowed, there is less scope for irony in this portrait. There are, however, a few examples, the most obvious being the comparison of the Summoner's inflamed face to that of a cherub:

> A Somonour was ther with us in that place,
> That hadde a fyr-reed cherubinnes face, (625-6)

Cherubim are second only to Seraphim in the nine orders of angels. The modern reader confuses cherubim with putti (the rather cute, chubby, winged babies with healthy ruddy faces), and it is tempting to identify the irony in the contrast between the corrupt Summoner and innocence of these angelic babies. However, this association of cherubim and putti dates only from the Renaissance period (see the two cherubs at the bottom of Raphael's *Sistine Madonna*); in the Middle Ages cherubim were normally depicted as celestial beings having four faces, multiple wings, and with human, animal, or birdlike characteristics, their many eyes denoting their all-seeing nature. The Poet's real point appears the be to draw a parallel between the all-knowing cherubim and the Summoner who knows everyone's secrets and sins, the difference being that the Summoner indulges them (for a bribe) and covers them up.

At the end of the portrait the Pilgrim gives some details of the Summoner's rôles in his parish without making any comment:

> In daunger hadde he at his owene gise
> The yonge girles of the diocise,
> And knew hir conseil, and was al hir reed. (665-7)

The Poet puts in this ironic detail: given what we have learned of the Summoner's corruption, it is entirely inappropriate that he should have such a dangerously corrupting influence over young people. One can just imagine the kind of advice he gives them. Finally, the Pilgrim rounds off the portrait with three lines giving details of the Summoner's accessories:

> A gerland hadde he set upon his heed
> As greet as it were for an ale-stake.
> A bokeleer hadde he maad hym of a cake. (668-670)

The garland of flowers is ironically incongruous since flowers represent the beauty and innocence of nature, but the simile comparing the garland to the sign outside an inn reminds us of the Summoner's drunkenness. The small shield made of bread implies cowardice and love of food. Bowden concludes, "The suggestion that he appears as an intensified, debauched Bacchus is strong" (*Guide* 116).

The Summoner and the Friar dislike each other intensely: the Friar tells a tale which exposes the wickedness of summoners and the

Summoner retaliates with a tale of a friar's dishonest and hypocritical exploitation of a bereaved family. Each man is criminally using his church office for financial gain, and they are in competition: a sinner who bribes the Friar to give him absolution evades the Summoner's threat of the archdeacon's court. At the same time, Keller points out that the Summoner must resent the fact that whilst his position gives him more status than a poor friar, in reality the friar appears to have accumulated more ill-gotten gains and to move in higher social circles. In addition, the Summoner knows he has no authority over the Friar who is licensed by his Order (Lambdin and Lambdin 309).

Lines 671-716: The Pardoner

There preached a pardoner as if he were a priest
He displayed a charter with the seals of the bishops on it,
And said that he himself could give the people absolution …
Simple folk believed him and liked his words,
And knelt down to kiss his seals;
…
Thus do you give your gold to gluttons to keep.
And part with it to such vulgar lechers.
(Langland. *The Vision of Piers Plowman* author's modernization)

The Protestant Revolution was begun, in 1516, by Martin Luther's objection to the sale of indulgences (i.e. pardons) by Johann Tetzel, a Dominican Friar licensed by the Pope to sell indulgences to raise money for the rebuilding of Saint Peter's in Rome. That was more than a century into the future, but it is evident from this portrait that Pardoners had been a target of criticism for some time.

The theory behind pardons was that an act of penance would allow the Pope to give the sinner remittance of time in purgatory by taking from the infinite 'treasury' of merit stored up by Christ and the saints. The Church soon found it expedient to make the necessary act of penance a monetary contribution. The system (even if one did not, like Luther, regard it as in itself an abuse) was open to corruption: not all those who claimed to be pardoners were actually authorized by the church, and not all of those so authorized were honest.

Bowden reports that, "The prior of St. Mary Roncevall in the early fourteenth century had a reputation as a pardoner … [and] made a great deal of money … the other brothers of the Order followed the prior's example to such an extent that the Crown felt it necessary in 1379 to seize the convent of St. Mary Roncevall and to arrest all those collecting arms. Although the convent was eventually restored to the Order, there occurred a further public scandal in 1387 concerning the sale of pardons" (*Guide* 73-4).

Pardoners also sold holy relics to the faithful. It was the fall of Jerusalem in 1099 which resulted in relics becoming much more common in Europe. Every church wanted as many relics as it could get. John Calvin later commented that there were enough pieces of the true cross scattered throughout Europe "to make a full load for a good ship,' and Guibert of Nogent was driven by the existence of two heads of John the Baptist to ask sarcastically, "Was this saint then bicephalous?" (quoted in Gies and Gies 294-5).

Pilgrim:
1. As with the Summoner, there is little for even the naïve Pilgrim to admire about this man who even looks absurd. Which words and phrases do suggest naïve approval by the Pilgrim?
Poet:
2. With what animals is the Pardoner compared in the portrait? What is the effect of these comparisons?
3. In what ways does the Pardoner seek to cut a fashionable figure as he rides along? What is the reality of his appearance?
4. What holy relics does he claim to carry? What are they in reality? How does he use them to make fools out of people?
5. What is the reason why he takes such care to appear to be a "noble ecclesiaste" in church (710)?
6. What conclusion does the Poet come to concerning the Pardoner's sexuality? What supporting evidence is provided in the portrait?

> With him there rode a noble Pardoner
> From the chapel of St Mary Roncevall [near Charing Cross, London], his friend and his companion,
> Who had come straight from the papal court in Rome [the Vatican].

He sang, "Come here to me my love," in a very loud voice
675 And the Summoner accompanied him with a powerful base;
There was never a trumpet that made half as much noise.
This Pardoner had hair as yellow as wax,
It hung down smoothly as a length of flax;
His hair fell down in thin clusters,
680 And he had spread it over his shoulders;
But it lay very thin, in strands here and there.
But for appearance sake he didn't wear a hood
Which was folded up in his saddlebag.
He thought he rode in the very latest fashion;
685 His hair hanging loose, he rode bareheaded, except for his skull-cap.
He had sewn onto his cap a pilgrim's badge of St. Veronica
showing a little picture of Christ's face.
He had bulging eyes like a hare.
His saddlebag lay in front of him on his lap
Full to the brim with pardons, fresh from Rome and still hot!
690 His voice was as high-pitched as a goat's.
He didn't have a beard, and never would have as long as he lived;
His chin was as smooth as if it had just been shaved.
I think that he was either a eunuch or a homosexual.
But as a seller of pardons, from Berwick-on-Tweed to Ware [from one end of the country to the other]
695 There was not another to compare with him.
For in his bag he had a pillow-case,
Which he said was the veil of Our Lady [Mary, Mother of Christ];
He said that he had a piece of the sail
That Saint Peter had, when he went
700 Upon the sea, until Christ called him to be a disciple.
He had a cross of brass, studded with false gems
And in a bottle he had some pigs' bones.
But with these relics, when he had found
A poor parson living in a country parish,
705 In one day he earned more money
Than the parson got in two months;
And thus, with false flattery and tricks,
He made apes [i.e., fools] out of the parson and his parishioners.
But to tell you the truth in conclusion,
710 When he was in church he was a noble cleric.
Very skillfully could he read a lesson or tell a story,
But best of all he sang the offertory hymn,

For he knew well that when that song was sung,
He was expected to preach and use his smooth tongue
715   To get as much silver as he knew how;
Therefore he sang the more merrily and loud.

In later portraits, the voices of the Pilgrim and of the Poet are less distinct than they originally were because the later pilgrims less effectively cover up their corruption at least from their companions on the pilgrimage. While the Prioress seems blissfully unaware that her conduct is inappropriate, and Monk feels it easy to justify his lifestyle, and the Friar boldly asserts his right to act as he does, the Pardoner appears to glory in his own cunning malevolence and to have total contempt for his victims. He manages to corrupt all three of the functions given to pardoners: he sells pardons which are (to say the least) suspect; he sells relics which he proudly acknowledges to be bogus; and he exploits his authority to preach to take money which the poor can ill-afford.

The Pardoner wears a vernicle, a pilgrims' badge associated with Rome. According to legend, Veronica wiped the face of Jesus on his way to Calvary and his features were miraculously impressed on the cloth. She later traveled to Rome to present the cloth to the Roman Emperor Tiberius, and so it came into the possession of the Popes. During the fourteenth century, it was the most venerated icon in Western Europe. The Pardonner's wearing of a vernicle, a representation of the original cloth, adds support to his claim to have just returned from Rome, a detail which strengthens the impression (or illusion) that his pardons are authentic. Once again, echoing the voice of the pilgrim himself, Rome is mentioned twice in the first half of the portrait:

> That streight was comen fro the court of Rome. (673)
> Bretful of pardoun, comen from Rome al hoot. (689)

This name-dropping is, however, undercut by the Poet's images of food. The Pardoner's "wallet" is like a cup overflowing with drink, and the pardons are like freshly baked goods (think pies or bread). The effect of these images is to reduce the Pardoner to the level of a common street hawker.

Bowden analyzes in detail the Poet's use of physiognomy in the description of the Pardoner (*Commentary* 275-6). On the Pardoner's hair, to which no less than seven lines are dedicated, she cites the

Anonyme de Physiognomonie liber Latinus to support her conclusion that the hair indicates "an impoverished blood, lack of virility, and effeminacy of mind, and the sparcer the hair, the more cunning and deceptive is the man" (275). The Pardoner's glaring eyes, reminiscent of those of the Monk and the Friar, suggest a shameless libertine given to folly, gluttony, and excessive drinking. Bowden quotes Polemon of Laodicea's *de Physiognomonia,* "When the eye is wide open and, like marble glitters or coruscates, it indicates a shameless lack of modesty" (276). In describing the Pardoner's appearance, the Poet first uses a simile which compares him with a hare, "Swiche glaringe eyen hadde he as an hare" (686), and then a second simile which compares him to with a goat, "A voys he hadde as smal as hath a goot" (690). The hare is traditionally a symbol of fertility and sensuality. The idea of fertility seems ironically inappropriate for "a gelding or a mare" (despite his boast later in the *Tales* that he has a girl in every town and that he has been considering getting married), but the implication that the Pardoner shows unbridled lust is apposite. Hares were also regarded in ancient times as hermaphrodite which is another hint at the ambiguity of the Pardoner's gender. The goat in Christian symbolism represents "oppressors, wicked men and demonic forces" (catholic-saints.info). The use of the noun 'goat' to mean 'a licentious man' is attested only from 1675 (Dictionary.com), but it seems reasonable to assume that the association of goats with uncontrolled sexual desire goes back much further.

In this portrait, the Pilgrim uses superlatives only twice. First he tells us that:

> But of his craft, fro Berwik into Ware,
> Ne was ther swich another pardoner (694-5)

Ware was the first town on the road out of London going north, and Berwick-upon-Tweed is situated just two and a half miles south of the Scottish border. The Poet, however, intends the reader to notice that what is missing from these lines is any word of approval or admiration. That there is no other pardoner like this one the entire length of the country does not actually imply that he is the best pardoner simply that he is the most shamelessly corrupt – the lines turn out not to be a true superlative. Contrast the true superlatives which the Pilgrim uses of the Monk, "A Monk ther was, a fair for the maistrie" (165) and the Friar, "Unto his ordre he was a noble post."

(214). Here, the apparent praise-lines merely indicates that the Pardoner is the most dishonest and devious pardoner, the only one who openly boasts of his ability to pass off a pillow-case as Mary's veil and pigs' bones as holy relics.

The only lines which embody naïve praise are those which describe the Pardoner in church:

> But trewely to tellen atte laste,
> He was in chirche a noble ecclesiaste. (709-10)

Notice that the structural device of the conjunction 'but' at the start of a line (which occurs an unprecedented six times in this portrait) is used to change the direction of the description. In most previous portraits, however, it has been used to turn the description from apparent praise to qualification (see the Knight 73, Prioress 142, Merchant 286, Cook 387, Summoner 661); here that is reversed, for up to this point the portrait has been massively negative (compare the Shipman 403). The Poet wishes us to understand that the essential paradox of the Pardoner's character is that he is an exceptional preacher – a point which will be re-enforced when he tells his tale. Had he used his God-given talents appropriately, he could have done much good. That he does not do so is implied by the qualification which the Poet puts into the superlative: the Pardoner is only "in chirche a noble ecclesiaste," unlike the Parson or the Ploughman whose Christian faith is expressed in the conduct of their lives outside of the Church, the Pardoner's faith is a mask which he puts on and off at will.

Just as the Friar is the best (i.e., most productive) beggar in his house, so is this Pardoner the most productive in the land and for the same reason: neither has any conscience in getting the last farthing from the poor and the gullible. Compare this description, in which we hear the scornful voice of the Pardoner himself, of how he makes monkeys (fools) out of honest folk:

> And thus, with feyned flaterie and japes,
> He made the person and the peple his apes. (707-8)

with this description of how the Friar achieves the same end:

> For thogh a widwe hadde noght a sho,
> So plesaunt was his 'In principio,'
> Yet wolde he have a ferthng, er he wente. (255-7)

Both men have the ability to use scripture to enrich themselves. The difference between the portraits is that the naïve Pilgrim who describes the Friar cannot find enough superlatives for him while the more aware Pilgrim who describes the Pardoner can find but two, and both are heavily qualified.

The Pilgrim seems openly confused on the subject of the Pardoner's sexuality, "I trowe he were a gelding or a mare" (693). Interestingly, the *Cambridge School Chaucer* offers no note at all on this line, as though its meaning were self-explanatory – which it clearly is not. Some editors gloss the terms as 'castrated eunuch' and 'congenital eunuch' respectively, but this appears to be splitting the term "gelding" into two meanings and applying one of them arbitrarily to "mare." McAlpine seems to me to be closer to the Pilgrim's meaning in defining the term "gelding" as including both castrated and congenital eunuchs. He goes on to speculate that "[mare] must be a term commonly used in Chaucer's day to designate a male person who, though not necessarily sterile or impotent, exhibits physical traits suggestive of femaleness," and suggests that, though Middle English did not have the word, the Pilgrim means "mare" to be understood as 'homosexual' (in George 127). The Pardoner's close friendship with the Summoner is described in terms which imply that it is homosexual in nature:

> With him ther rood a gentil Pardoner
> Of Rouncivale, his freend and his compeer,
> That streight was comen fro the court of Rome.
> Ful loude he soong 'Com hider, love, to me!'
> This Somonour bar to him a stif burdoun; (671-5)

The word "compeer" suggests that the two are more or less constant companions (in which case the Pardoner's claim to have come straight from Rome seems unlikely). There is no doubt that the Pardoner is singing a popular love song and that the Summoner "bar to him a stif burdoun" which appears to mean that he offers a strong base accompaniment, but the word "stif" surely contains a sexual innuendo (compare the description of the leacherous Friar as "a noble post" 214). Similarly, the contrast between the voice of the Summoner, as loud as a trumpet, "Was nevere trompe of half so greet a soun" (676), and the high-pitched voice of the Pardoner, "A voys he hadde as smal as hath a goot." (690), suggests that the latter is the passive, 'female' partner in their sexual relationship.

One could go on and on with this, but frankly it all gets a bit distasteful: sadly, there is no reason to assume that even a great poet like Chaucer was immune to the sexual and gender prejudices of his day (though it is to be regretted that so many critics appear to share the same prejudices). The fact is that the Pilgrim has given plenty of evidence of his admiration for 'manliness' in the *Prologue*: the Monk is a "manly man" (167), the Knight and Friar is each "a worthy man" (43 & 243), the Parson "a good man" (479), and the Host a "seemly man" (753). The Pardoner disturbs the Pilgrim because he is so obviously unmanly; sexual and gender ambiguity are together presented as outward manifestations of the Pardoner's moral corruption.

We have noted that the idea that victims are entirely absent from the *Prologue* is an exaggeration. It is significant, for example, that the Poet does not repeate the accusation of Langland that often the parish priest is in league with the pardoner and split between them money which would otherwise go to the poor (*The Vision of Piers Plowman*). In this portrait, it is specified that the Pardoner searches out parishes in the countryside because there the people will be more uneducated, more trusting and more gullible, and that it is also the representative of the secular clergy who suffers:

> But with thise relikes, whan that he fond
> A povre person dwellinge upon lond,
> Upon a day he gat him moore moneye
> Than that the person gat in monthes tweye; (703-6)

It is surely no coincidence that the Poet uses a line which parallels the description of the only pure cleric described, the "povre person of a toun" whose parish is described as being in the country (480). There could be no greater contrast between the Parson who would rather pay his parishioners' tithes himself than excommunicate them for non-payment and the Pardoner who earns more in a day than the Parson would in two months even if everyone was able to pay their tithes. Just as the consistency of the Parson's words and deeds is emphasized:

> But Christes lore and his apostles twelve
> He taughte, but first he folwed it himselve. (529-30)

so too is the hypocrisy of the Pardoner who wins the confidence of his victims with "feyned flaterie and japes" (707). Affectation in speech appears almost to be a defining feature of all clerics except the Parson. The Prioress sings divine service. "Entuned in her nose ful seemly / [and French] ful faire and fetisly" (123-4); the Friar, "lipsed, for his wantownesse, / To make his Englissh sweete upon his tonge" (266-7); the Clerk speaks, "in form and reverence / And short and quik and ful of hy sentence" (307-8). (Only the hunting Monk escapes the charge of affectation in speech.) In contrast, the most agricultural language (in every sense of that phrase) comes from the plain-spoken Parson who thinks that you cannot have, "A shiten shepherde and a clene sheep" (506) and who, upon finding an obstinate sinner, "wolde he snibben sharply for the nonis" (525). Again, in contrast to the Parson, the Pardoner smooths his tongue knowing that he is about to preach "wel affile his tonge / To winne silver, as he ful wel koude" (714-5). With this smooth-tongued churl, both the Pilgrim and the Poet have reached the bottom of the moral barrel!

Chapter Eleven: Building Upon the Frame Story

Lines 717-748: The Apology

1. For what two aspects of his writing does the narrator ask the reader's forgiveness and indulgence (727-748)?
2. What justifications/excuses does the Pilgrim offer?

Now have I told you truthfully and briefly,
The social rank, the dress, the number, and the reason
Why this company was assembled
720   In Southwark, at this fine hostelry
Called the Tabard Inn, adjacent to the Bell.
But now the time is come to tell you
How we all conducted ourselves that same night,
When we arrived at that hostelry;
725   And afterwards I will tell you about our journey
And all the remainder of our pilgrimage.
But first, I pray you, of your courtesy,
That you will not ascribe it to my lack of culture,
Even though I speak plainly of this narrative,
730   Presenting to you their words and describing their behavior;
Even if I use their exact words.
For this you know as well as I do:
Whoever repeats a tale told by another man,
He must report, as nearly as he is able,
735   Every single word, if he can,
Even if that means that he speaks very rudely and directly,
Or else he must tell his tale inaccurately,
Or make something up, or substitute different words.
He may not refrain from telling the truth, even about his own brother;
740   Otherwise he might just as well say one word as another.
Christ expressed himself pretty plainly in holy writ,
And, you know well, there's nothing low in it.
Also Plato says, whoever is able to read him,
"The words must be closely related to the deed."
745   Also, I pray that you will forgive me,
If I have not set folk in their proper social rank
Here in this tale, as they should stand.
My intelligence is limited, you understand.

The Poet now turns his comic irony directly against the one person who has so far escaped – Chaucer the Pilgrim, the man who looks like Geoffrey Chaucer but has none of the intelligence of a poet with a Europe-wide reputation. The Pilgrim here apologizes for the very stylistic techniques which the Poet has deliberately adopted and which make *The Canterbury Tales* the innovative and lively work that it is.

The first apology is for the use of strong, occasionally lewd, language in links and in tales which will describe base human actions. The Pilgrim's defense, which he presents seriously, is as patently absurd as is the Monk's justification for ignoring the rules of his Order. Firstly he claims that he is under an artistic obligation to use the words used by the original speaker, for to do anything else would be to "telle his tale untrewe, / Or feyne thing" (737-8). The joke here, of course, is that the reader knows that the whole narrative is fiction; there were no original pilgrim storytellers to whom the Pilgrim must be faithful. The second defense is the use of analogy: Christ "spak hymself ful brode in hooly writ" (741), and nobody criticizes Christ; and Plato, no less, wrote in *Timaeus* that "The words moote be cosin to the dede" (743). This is equally absurd for what unites Christ and Plato is that both used parables or myths to speak about an eternal ideal which it is beyond the ability of human language to describe directly. Plato's statement is specifically about the inadequacy of language to describe abstract philosophical concepts and realities which go beyond empirical experience. The Pilgrim's analogy is absurd because, though Christ and Plato did use stories from everyday life to illustrate their ideas, neither used the kind of foul language which, for example, comes out of the mouth of the Miller who has no idea of telling his story to illustrate a divine or ideal truth. His aim is simply to mock the Reeve.

The second apology is for not having "set folk in hir degree" (746), that is for not presenting the pilgrims correctly in order of their social status in the *Prologue*. In contrast to the long and complicated defense against the charge of using bad language, the Pilgrim offers one line, "My wit is short, ye may wel understonde" (748). This defense comes as a comic anti-climax to the apology. There is also humor in the paradoxical idea of someone called Geoffrey Chaucer being too intellectually challenged to arrange his characters properly.

In fact, it is essential to the Poet that the *Prologue* and the *Tales* should have a spontaneous, chaotic feel.

Lines 749-770: Introducing Harry Bailey

1. The portrait of the Host (749-762) is entirely complimentary. Can you guess why?

> Great hospitality our host showed to us all,
> 750 And straight away set us down to a supper.
> He served us with food that was of the best;
> Strong was the wine, we were all pleased to drink it.
> Our good host was altogether an impressive man
> Fit to have been a master of ceremonies in some nobleman's hall.
> 755 He was a large man, with prominent, gleaming eyes –
> A finer businessman is not to be found in Cheapside -
> Forthright in his speech, and wise, and well mannered,
> And, as to the manly qualities, lacking in nothing.
> Also, he was a very merry man,
> 760 And after supper, he began to joke with the company,
> Speaking of mirth among other things,
> When all of us had paid our bills,
> And saying thus: "Now masters, truly
> You are all heartily welcome here,
> 765 For on my oath, I must say that,
> I have not seen, this year, such a merry company
> Together in this inn as I see now.
> Fain would I entertain you, if I knew how to.
> And I have just this moment thought of a scheme,
> 770 To give you pleasure, and it shall cost you nothing.

Helen Cooper tells us that "there was in Southwark in the early 1380s a 'Henri Bayliff, ostyler', probably the same man who represented the borough in Parliament in 1378-9 and acted as tax collector" (60). Harry Bailly "is identified as another sanguine character by his good humour, manly physique and love of company" (Hussey et al. 161). Winny identifies his controlling planet as the Sun and quotes Bartholomaeus Anglicus (c.1203–1272), the Franciscan encyclopaedist:

> The sun maketh a man corpulent, great of body, fair of face and well coloured, with great eyen … [It] hath virtue of unity and accord, for he joineth, concileth and accordeth the

planets in their own effects anf doings. Also, he accordeth
together elements that be contrary. (Hussey et al. 165)

As Winny points out, this is exactly the Host's rôle in relation to the diverse company of pilgrims whom he unifies into the structure of the game.

The Host is very much what he appears to be. Since he is the only character in *The Canterbury Tales* who can be identified with a historical figure with something approaching certainty, Chaucer is here talking about a person whom he and the members of his audience knew or knew of. Thus, there is no dark secret about him, but even so the Pilgrim sees without fully understanding. He seems the ideal host, jolly, sociable and welcoming and his description echoes his earlier praise-lines:

A semely[1] man Oure Hooste was withalle
For to han been a marchal in an halle[2].
A large man he was with eyen stepe[3] –
A fairer burgeys[2] is ther noon in Chepe –
Boold of his speche, and wys, and wel ytaught[4],
And of manhod hym lakkede right naught[5].
Eek therto he was right a mirie man[6], (753-9)

Compare these phrases with the following descriptions:

[1] Ful semely after hir mete she raughte. (Prioress 136)
[2] Wel semed ech of hem a fair burgeys
To sitten in a yeldehalle on a deis. (Guildsmen 371-2)
[3] His eyen twinkled in his heed aright,
As doon the sterres in the frosty night. (Friar 269-70)
[4] And that was seyd in forme and reverence,
And short and quik and ful of hy sentence; (Clerk 307-8)
[5] A manly man, to been an abbot able. (Monk 167)
[6] A Frere ther was, a wantownc and a merie, (Friar 208)

These careful parallels indicate that, for the Pilgrim, the Host embodies all of those qualities which he has naïvely most admired in the other pilgrims. What he fails to appreciate, even as he observes and records the evidence of it, is the acute businessman, the man who makes sure that his guests have paid their "rekeninges" (762) before he begins to flatter them and talk to them about his scheme. Harry is careful to explain to the pilgrims that the story-telling game will "coste noght" (770), even though this is not strictly speaking true since each pilgrim will have to contribute to the winner's prize, "a soper at oure aller cost" (801). More importantly, the scheme ensures that the company will all return to the Tabbard and stay there for at least an evening: Harry is very effectively drumming up trade with, Baldwin comments ironically, "all the spontaneity of a sideshow barker" (63). This aspect of the Host, of which the Pilgrim remains blissfully unaware, the Poet makes crystal clear to the reader.

Lines 771-823: Harry Bailey's Plan

1. Explain briefly the Host's proposal. What details do the pilgrims add in agreeing to his idea?
2. In what ways does the Host establish his authority over the pilgrims?

> You go to Canterbury; may God speed you,
> And may the blessed martyr reward you as you deserve!
> I know well that as you go on your way,
> You plan to tell tales and amuse yourselves;
> 775   For truly, there is neither comfort nor enjoyment
> Riding along the way as dumb as a stone;
> And therefore will I provide you with amusement,
> As I said before, to give you some pleasure.
> And if you all agree unanimously
> 780   To be ruled by my judgment,
> And to do exactly as I direct you,
> Tomorrow, when you ride upon your way,
> Then, by my father's soul, who is dead,
> If you do not enjoy yourselves, I will give you my head!
> 785   Hold up your hands, without any more talk."
> Our decision was not difficult to reach.
> We thought it was not worth thinking too seriously about,
> And we granted him his way without further discussion,
> And bade him tell his plan if it pleased him.
> 790   "Masters," stated he, "listen carefully to something for your own advantage;
> But do not, I beg of you, receive it scornfully.
> This is the point, to put it briefly and plainly,
> That each of you, to make our journey seem shorter,
> Shall tell two stories as you wend your way
> 795   Towards Canterbury, that is my point,
> And on the return journey shall tell another two,
> All of adventures which have happened in olden times.
> And he who does this the best of all,

That is to say, who tells in this competition
800   The most morally meaningful and most entertaining tales,
        Shall have a supper paid for by the others
        Here in this place, sitting by this very post,
        When we come back again from Canterbury.
        And in order to add to your enjoyment,
805   I will myself gladly ride along with you,
        Completely at my own cost and be your master of ceremonies;
        But whosoever shall go against my rules
        Shall pay for all that we spend along the way.
        And if you are agreed to those conditions,
810   Tell me at once, without more discussion,
        And I will plan to rise early to be ready to start."
        This thing was granted, and we pledged our agreement to his terms
        With very glad hearts, and we prayed him also
        That he would consent to play his part,
815   And that he would be our governor,
        And judge and score keeper of our tales,
        And set a supper at a certain price,
        And we would abide by his rules
        In all things; and thus unanimously
820   We accepted his authority.
        And, to seal the agreement, the wine was fetched immediately;
        We drank, and each one of us went to rest,
        Without tarrying any longer.

If we accept that the company consists of twenty-nine (including the Pilgrim, but not including the Host), then Harry Bailey's plan envisages at total of one hundred and sixteen stories, though Chaucer only completed twenty-four of them before he abandoned the work. The tales exist in eighty-two different manuscripts, but the order of the tales varies and the links between them, which develop the frame story of the journey to Canterbury and the reactions and interactions of the pilgrims, are incomplete.

The presentation in the text of the Host's plan can be seen on two levels: realism and allegory. On the level of psychological realism, Harry seems to protest too much about his rôles as ultimate authority on the pilgrimage: three times he insists that the pilgrims must agree to his plan unanimously and without discussion (779, 785 & 809-10), and twice he stresses that his word as master of ceremonies will be final (780-1 & 807-8). He will remind them twice more on the following morning before the competition actually begins (see 831 and 835-6). The Poet extracts some humor from his portrait of this socially assertive control-freak, but there is nothing sinister here: the fact is that Harry is inferior in status to at least half of the pilgrims, and this explains his desire to establish his authority from the very beginning. In fact, as Kittredge points out, several times he will lose control of the game which he has set in motion, and twice the Knight will use his universally acknowledged status to bring order to the quarreling pilgrims, the first instance being when the Host, who has no problem interrupting Chaucer the Pilgrim, cannot interrupt the Monk's tedious tale, and the second when the Knight intervenes to reconcile a quarrel which erupts between the Host and the Pardoner (163-6).

At the level of allegory, Blamires sees a "monarchal analogy" in the lines which establish the authority of the Host. Such a reading is supported firstly by the writer of SparkNotes who points out that Harry uses "very legalistic terms" to define his rôles: "juggement" (780), "juge and reportour" (816), and that the pilgrims echo this language appointing him their "governour" (815); and secondly by Pollard who quotes Tyrwhitt's opinion that the phrase "In heigh and lough" (819) derives from Latin and French phrases meaning "entire submission on one side and sovereignty on the other" (101). Blamires argues that the presentation of the agreement "affirms that a people's assent can be 'glad' and even almost unconditional (*in heigh and lough*) to a monarch with the right combination of consultative instincts, social wisdom and accomplishment" (Brown ed. 146). He adds that the lines' "overriding implication concerns the politically resonant establishment of a harmonious social contract about government and leadership … a proper working relationship between ruler and ruled" (Brown ed. 144-5). That some allegory of governance is intended appears beyond dispute. Also clear is the Pilgrim's enthusiastic approval of the agreement and the process by which it is reached. If, as Blamers claims, the lines present some sort of ideal view of kingship which combines both divine right and free assent, then we should associate this idealization with the Pilgrim. Since the agreement, as already stated, begins to break down after the end of the very first story, we may see the Poet as more skeptical.

Harry Bailey is the only one of the group whose motivation for making the journey has nothing at all to do with pilgrimage. Indeed, his dominant personality effectively diverts the focus of the pilgrimage from the tomb of St. Thomas Becket in Canterbury to the story-telling competition which will end back at the Tabard Inn.

Lines 824-860: The Pilgrims leave London

1. However it comes about, it is entirely appropriate that the storytelling should begin with the Knight. Why?

On the morrow, when day had begun to spring,
825   Up rose our Host, and was the cockerel for us all.
And gathered us together all in a flock,
And forth we rode at little more than a walk
Unto the watering place named for Saint Thomas;
And there our Host stopped his horse
830   And said, "Gentlemen, listen, if you please.
You know your prior agreement, and I remind you of it.
If what you said last night accords with what you say this morning,
Let's see now who shall tell the first tale.
As ever I may drink wine or ale,
835   Whosoever may rebel against my judgment
Shall pay for all that is spent along the way.
Now draw straws, before we continue our journey;
He who has the shortest shall begin.
Sir Knight," said he, "my master and my lord,
840   Now draw a straw, for that is my decision.
Come nearer," he said, "my lady Prioress.
And you, sir Clerk, put aside your modesty,
And no more studying; lay hand on, every man!"
Immediately, every person began to draw,
845   And shortly to tell it as it happened,
Whether by chance, or fate, or luck,
The truth is this: the draw was won by the Knight,
For which everyone was very happy and glad,
And he must tell his tale, as was reasonable,
850   By our previous promise and by our formal agreement,
As you have heard; what more needs to be said?"
And when this good man [the Knight] saw that it was so,
Like a wise and obedient man
Keeping his agreement by his free will,
855   He said, "Since I must begin the game,
What! Welcome is the draw, in God's name!

Now let us ride, and listen to what I say."
And with that word we rode forth on our way,
And he began with a truly merry demeanor
860   To tell his tale straightaway, and said as you may hear.

This section begins with two animal images. The Host is a cockerel waking the pilgrims, an appropriate metaphor given the Pilgrim's emphasis on his manliness. The pilgrims are a flock, perhaps of birds (this metaphor will soon be repeated) or of sheep with the Host, by implication, their shepherd. The phrase "gadrede us togidre" (826) with its strong, active verb, conveys the degree of control which he exerts over them and which they (for the moment) accept.

The Host is at pains to remind the company of the terms of their social contract:

And seyde, "Lordinges, herkneth, if yow leste.
Ye woot youre foreward, and I it yow recorde.
If even-song and morwe-song accorde,
Lat se now who shal telle the firste tale.
As evere mote I drinke wyn or ale,
Whoso be rebel to my juggement
Shal paye for al that by the wey is spent." (830-6)

He reminds them of their prior agreement (effectively an oath of loyalty), applies the principle of consistency by using a metaphor which compares the pilgrims to birds (832), and reminds his 'subjects' of the penalty for disobedience. The use of the word "rebel" not a decade after Wat Tyler's Rebellion in 1381, enforces the political analogy.

The Host is precise in the way that he addresses the pilgrims. He politely calls them collectively "Lordinges" meaning gentlemen or masters, but he is careful to speak first to those of high status, beginning with the Knight who he calls "my maister and my lord" (839), then the Prioress who he calls "my lady" (841), and finally the Clerk who he calls "sire" (842). The Host's address to the Knight establishes his preeminent status, that to the Prioress recognizes her own view of herself as a gentile lady (we should recall the desire of the Guildsmen's wives to attain precisely this level of respect, "It is full fair to been ycleped 'madame,'" [378]), and that to the Clerk shows deference. Pollard notes the importance of the verb form which the Host uses to indicate that these three pilgrims should participate in picking straws, "draweth … Cometh … studieth noght" (840-3) which he calls "polite plural imperatives (101). In contrast, in speaking to the remainder of the company, the Host uses the blunt imperative, "ley hond to, every man!" (843).

The Poet's final joke at the expense of the Pilgrim is the latter's naïve reaction to the fact that the Knight, the highest status pilgrim, just happens to pick the shortest straw:

> Were it by aventure, or sort, or cas,
> The sothe is this, the cut fil to the Knight (846-7)

Clearly Harry Bailey has manipulated the drawing of lots to ensure the most socially appropriate outcome. The Pilgrim's inability to see this, or perhaps his awkward attempt to cover it up, are equally disingenuous since the Pilgrim similarly fixed the order of the portraits by putting the Knight first. Thus, the *Prologue* ends on a note of appropriateness and accord:

> The sothe is this, the cut fil to the Knight,
> Of which ful blithe and glad was every wight,
> And telle he moste his tale, as was resoun,
> By foreward and by composicioun, (847-50)

The Pilgrim repeats the word "resound" (a medieval term from rhetoric meaning order, the proper sequence of parts in a speech) from line 37. He leaves us with an idealized picture of a company united by agreement under a firm leader whose powers (including the power of punishment) are acknowledged and accepted by all.

The Poet's irony in the repetition of "resound" is that just as the Pilgrim was not able to stick to "resound" either in the manner in which he described the pilgrims or in the order in which he presented them, so the Host's powers of control will evaporate when, seeking to preserve the decorum of status, he nominates the Monk to tell the second tale only to have the Miller successfully rebel against his authority:

> Our Host laughed, and swore, "As I might live,
> This goes very well, the bag is open,
> Let's see now who shall tell another tale,
> For truly, the game is well begun.
> Now tell on, sir Monk, if you can
> Something to equal the Knight's tale."
> The Miller, who having drunk too much was all pale,
> So that he sat upon his horse unsteadily,
> He would not doff either his hood nor his hat,

Nor wait behind any man out of courtesy,
But in a voice like Pilate's he began to shout,
And swore by the arms and blood and bones of Christ,
"I can tell a noble tale for the occasion,
With which I will now top the Knight's tale."
Our Host saw that he was drunk on ale,
And said, "Wait on, Robin, my dear brother,
Some better man shall first tell another tale,
Wait, and let us do this sensibly."
"By God's soul," he cried, "that I will not,
For I will speak, or else go my way."
Our Host answered, "Tell on, and go to the devil!
You are a fool, your wit is overcome!"
"Now listen up," said the Miller, "each and every one,"
("The Miller's Prologue" author's modernization)

In this way, the much celebrated unity of the company under the governance of the Host, who clearly plans for each pilgrim to tell his tale "in hir degree" (746), disintegrates.

Appendix One: Guide to Further Reading

As I wrote in the Preface, the Chaucer literature is vast, but much of it is written by specialists for specialists. An additional problem for the reader/ student seeking an introduction to The General Prologue is the fact that, since most books deal with the whole of The Canterbury Tales (if not the whole of Chaucer's literary output), they tend to contain only a chapter on the Prologue. The works selected appear to me to offer a great place to start.

John Matthews Manly's *Some New Light on Chaucer* - the printed text of his Lowell Lectures, 1924 - the style is clear and readable - purist literary critics who stress the absolute primacy of the text find Manly's approach archaic, but his actual thesis (that in constructing his portraits Chaucer drew upon his observation of real individuals) seems to be self-evidently true.

George Kittredge's *Chaucer and His Poetry* - the printed text of his Johns Hopkins Lectures, 1915 - clear and readable - modern criticism has been harsh on Kittredge's thesis (that the *Prologue* introduces the characters in a coherent and consistent dramatic poem in which the tales are extended speeches matching the characters of the tellers), but there seems no doubt that this was a part of Chaucer's artistic intention.

Laura and Robert Lambdin's *Chaucer's Pilgrims A Historical Guide to the Pilgrims in The Canterbury Tales* (1999) - brings Manly's approach up to date.

Muriel Bowden's *A Commentary on the General Prologue* - the best single volume on the *Prologue* - emphasizes the historical background to the pilgrims – exhaustively documented.

Hussey, Spearing and Winny's *An Introduction to Chaucer* (1965) - a clearly written primer to Chaucer's world.

Terry Jones' *Chaucer's Knight - The Portrait of a Medieval Mercenary* (1985) - the section on the portrait of the Knight in the *Prologue* is well worth reading, even if you do not end up accepting Jones' thesis.

Peter Brown's *A Companion to Chaucer* (2002) - a huge book but, read selectively, has excellent material on the *Prologue*.

Jodi-Anne George's *Geoffrey Chaucer The General Prologue to the Canterbury Tales* (2000) - offers a comprehensive overview of writing about the *Prologue* from 1368 to 1996 - obviously intended for the advanced student - provides well-chosen extracts with helpful introductions so that the reader is able to follow the evolution of critical responses to this text.

Bibliography

Note: To keep the Bibliography a reasonable length, I compromised. Wherever I quoted or consciously paraphrased ideas from other works, I gave in-text citations. However, I have not cited ideas I regarded as 'common knowledge' or ideas I came up with myself and only subsequently found in secondary sources. If an in-text citation does not appear in the Bibliography, the source is a small website. Google the quote together with the citation to find the source.

Baldwin, Ralph. *The Unity of The Canterbury Tales*. 1st ed. Copenhagen: Rosenkilde and Bagger, 1955. Print.

Benson, C. David. *Chaucer's Drama of Style Poetic Variety and Contrast in the Canterbury Tales* . 1st ed. Chapel Hill: University of North Carolina Press, 1986. Print.

Bloom, Harold, ed. *Geoffrey Chaucer*. 1st ed. Broomall: Chelsea House Publishers, 1999. Print.

Bloom, Harold, ed. *Bloom's Modern Critical Interpretations: Geoffrey Chaucer The Canterbury Tales*. New Edition. New York: Infobase Publishing, 2008. Print.

Bloom, Harold, ed. *Modern Critical Interpretations: Geoffrey Chaucer's The General Prologue to the Canterbury Tales*. 1st ed. New York: Chelsea House Publishers, 1988. Print.

Boitani, Piero, and Jill Mann, eds. *The Cambridge Companion to Chaucer*. 5th printing. Cambridge: Cambridge University Press, 2008. Print.

Bowden, Muriel. *A Reader's Guide to Geoffrey Chaucer*. 1st ed. New York: Farrar, Straus and Giroux, 1964. Print.

Bowden, Muriel. *A Commentary in the General Prologue to the Canterbury Tales*. 2nd ed. London: MacMillan Company, 1969. Print.

Brewer, Derek. *Chaucer and His World*. 1st ed. New York: Dodd, Mead & Company, 1978. Print.

Brown, Peter, and Andrew Butcher. *The Age of Saturn: Literature and History in The Canterbury Tales*. 1st ed. Cambridge: Basil Blackwell, 1991. Print.

Brown, Peter ed.. *A Companion to Chaucer*. 1st ed. Malden: Blackwell Publishing, 2002. Print.

Chaucer, Geoffrey. *The General Prologue to the Canterbury Tales*. Ed. David Kirkham and Valerie Allen. 7th Printing. Cambridge: Cambridge University Press, 2005. Print.

Clements, John. "The Sword & Buckler Tradition - Part 1." *ARMA*. The Association for Renaissance Martial Arts, 1999. Web. 17 Jun 2012.

J.S. Cockburn, H.P.F. King, K.G.T. McDonnell (Editors). "Religious Houses: House of Benedictine nuns." A History of the County of Middlesex: Volume 1: Physique, Archaeology, Domesday, Ecclesiastical Organization, The Jews, Religious Houses, Education of Working Classes to 1870, Private Education from Sixteenth Century (1969): 156-159. British History Online. Web. 06 June 2012.

Cooper, Helen. *Oxford Guides to Chaucer: The Canterbury Tales*. 2nd ed. New York: Oxford University Press, 1996. Print.

Curry, Walter. "Chaucer's Reeve and Miller." *PMLA* , 35.2 (1920): 189-209. Print.

---. "The Malady of Chaucer's Summoner." *Modern Philology* . 19.4 (1922): 395-404. Print.

Del Dotto, Darcy, and Hailey Prescott. "Rouncy." *Horses in Medieval Times*. Massachusetts Academy of Math and Science, n.d. Web. 22 May 2012.

Forkin, Thomas. "Essays in Medieval Studies." *Essays in Medieval Studies* . Volume 24. (2007): 31-41. Print.

Gastle, Brian. "Chaucer's 'Shaply' Guildsmen and Mercantile Pretensions." *Neuphilologische Mitteilungen*. (1998): 211-16. Print.

Gies , Frances, and Joseph Gies. *Daily Life in Medieval Times*. 1st ed. New York: Barnes & Noble Books, 1990. Print.

Gilbert, Rosalie. "Sumptuary Laws." *ROSALIE'S MEDIEVAL WOMAN*. Rosalie Gilbert, n.d. Web. 26 Nov 2012.

Gravett, Christopher. *Knight: Noble Warrior of England 1200-1600*. 1st ed. Westminster: Osprey Publishing, 2008. Print.

Hall, Francine. "Chaucer and Chivalry." Knight Templar Magazine, Aug 2001. Web. 6 Nov 2012.

Hallissy, Margaret, *A Companion to Chaucer's Canterbury Tales*. 1st ed. Westport: Greenwood, 1995. Print.

Halveron, John. *Geoffrey Chaucer The Canterbury Tales*. 1st ed. Indianapolis: Bobbs-Merrill Company, 1971. Print.

Hirsh, John. *Chaucer and the Canterbury Tales A Short Introduction*. 1st ed. Malden: Blackwell Publishing, 2003. Print.

Hodges, Laura. *Chaucer And Clothing: Clerical And Academic Costume In The General Prologue To The Canterbury Tales*. 1st ed. Cambridge: D. S. Brewer, 2005. Print.

Howard, Donald. "The Idea of *The Canterbury Tales*." *Modern Critical Views: Geoffrey Chaucer*. Ed. Harold Bloom. 1st ed. New York: Chelsea House Publishers, 1985. 79-104. Print.

Hussey, Maurice, A. C. Spearing, and James Winny. *An Introduction to Chaucer*. 1st ed. Cambridge: Cambridge University Press, 1965. Print.

Johnston, Ian. "Introduction to 'The General Prologue' of *The Canterbury Tales*." *johnstonia*. N.p., 05 1995. Web. 6 Nov 2012.

Johnson, Jason. "Chaucer's Canterbury Tales: Contrasting Clergy Compare and Contrast the Parson and the Friar." *Entertainment Books*. Yahoo! Voices, 10 2003. Web. 13 Nov 2012.

Jones, Terry. *Chaucer's Knight - The Portrait of a Medieval Mercenary*. New York: Methuen, 1985.

Kittredge, George. *Chaucer and His Poetry*. 55th Anniversary Edition. Cambridge: Harvard University Press, 1970. Print.

Lambdin, Laura, and Robert Lambdin, eds. *Chaucer's Pilgrims A Historical Guide to the Pilgrims in The Canterbury Tales*. 1st ed. Westport: Praeger, 1999. Print.

Manly, John. "A Knight Ther Was." *Transactions and Proceedings of the American Philological Association*. 38. (1907): 89-107. Print.

Manly, John. *Some New Light on Chaucer*. Reprint of 1st ed. Gloucester: Peter Smith, 1959. Print.

"Medieval Estates and Orders - Making and Breaking Rules: Texts and Contexts." *The Norton Anthology of English Literature*. W.W. Norton and Company. Web. 27 Nov 2012.

Miller, Robert. *Chaucer Sources and Backgrounds*. 1st ed. New York: Oxford University press, 1977. Print.

Patterson, Lee. *Geoffrey Chaucer's The Canterbury Tales: A Casebook*. 1st ed. New York: Oxford University Press, 2007. Print.

Phillips, Jonathan. *Holy Warriors: A Modern History of the Crusades*. 1st ed. New York: Random House, 2009. Print.

Pollard, Alfred. *Chaucer's Canterbury Tales: The Prologue*, 1st ed. London: Macmillan, 1903. Print.

Prestwich, Michael. *Knight The Medieval Warrior's (Unofficial) Manual*. 1st ed. New York: Thames & Hudson, 2010. Print.

Sainty, Guy. "THE TEUTONIC ORDER OF HOLY MARY IN JERUSALEM." *THE PAPAL ORDERS*. N.p.. Web. 7 Nov 2012.

Shuster, Allison, Kristen Zaki, and Arianne Traurig. "Chaucer's Pilgrims and Their Clothing." *Medieval Literature and Material Culture* . N.p.. Web. 13 Nov 2012.

Urban, William. *Medieval Mercenaries: The Business of War*. 1st ed. St Paul: MBI Publishing Co., 2006. Print.

Vigneswaran, Krish. "An Analysis of Geoffrey Chaucer's Understanding of Medicine and its Influence on His Work." *Vanderbilt Undergraduate Research Journal*. 3.1 (2007): 1-5. Print.

Wetherbee, Winthrop. *Geoffrey Chaucer: The Canterbury Tales*. 2nd ed. Cambridge: Cambridge University Press, 2004. Print.

Wilcockson, Colin. *Geoffrey Chaucer: The Canterbury Tales A Selection*. 1st ed., London: Penguin Books, 2008. Print.

Williams, David. *The Canterbury Tales: A Literary Pilgrimage*. 1st ed. Boston: Twayne Publishers, 1987. Print.

About the Author

Ray Moore was born in Nottingham, England in 1950. He obtained his Master's Degree in Literature at Lancaster University in 1974 and then taught in secondary education for twenty-eight years before relocating to Florida with his wife in 2002. There he taught English and Information Technology in the International Baccalaureate Program at Vanguard High School in Ocala.

He retired in June 2012 and is now a full-time writer and fitness fanatic.

You can contact the author by email: mooreray1@yahoo.com

Also by Ray Moore:

Fiction:

Investigations of The Reverend Lyle Thorne (published October 2012)

Further Investigations of The Reverend Lyle Thorne (published March 2013)

Non-fiction:

"The Stranger" by Albert Camus: A Critical Introduction (published October 2012)

Printed in Great Britain
by Amazon.co.uk, Ltd.,
Marston Gate.